AN INTRODUCTION TO THE *GAWAIN*-POET

LONGMAN MEDIEVAL AND RENAISSANCE LIBRARY

General Editors:
CHARLOTTE BREWER, Hertford College, Oxford
N. H. KEEBLE, University of Stirling

Ad Putter

AN INTRODUCTION TO THE *GAWAIN*-POET

LONGMAN
LONDON AND NEW YORK

Addison Wesley Longman
Edinburgh Gate
Harlow
Essex CM20 2JE
England
and Associated Companies throughout the world.

Published in the United States of America
by Addison Wesley Longman Inc., New York.

First Published 1996

ISBN 0 582 22575 2 CSD
ISBN 0 582 22574 4 PPR

British Library Cataloguing-in-Publication Data
A catalogue record for this book is
available from the British Library

Library of Congress Cataloging-in-Publication Data
A catalog entry for this title is available from the
Library of Congress

Set by 8 in 10/12pt Bembo
Transferred to digital print on demand, 2002
Printed and bound by Antony Rowe Ltd, Eastbourne

Contents

Preface

This book is an introduction to the *Gawain*-poet's four surviving works: *Sir Gawain and the Green Knight, Patience, Pearl,* and *Cleanness.* Its purpose is to make all four poems accessible to students by setting the poet and his works in their relevant historical and cultural context, and, above all, by developing some lines of critical argument that, I think, bring out the best in the *Gawain*-poet's works.

My studies of the poems and their context are based on fresh research and ideas. I have not wanted merely to rehearse existing opinion about the *Gawain*-poet. Anyone interested in 'what the critics have said' about the poet and his oeuvre should consult the annotated bibliographies of criticism on the *Gawain*-poet by Andrew (1979); Foley (1989); Blanch (1990); and Stainsby (1991). In this book, secondary literature is referred to selectively, where it is relevant to my own argument, or where I am indebted to it.

In order to make this book easier to use for the general reader, quotations from the *Gawain*-poet have been translated into modern English. Both in my translations from Middle English and in my translations from foreign languages, I have opted for literal rather than elegant renderings; it is hoped that they will be used as an aid to reading the original passages, rather than as a substitute for it. All translations are my own; but in the bibliography of primary sources I also list references to published translations of important (non-English) medieval texts that are cited in this book. It may be reassuring to know that quite a few of the Latin, French, and Italian texts referred to in this book are available in translation.

Finally, a word of thanks for the time and mental energy which friends and colleagues have put into this book. Alun David taught me a thing or two about how to read the *Gawain*-poet's biblical sources.

During the many weeks it took me to write the chapter on *Sir Gawain and the Green Knight*, Myra Stokes listened every day to my work in progress and gave me lots of ideas for next day's instalment. Charlotte Brewer, John Burrow, Jane Gilbert, Jill Mann, James Simpson, and Myra Stokes read most of this book in draft, and made valuable suggestions and corrections. I share with these learned and faithful readers the horrible secret of what this book would have looked like without their intervention, and I am very grateful to them for ensuring that this secret has not become public knowledge.

A.P.

Note on references and abbreviations

The reference system adopted for *secondary sources* is the author-date system, where the date is the year of publication. When more than one work by the same author appeared in the same year, the year of publication is followed by a, b, c, etc. Full bibliographical details for author-year references can be found by checking the bibliography at the end of this book. In the case of citations from *primary sources*, I have given full bibliographical details in footnotes. My numerous quotations from the *Gawain*-poet and from Chaucer are from the following editions: *Cleanness*, ed. J.J. Anderson (Manchester: Manchester University Press, 1977); *Patience*, ed. J.J. Anderson (Manchester: Manchester University Press, 1969); *Pearl*, ed. E.V. Gordon (Oxford: Clarendon Press, 1974); *Sir Gawain and the Green Knight*, eds J.R.R. Tolkien and E.V. Gordon, revised by Norman Davis (Oxford: Clarendon Press, 1967); and *The Riverside Chaucer*, ed. Larry D. Benson et al. (Boston: Houghton Mifflin, 1987).

The following abbreviations are used in the text and in the bibliography:

CC	*Corpus Christianorum, Series Latina*
CFMA	Classiques Français du Moyen Age
ChR	*Chaucer Review*
CSEL	*Corpus Scriptorum Ecclesiasticorum Latinorum*
EETS ES	Early English Text Society, Extra Series
EETS OS	Early English Text Society, Original Series
ES	*English Studies*
LCL	Loeb Classical Library
MED	*Middle English Dictionary*

MLN	*Modern Language Notes*
MLR	*Modern Language Review*
MP	*Modern Philology*
MS	*Mediaeval Studies*
N&Q	*Notes and Queries*
PL	*Patrologia Latina*
PMLA	*Publications of the Modern Language Association of America*
RES	*Review of English Studies*
SAC	*Studies in the Age of Chaucer*
SATF	Société des Anciens Textes Français

For

Ruth, Hein, and Esther

Chapter 1

The *Gawain*-poet in context

INTRODUCTION

The works of the *Gawain*-poet have come down to us in a single manuscript: British Library, Cotton Nero A.x. This manuscript had been gathering dust for centuries before the poems it contains began to attract a wide readership. Only in 1839 did the whole of *Sir Gawain and the Green Knight* first appear in print. The *Gawain*-poet's other works—*Pearl, Cleanness,* and *Patience*—had to suffer neglect longer still, until 1864, when Richard Morris edited the four poems of Cotton Nero A.x. in the first volume of the Original Series of the Early English Text Society (Turville-Petre 1977, 127). Since then, the *Gawain*-poet has been read and re-read, and his works have been the subject of lively critical debate. Today, *Pearl* and *Sir Gawain and the Green Knight* are also inspiring contemporary literature and art in a way they never seem to have done in the poet's own lifetime.[1]

The fortunes of the disappointingly small and unimpressive manuscript reflect the *Gawain*-poet's recent rise to fame.[2] Its first known owner was Henry Savile of Bank (1568–1617), a lesser Yorkshire gentleman. From him it passed into the hands of Sir Robert Cotton, the famous antiquary and book-collector. Cotton seems not to have recognized the *Gawain*-poet for the genius he was, and his librarian bound the manuscript of his works in with two unrelated Latin moral treatises. Still unrecognized, the *Gawain*-poet's works might well have perished forever when a fire raged through the Cottonian library in 1731, destroying

---

1. Some recent examples are Iris Murdoch's novel *The Green Knight* (1993), Harrison Birtwistle's opera *Gawain* (1994), and Douglas Oliver's poem 'The Infant and The Pearl', in *Kind* (London: Agneau 2, 1987), 127–62.
2. For a history of the manuscript see Salter (1983, 83–4), and Vantuono (1984, I, xvii–xix).

many texts that might have shed more light on the *Gawain*-poet. Fortunately, Cotton Nero A.x. escaped with little damage and, along with other survivors of the fire, the original manuscript was transferred to the British Library. In 1964, the manuscript containing the *Gawain*-poet's works was rebound into a separate volume, as it was originally, and Cotton Nero A.x. has now made its way into the display cabinets of the British Museum, where it belongs.

The particular qualities and characteristics of the *Gawain*-poet's works, to which the manuscript owes its present visibility in the British Museum, are the subject of the four main chapters in this book, which are devoted to *Sir Gawain and the Green Knight*, *Patience*, *Pearl*, and *Cleanness* respectively. In this chapter I will be concerned with the *Gawain*-poet's works only in so far as they shed light on the issue of the *Gawain*-poet's social circumstances and historical situation. The questions that will occupy me here are what kind of background and what kind of milieu we should be imagining for the *Gawain*-poet.

If in trying to answer these questions we were to limit ourselves only to incontrovertible 'facts', this chapter would be very brief, for one of the surest facts about the *Gawain*-poet is that there are not many. The '*Gawain*-poet' (or '*Pearl*-poet') is himself a scholarly invention, merely a convenient name given to the single author who is now commonly accepted as having written all four poems in Cotton Nero A.x.[3] Attempts to unmask the '*Gawain*-poet' have so far failed to gain wide acceptance. The idea that the *Gawain*-poet might be a certain 'Massey' (a common Cheshire name) is the most recent conjecture and the only one with any serious support, but it depends on straining one's eyesight (and perhaps one's credulity) in order to see an anagram of the poet's name in selected words from *Pearl* (Peterson 1974), or a signature in the doodles underneath an ornamental letter in the manuscript (Vantuono 1975). Whilst many would dispute the identification of the *Gawain*-poet with John (or Hugh) Massey, the Cheshire origin of the *Gawain*-poet is well attested by the poet's dialect, which has been localized near Holmes Chapel in east Cheshire (McIntosh 1963).

In addition to his dialect, we also know, with some degree of certainty, when the *Gawain*-poet's works were composed. The latest possible date is that of the manuscript, which can be dated on the basis

---

3. *St Erkenwald*, which used to be attributed to the *Gawain*-poet on grounds of similarities in dialect and phraseology, is now generally taken to be by a different author (Benson 1965a). As well as surviving in a different manuscript, *St Erkenwald* does not have the rich vocabulary of the *Gawain*-poet's works.

of the handwriting and the manuscript illuminations to about 1400. The presence of scribal errors in the manuscript suggests that Cotton Nero A.x. is some stages removed from the author's original, which must therefore have been written some time before 1400. For the earliest possible date we must turn to internal evidence from the poems themselves. The most revealing clue comes from *Cleanness*, where the poet probably used *Mandeville's Travels* for his descriptions of the Dead Sea and the vessels at Belshazzar's feast (Brown 1904, 149–53). *Mandeville's Travels*, which purports to be a first-hand account in French of an amazing journey around the world, was compiled by an armchair traveller on the continent in about 1357, and soon became an international best-seller. The French version of *Mandeville's Travels* known to the *Gawain*-poet was the so-called Insular Version, which presents a slightly later text than the Continental Version, though at least one copy is known to have circulated in England before 1390 (Seymour 1993, 8). This would place *Cleanness* in the last decades of the fourteenth century. Certain descriptive details—such as the architecture of Castle Hautdesert in *Sir Gawain* —likewise point to the end of the fourteenth century. Going about as far as the evidence allows, the *Middle English Dictionary* dates the *Gawain*-poet's works to about 1390. This means that the *Gawain*-poet must have been writing his poems at around the same time that Geoffrey Chaucer was working on his *Canterbury Tales*, that John Gower was completing his first version of the *Confessio Amantis*, and that William Langland was rewriting *Piers Plowman*.

The facts thus far: somewhere in England, towards the end of the fourteenth century, an unknown Englishman wrote four poems in a north west Midlands dialect. In order to say more about the poet and his milieu it will be necessary to make informed guesses on the basis of clues from the *Gawain*-poet's own works, or on the basis of similar works that might furnish some point of comparison. In the rest of this chapter I shall be trying to reconstruct a picture of the *Gawain*-poet, building first of all on the poet's reading, secondly on the poet's self-presentation and outlook in his works, and finally on evidence about the milieux and audiences of other alliterative poets. With the exception of pp. 25–6, which will help to acquaint first-time readers of the *Gawain*-poet with the basic principles of alliterative metre, this discussion is not meant to be introductory to the later chapters, nor should it be seen as a necessary preliminary to reading the poems. The *Gawain*-poet left us no life records apart from his literary oeuvre, so that, like all research into the *Gawain*-poet's social background, my own argument cannot avoid leaning heavily on the poems themselves. In what follows I am therefore already presupposing in my reader some familiarity with the *Gawain*-poet's characteristic voice. Newcomers to the *Gawain*-poet might prefer to move straight to the chapters on the poet's works, each of which is an accessible and more or less self-contained study, and return to the following discussion afterwards.

THE POET'S READING

One source of evidence that sheds some light on the poet's social position is formed by the kind of reading that went into the making of his poems. What we know about the sources for the *Gawain*-poet's works, about his reading, strongly suggests a clerical background and education. It is true that many of the books which the *Gawain*-poet knew, particularly those in French, were mainstream enough. *Mandeville's Travels*, a source for *Cleanness*, was widely disseminated. Another popular French source for the *Gawain*-poet was the *Roman de la Rose* (Pilch 1964), an early-thirteenth-century allegorical dream vision by Guillaume de Lorris and Jean de Meun, whom the poet refers to as 'Clopyngnel' (Jean de Meun's birthplace) in *Cleanness* (1057). Even more so than *Mandeville's Travels*, the *Roman de la Rose* took later medieval England by storm: it was, for instance, translated by Chaucer, who incidentally also knew the version of *Mandeville's Travels* which the *Gawain*-poet used in *Cleanness*. The poet's main sources (again French) for *Sir Gawain and the Green Knight* were Arthurian romances, the favourite reading matter of the well-to-do of fourteenth-century England. The *Gawain*-poet shows a deep familiarity with the conventions of the genre, and occasionally in *Gawain* it is possible to detect borrowings from specific romances, such as Chrétien de Troyes's *Erec et Enide* (c. 1170), the *First Continuation* of Chrétien's *Perceval* (c. 1195), or the *Prose Lancelot* (c. 1220) (Putter 1995). In the last lines of *Gawain* the poet also alludes to 'þe Brutus bokez' (2523), which are called on as witnesses to the fabulous story he has just narrated. The mention of books about the history of Britain and its mythical founder Brutus may allude to Wace's French *Brut* (c. 1160), which made available to a wide readership Geoffrey of Monmouth's Latin 'history' of the founding of Britain and King Arthur's glorious reign. But again the *Brut* was too widespread to tell us much about the *Gawain*-poet's background. In the fourteenth century, the *Brut* sparked off a host of adaptations and translations in Anglo-Norman and English.

The sources mentioned so far were immensely popular, and anyone in later-medieval England who was educated, and who had access to manuscripts—precious commodities, let us not forget—might sooner or later have come across them. But things are different for the (in contemporary terms) *avant garde* sources that have been suggested for *Pearl*: Boccaccio's *Olympia* and Dante's *Divina Commedia*. The first of these is a pastoral elegy in Latin in which Boccaccio, through the persona of a shepherd named Silvius, mourns for the death of his small daughter.[4] Like the *Pearl*-poet's daughter, she appears to him in a vision of Paradise, and reminds her father that virtuous behaviour may bring him to heaven as well. The similarities in situation and (possibly hence) expression between *Pearl* and Boccaccio's *Olympia* are close, and scholarly opinion might well have embraced *Olympia* as one of the *Gawain*-poet's sources if it were not for the fact that no manuscript of Boccaccio's *Olympia* is known to have circulated in England when *Pearl* was composed (Carlson 1987). Nor is this surprising: when the *Gawain*-poet was writing his poems Boccaccio had only just died (in 1375), and *Olympia* was completed only a few years before this date. These facts seriously weaken the case for a direct link between *Pearl* and *Olympia*, though the case need not perhaps be closed: why, for instance, might not the *Gawain*-poet, like Chaucer, have travelled to Italy? Or why could he not have gone to London, where, among the thriving community of Italian bankers and merchants, the latest Italian literature seems to have been available (Childs 1983)? True, these possibilities would conflict with the old view of the *Gawain*-poet as a provincial and isolated poet, but, as I shall argue later, the latest research does little to support that view.

Dante's *Divina Commedia* is a far more likely source for *Pearl* than Boccaccio (see below pp. 188–9). There is some evidence—which is more than can be said for Boccaccio's *Olympia*—that Dante's masterpiece was known in fourteenth-century England. Chaucer had read it, and another alliterative poet from Cheshire, the poet of *St Erkenwald*, may also have known the *Divina Commedia* in a glossed version (Whatley 1986). Even so the *Gawain*-poet's acquaintance with Dante would place him in a very small company. However, the grounds for supposing that he belonged to that company are solid. Like Dante in *Purgatorio*, the

---

4. Gollancz (1921a) offers a text and translation of *Olympia*. See Finlayson (1983) for a recent appraisal of the relationship between *Pearl* and Boccaccio.

Gawain-poet in *Pearl* describes his vision of the beautiful landscape surrounding heaven. Walking through this setting, the paths of both Dante and the *Gawain*-poet are blocked by a stream, which marks the boundary between the earthly paradise and heaven. Across the stream the poets see the figures of deceased friends: the Pearl-maiden in *Pearl*; Matelda and then Beatrice in Dante. More striking still than the correspondences in scene and setting is the chillingly cold reception that awaits both Dante and the Dreamer in *Pearl*, who receive a series of stinging rebukes from the women they loved and still love. Perhaps these parallels are ideas which Dante and the *Gawain*-poet arrived at independently as they sought to convey the contradictory truths about heaven that formed part of their common intellectual inheritance: that heaven was beautiful but inaccessible to mortals (hence the motifs of the pastoral landscape and the barrier of the river); that heaven accommodated the virtuous dead but also de-humanized them (hence the cold *distance* of Beatrice's responses to Dante and the Pearl-maiden's responses to the Dreamer). But, like many other critics, I cannot help thinking of Dante when reading *Pearl*, and, with them, I should like to believe that the *Gawain*-poet was thinking of Dante as well. Because Dante was little known in later-medieval England, the *Gawain*-poet's use of it would reveal more about him than any of the French sources. For if the *Gawain*-poet did know Dante he must have been a more cosmopolitan poet than he is usually given credit for.

Also of interest is the poet's knowledge of Latin texts, which is borne out by far more than his putative use of Boccaccio's *Olympia*. There is first of all his knowledge of the Bible. For readers with no Latin, translations of the Vulgate were to be had. Rhymed Bibles (in English, but mainly in French) were popular in aristocratic circles, and Wycliffe's followers were translating the Latin Vulgate into English prose so as to make the letter of scripture accessible to the ordinary layman. But the *Gawain*-poet had no need for translations. A comparison between the Vulgate and his retellings of the Old Testament in *Patience* and *Cleanness* makes it very clear that he had the precise wording of the Latin Bible in his eye or in his mind.

The *Gawain*-poet's literacy in Latin (as opposed to vernacular languages) has some value as a social marker, for in later-medieval England proficiency in Latin continued, at least formally, to distinguish the cleric from the layman. Thus, when charged with a criminal offence, the accused could establish his clerical status by reading out some lines from the Latin Vulgate, and, if successful, claim 'benefit of clergy', the right to be punished by the appropriate ecclesiastical rather than secular authorities. Now, evidently, the cases of the laymen John Gower and Geoffrey Chaucer, both enviably fluent in Latin, show that this test was no longer watertight in the later fourteenth century; but, then, it would be an understatement to say that the *Gawain*-poet could read the Latin Bible: he really *knew* it. The most impressive testimony to this is the story in *Cleanness* about the sacred vessels defiled by Belshazzar, the history of which the *Gawain*-poet traces effortlessly from one historical time and place to another. As told by the *Gawain*-poet, the chronology of events, and the connections between them, are faultless; yet, remarkably enough, this continuity of action is achieved by the poet through an intelligent selection and combination of a bewildering variety of Old Testament sources.[5] To get an impression of how well the poet knew his way around the Bible, we can follow him briefly on his tour around the Old Testament. The *Gawain*-poet's history first follows Jeremiah 52: 1–27, as he tells of the destruction of Jersualem under Zedekiah, and the sacking of the Temple, the spoils of which are presented to the King of Babylon, Nebuchadnezzar (*Cleanness*, 1157–1312). But while following Jeremiah, small changes in emphasis show that the poet occasionally reached back beyond Jeremiah to the slightly shorter account of the sacking of Jerusalem in II Chronicles 37: 11–20. The rest of the poet's story, from the death of Nebuchadnezzar to the death of his son (*Cleanness*, 1313–1804), has yet another Old Testament source: the Book of Daniel. Following Daniel 5: 1–24, the poet narrates how Nebuchadnezzar's proud son Belshazzar comes to the throne and angers God by desecrating the holy vessels from the Temple. A hand appears from nowhere to write mysterious letters on the wall, which Daniel, the prisoner-prophet, is called upon to interpret. Daniel predicts a violent end for Belshazzar, putting him in mind of the instructive example of his father Nebuchadnezzar, whom God briefly turned into a beast to punish his pride. In Daniel 5, the description of Nebuchadnezzar's miraculous metamorphosis into a wild beast is brief, and the *Gawain*-poet expanded it by going back to Daniel 4: 27–33, before returning again to Daniel 5 in order to show how Daniel's prophecies come true. In the course of this already intricate interweaving of scattered biblical sources, the *Gawain*-poet occasionally added relevant details from other places in the Old Testament. Thus he looked up—or, more probably, remembered—

---

5. The edition of *Cleanness* by Gollancz (1921b) gives the relevant passages from the Vulgate Bible in an appendix.

the names of the Jewish prophets handed over to Nebuchadnezzar (*Cleanness*, 1301–2; cf. Daniel 1: 6); and he fleshed out the description of the vessels in the Temple (*Cleanness*, 1269–92 and 1441–88) with some apposite details recollected from other places in the Bible where the Tabernacle or the Temple are portrayed (Exodus 37: 17–27 and II Chronicles 3: 15–4: 22). The strands in this rich tapestry of biblical sources are imperceptible to the eye that has not studied the sources, and this has kindly protected readers from having to take too much notice of the poet's scholarship. The *Gawain*-poet's statement that his *exemplum* is taken straight from the Book of Daniel (1157) suggests that he might not have noticed his own scholarship himself, that the biblical history had simply formed itself in his mind without him needing to look again at the various sources, as I have just done. Yet although the *Gawain*-poet wears his scholarship lightly, the story of the vessels remains a remarkable feat of compilation, one which warrants the conclusion that its author must have had the Bible at his fingertips.[6] And even for the fourteenth century, when the Bible was read (or listened to) far more often than it is today, it is difficult to imagine a layman with the confidence or ability to have undertaken a work of this kind.

Some other Latin texts, apart from the Bible, were used by the *Gawain*-poet. For *Patience*, the poet's retelling of the story about Jonah and the Whale, he relied not only on the Bible, but also on a delightful Latin verse rendition of the Book of Jonah by the accomplished early-twelfth-century poet Marbod of Rennes.[7] The influence of the late-classical poem *Carmen de Jona propheta* (once attributed to Tertullian) has

6. The *Gawain*-poet's 'edition' of biblical episodes may of course go back to an earlier text. However, I have not been able to find a source for the *Gawain*-poet's biblical compilation in any of the biblical retellings that were influential in later-medieval England: Peter Comestor's *Historia Scholastica*, Peter Riga's *Aurora*, Lawrence of Durham's *Hypognosticon*, Herman de Valencienne's *Bible*, the *Bible anonyme*, the *Cursor Mundi*, and the *Strophic Versions* of the Old Testament. The closest analogue to the *Gawain*-poet's continuous history that I have found is Josephus's *De Antiquitatibus Judaicis* (see especially X, 7–11), a history of the Jews, known to the Middle Ages in a sixth-century Latin translation. *Cleanness*'s faithfulness to the Old Testament, and its failure to follow Josephus at points where it departs from the Bible, suggest that the *Gawain*-poet's compilation is his own. A remaining possibility is that the *Gawain*-poet availed himself of the clerical aids (such as biblical dictionaries and biblical concordances) that the thirteenth-century scholastics produced. This possibility would of course only confirm the poet's clerical background.

7. Attila Fày, who first proposed Marbod of Rennes's *Naufragium Jonae prophetae* as a source (1975), did not present as strong a case as he might have done, for reading his article one might come away with the impression that Marbod of Rennes was an obscure Church Father. But as Elizabeth Salter later made clear (1988, 12–13, 17, 73–4), some

also been detected in *Patience*, particularly in the dramatic description of the storm (129–68) which the poet added to the biblical matter (Vantuono 1972), but it is more likely that the anonymous poet of *Carmen de Jona propheta* and the *Gawain*-poet went back independently to classical models for the storm-scene. Both Middle English and Latin poets seem to have seized upon a storm at sea as an opportunity to show off their knowledge of the literary conventions which had built up around this theme—a knowledge which, in the case of the *Gawain*-poet, certainly included classical precedents, particularly Virgil (Chapman 1945; Jacobs 1972).

Sir Gawain and the Green Knight contains a similarly conventional passage, which for all its rhetorical fireworks is beautifully adjusted to the plot: the description of the passing seasons (500–33). Influential medieval handbooks on the art of poetry recommended the theme of the passing seasons as an elegant variation on the literary topos of the *descriptio temporis*, and the *Gawain*-poet proved himself in every respect a master of the craft (Pearsall 1955). The description of the fleeting year that lies between Gawain's promise to seek out the Green Knight and its execution sets many familiar motifs to work. We find in it, for instance, the conflict between summer and winter, which are often personified in Latin poetry as two quarrelling opponents, and which in *Gawain* literally fight for supremacy: 'þenne þe weder of the worlde wyth wynter hit þrepez' (504). The *Gawain*-poet also mobilizes the old associations between the passing of natural time and human mutability and death, sharpening our awareness of time as something that is *running out* for the protagonist. And 'running' here is to be taken literally, for that is exactly what the year does in *Gawain*:

> A ȝere ȝernes ful ȝerne, and ȝeldeȝ neuer lyke,
> Þe forme to þe fynisment foldez ful selden.
>
> (498–9)

(A year runs by very eagerly, and never yields the same, the beginning corresponds only rarely with the end.)

Once more the poet's ingenious word-play on 'ȝere' (year) and 'ȝerneȝ' (from Old English *ge-irnan* > by metathesis *ge-rinnan*, 'run') shows the

---

of the poems by this humanistic bishop circulated at the court of Henry I of England, and were translated into Middle English; all the more reason to accept Salter's judgement that 'the poet of *Patience* used the alliterative Latin of Marbod of Rennes's *Naufragium Jonae prophetae* ... as part of his source material' (320, n.2). In a future article I hope to present some further evidence that Marbod of Rennes's poem *Naufragium Jonae prophetae* was read and admired in England and on the continent.

mind of someone who is momentarily thinking in Latin, where the pun probably has its roots (Silverstein 1964). In Latin the courses of the seasons were called *curricula*, and the year *curriculum* because, as the Latin encyclopedists pointed out, the seasons and the sun run (*currunt*). It would seem impossible to render into English this etymological pun whereby the act of 'running' (*currere*) comes to define the very nature of a year (*curriculum*), but the *Gawain*-poet manages: a 'ȝere ȝemes'.[8]

That the *Gawain*-poet was indeed thinking of the Latin is suggested by the next line: 'þe forme to þe fynisment foldez ful selden'. Again the line seems utterly original to the alliterative poem, for the propositional content that beginnings do not correspond with endings is neatly reinforced by the formal operations of alliteration, where sounds (as in *forme* and *fy*nisment) always correspond at the beginning but never at the end. But the *Gawain*-poet probably remembered this maxim from Cato's *Distichs* (Silverstein 1964), which he and other educated Englishmen would have read at school, where it was used for teaching Latin:

> Cum fueris felix, quae sunt adversa caveto:
> non eodem *cursu* respondent ultima primis.
> (Cato's *Distichs*, I, 18)[9]

(If you have been fortunate, watch out for adversity: the beginning and the end do not follow the same course.)

Note how in the Latin a cognate of *currere* reappears in the word *cursu*, a fact which might explain why Cato's distich came to the *Gawain*-poet's mind. One can rest assured that an appreciation of *Gawain* in no way depends on knowing all of this; however, quite apart from establishing the poet's Latinity, it does lead one to marvel at how strongly the *Gawain*-poet's equivalent to Cato's distich and the pun on *curricula* have come into their own, how fully independent they have become of the Latin ideas that first inspired them.

In *Cleanness*, the poet's consciousness of textual precedent comes across in his expansive treatment of the Flood, a theme which, like that of the passing seasons, had become a recognized topos for literary elaboration. Here, too, the *Gawain*-poet worked in an established Latin tradition, formed by Ovid's legend of Deucalion's Flood in the *Metamorphoses* as well as Avitus of Vienne's *De diluvio mundi*, the closest

---

8. Cf. l. 529: 'þus ȝirnez þe ȝere in ȝisterdayez mony'.
9. Cato's *Distichs*, in *Minor Latin Poets*, Loeb Classical Library, eds J. Wight Duff and Arnold M. Duff (Cambridge, Mass.: Harvard University Press, 1934).

analogue to the *Gawain*-poet's famous Flood description that I know of (Putter forthcoming). A final Latin poem which may have been known to the *Gawain*-poet is the anonymous *Carmen de Sodoma* (also attributed to Tertullian), which has one or two lines strikingly similar to *Cleanness*, though not enough to clinch the case for the *Gawain*-poet's direct use of it (Vantuono 1984, I, 383–5). It is worth noting that the influence of exegetical works is minimal: the *Gawain*-poet fortunately did not see his role as being that of a biblical commentator. When in *Cleanness* and *Patience* he took the Bible as his main source, he remained first and foremost a story-teller and a poet. Since, in that capacity, the *Gawain*-poet had a distinguished line of biblical poets behind him—stretching back through the English compiler of the *Cursor Mundi* to the early Christian epic poets—it should not surprise us that the *Gawain*-poet was occasionally conscious of his own belatedness, and sometimes glanced back to his literary precursors.

It may be possible to detect some more general intellectual influences on the *Gawain*-poet's work that imply a clerical training. Jill Mann (1986) has argued that the poet was *au fait* with Aristotelian economic theory and, certainly, from the perspective of this theory, the Exchanges of Winnings look like playful thought experiments about value and exchange. The *Gawain*-poet also knew a certain amount of legal jargon (Blanch and Wasserman 1984). An interesting example of this is the Green Knight's reassurance that he has not come 'in fere in fe3tyng wyse' (*Gawain*, 267), which probably derives from the Anglo-Norman 'a fuer de guerre' (with violent intent), a technical legal term used in chancery documents of the time (Legge 1936). But a smattering of law does not necessarily make our poet a trained lawyer or a chancery clerk. In the extraordinarily litigious age of the *Gawain*-poet, men and women of the world could scarcely avoid coming into contact with the courts. By comparison with his contemporaries Chaucer and Langland, the *Gawain*-poet's knowledge of the law hardly stands out.

THE POET'S WAY OF READING

The non-specialist nature of the poet's knowledge is worth emphasizing, because the survey of sources and analogues, and my suggestion that he was a cleric, may have created the false impression that the *Gawain*-poet was an especially bookish or pious poet. He was neither of these two.

As regards the reading that he presumed in his audience, he is if anything more accessible than Chaucer or Langland. The *Roman de la Rose* is the only non-biblical work which the poet mentions in his entire oeuvre and, significantly, this work was so well known that far from excluding anyone in his audience, it must have brought everyone together on the field of common knowledge. Moreover, the *Gawain*-poet was not a slave to his sources; quite the contrary, he did with the *Roman de la Rose* what he did with that handful of sources which he did not care to name: he swallowed them up, absorbed them, and usually left only the slightest trace of his own indebtedness.

In the chapters on the poet's individual works, I shall have more to say about the *Gawain*-poet's independent way with his sources, but for the purposes of this general chapter we can stick with the example of the *Roman de la Rose*, which the poet used in all his poems—and I mean 'used' here in the strong sense of the word. Thus the *Roman de la Rose*, a work which boasts one of the most obscene endings of world literature, is transformed by the poet into the 'clene Rose' (1057) of *Cleanness*.[10] The *Rose* is honoured with this epithet because the poet gives the Friend's advice in the *Roman* a very different application. In the *Roman de la Rose*, the Friend convinces the Lover that the best way to ingratiate himself with his lady is to imitate her ways; in precisely this way, adds the *Gawain*-poet, the Christian should seek to make himself pleasing to Christ:

If þou wyl dele drwrye wyth dryȝtyn þenne,
And lelly louy þy lorde and his leef worþe,
Þenne confourme þe to Kryst ...

(1065–7)

(Thus, if you want to have love-dealings with God, and faithfully love your lord and wish to become his lover, then conform yourself to Christ ...)

The *Gawain*-poet's appropriation of the *Roman de la Rose* seems wildly eccentric, but in the context of *Cleanness* it works. To see why, it may not be enough to note that the poet followed a typically medieval line of interpretation of the *Rose*, which 'cleansed' the work by moralizing it. For I suspect that, unlike many embarrassed commentators, the *Gawain*-poet approved of the *Roman de la Rose* at a basic level. Only slightly earlier in *Cleanness*, the poet may be found extolling the joys of

10. The exact source passage from the *Roman de la Rose* and the *Gawain*-poet's use of it in *Cleanness* have recently been discussed by Twomey (1994).

heterosexual intercourse, and damning any other variety. The *Roman de la Rose* thus also ranks as 'clean' in the main sense which the poet gives to the word: the love and sex it portrays are between a man and a woman, as opposed to what the poet condemns as 'unclean' love, such as that practised by the Sodomites.

While in *Cleanness* the *Roman de la Rose* is pressed into the service of morality and the promotion of sexual 'cleanness', the same advice by the Friend becomes a source of light comedy in *Patience*, where the poet personifies the eight beatitudes as eight sparkling ladies:

> These arn þe happes alle aȝt that vus bihiȝt weren,
> If we þyse ladyes wolde lof in lyknyng of þewes:
> Dame Pouert, dame Pitee, dame Penaunce þe þrydde,
> Dame Mekenesse, dame Mercy and miry Clannesse,
>
> And þenne dame Pes and Pacyence put in þer-after ...
> (29–33)[11]

(These are all the eight blessings that were promised to us, if we would court these ladies by copying their manners: lady Poverty, lady Pity, lady Tribulation the third, lady Meekness, lady Mercy, and pleasing Cleanness, and then added to them lady Peace and Patience.)

In other medieval works, readers might have had to brace themselves for a long exposition about how precisely these virtues should be cultivated. In *Patience*, however, the personification of the virtues as ladies enables the poet to rephrase this question in a more interesting and lighter vein: how does a man go about courting a woman? At this point the Friend's advice from the *Roman* sneaks in once again: the way to a woman's heart lies in imitating her ways: 'if we þyse ladyes wolde lof *in lyknyng of þewes*'.

Comparing this with the poet's very different use of the same idea in *Cleanness*, one gets a sense of how infinitely adaptable the *Roman de la Rose* was for the *Gawain*-poet. A brief list of the poet's transformations of other bits from the *Rose* in *Pearl* and *Gawain* completes and confirms the picture. Thus the description of the celestial woodland in *Pearl* draws on the Garden of Love in the *Rose* (see pp. 154–6 below); the phrases that express the unsurpassable beauty of the Pearl-maiden come from Jean de Meun's portrait of the goddess Nature (Pilch 1964); the description of Arthur in *Gawain* is reminiscent of that of Youth in the *Roman de la Rose*

---

11. Anderson (1969) draws attention to the use of the *Roman de la Rose* in this passage in his editorial note to line 30.

(Putter 1995, 75). Thus several snippets from the *Rose* usefully render their services to the poet, and the best sign of their subordination to the poet's design is that these services tend to look unlikely only when one examines their original function in the text from which the poet culled them.

The source-materials of the *Gawain*-poet do not stick out as foreign elements in the poet's text, as learned references or allusions. They are fully integrated into the *Gawain*-poet's text, so that quite often they are no longer recognizable as borrowings at all. The unusual degree of uncertainty about whether some texts were sources for the *Gawain*-poet's works or not may be due precisely to this ability of the poet to change whatever he touches.

THE POET IN THE TEXT: A HUMBLE CLERIC

The *Gawain*-poet's complete assimilation of his sources may make his works a difficult terrain for source-hunters, but it also recommends him to the general reader, who need not be afraid of stumbling over allusions to classical or medieval writers and works which he or she is presumed to know. This may in turn reveal something about the kind of audience which the *Gawain*-poet had in mind. On the evidence of his poems, this audience need not have been very learned or widely read. Not all critics would accept this. Ordelle Hill (1968), for example, believes that *Pearl* and *Patience* were meant for a 'select group' of priests and preachers, and written by someone from within the ranks of this clerical élite. My own view of the poet is very different, and I would like to advocate it by looking briefly at the way the poet presents himself and his audience in his own text.

First, however, a fact about the clerical estate that has important implications for what a clerical background might imply about the *Gawain*-poet. The clerical estate was an extremely diverse group of people who, in theory, had no more in common with each other than a basic education, and in practice not even that.[12] The class consisted on the one hand of 'regular clerics', who lived a cloistered life (monks) or had taken a vow of poverty (friars), and on the other hand of secular clerics, a calling in which men could progress through several orders: first

---

12. My discussion of the clerical estate draws on Keen (1990, 240–70).

the minor orders and then the major orders, which in the West culmin-
ated in the orders of deacon and priest. Only clerics of the rank of
deacon and above were allowed to preach, and only priests could celebrate the mass. While regular clerics were typically in priests' orders,
many secular clerics never took major orders at all: one strong disincen-
tive for doing so was that it entailed a vow of celibacy. Moreover, not all
secular clerics were churchmen engaged in liturgical or pastoral work.
The skills that went with a formal education made clerics obvious candi-
dates for secretarial and administrative jobs, whether it was in the
employment of the Crown, or in the service of an important nobleman
or prelate.

This simplified outline makes it painfully clear that my proposition
that the *Gawain*-poet was a cleric does not actually say very much. We
need to know what *kind* of cleric the *Gawain*-poet was. It seems to me
that the weightiest argument against Hill's suggestion that he was a
preacher or priest (i.e. a deacon or higher) is that the *Gawain*-poet consistently describes himself in his works not as *dispensing* sermons or the
eucharist in the way a priest might, but as being on the *receiving* end of
priests and preachers. Thus in *Patience* the poet represents himself as the
average church-goer, who hears his sermons from the pulpit:

I herde on a halyday, at a hyȝe masse,
How Mathew melede þat his mayster his meyny con teche ...   (9–10)

(I heard on a holy day, at high mass, how Matthew spoke about his master's
teachings to his following ...)

In *Pearl*, too, he imagines himself, interestingly, as someone receiving
rather than administering the eucharist:

And syþen to God I hit bytaȝte
In Krysteȝ dere blessyng and myn,
Þat in þe forme of bred and wyn
Þe preste vus scheweȝ vch a daye.   (1207–10)

(And then I committed it to God, with my blessing and the blessing of
Christ, who is shown to us by the priest every day in the form of bread and
wine.)

In this 'vus' in the final line of the passage, the poet and his imagined
audience merge without distinction to form the congregation, the
ordinary people that are at the other side of the altar from the 'preste'
who consecrates the host.

Cleanness is no exception to my case, and it seems to me that the whole character of the poem militates against the view that it was intended for (or composed by someone from) a 'select' clerical group. For the most notable feature of *Cleanness*—which will be taken up in detail in my chapter on the poem—is that it addresses moral issues as if they were simply matters of good or bad taste. The poet, that is, does not combat what he sees as vices with church doctrine or with citations from 'authorities'; his main strategy, and one which he is dangerously good at, is to present these vices in intensely physical terms, as behaviour that is 'dirty' or 'filthy', and by doing so to elicit from his audience a knee-jerk reaction against them. Nothing could therefore be further from the mark than calling *Cleanness* a theologians' text. Far from seeking to convince through sustained argument, the poet addresses or projects what Stanley Fish (1984) memorably calls a '*community of the same*'; the poet speaks, or pretends to speak, only for 'common sense'; he speaks *for* rather than *at* his audience, who, to put it crudely, are simply expected to share the poet's basic standards of cleanliness and personal hygiene.

In this light, the poet's reference in *Cleanness* to 'hyʒe clerkes' makes perfect sense:

> Bot I haue herkned and herde of mony *hyʒe clerkeʒ*,
> And als in resouneʒ of ryʒt red hit myseluen,
> Þat þat ilk proper prynce þat paradys weldeʒ
> Is displesed at vch a poynt þat plyes to scaþe ...   (193–6)

> (But I have learnt and heard from many scholars, and have also read it myself in true writings, that the excellent prince who rules paradise is displesed by anything which tends to harm ...)

While the poet goes so far as to represent himself consulting church doctrine ('I ... red hit myseluen'), he also draws an implicit distinction between 'hyʒe clerkeʒ' and an insignificant person like himself, between the clerical élite that has the authority to tell him what he should believe, and the run-of-the-mill cleric with enough reading to discover for himself that the 'hyʒe clerkeʒ' were right.

In *Sir Gawain and the Green Knight*, finally, the poet has nothing significant to say about himself at all. All I would remark about *Gawain* is that it is as secular as one could reasonably wish from a cleric. True, there is a great deal of church-going, but in the joyful world of *Sir Gawain and the Green Knight* dancing, hearing mass, and dining in grand style follow on from one another so quickly that one never gets the sense that these activities are discontinuous, or the sense that it is improper that the celebration of court-life should begin in the hall and end in the chapel. After his ordeal is over, Gawain might possibly be more solemn at mass than he was before, but on the whole religious observances in *Gawain* do not stand as a reproach to good living but are meant to enrich it.

The *Gawain*-poet, then, does not speak as a priest, or as a preacher; he does not really speak as a cleric at all. In his poems he is someone who is among the congregation listening to a sermon; someone who joins 'vus' in the nave to watch the priest elevate the host; who is enlightened by the wisdom of 'hy3e clerke3'; and who in *Gawain* enthuses about the joys of life at court. He is, in other words, like the 'intelligent layman' of the fourteenth century. A cleric in minor orders, employed in some administrative capacity, would fit the bill nicely.

It might be objected at this point that the author inside the poem may be dissimilar from the one outside it, and that to confuse the two is tantamount to committing the 'autobiographical fallacy'. Who knows, the *Gawain*-poet might have been an important cleric after all, only pretending for the purposes of his fiction to be a humble one. The principle of the autobiographical fallacy can open any number of doors, but, lacking any corroborating life records for our poet, they only lead to idle speculation. Moreover, the public identity of any poet, both the way he is and the way he is known by others, inevitably puts constraints on the extent to which he can plausibly and effectively reinvent himself, especially in the medieval period. A degree of misfit between the poet as he represented himself and as he really was could have been part of the entertainment— think, for example, of Chaucer's fictionalization of himself as a round and dull-witted bibliophile—but only if the audience was capable of recognizing the poet's self-presentation as an *approximation* of the truth. For these reasons it does not seem useful to cling to an image of the *Gawain*-poet that is irreconcilable with the worldly and humble cleric that appears in his fictions.

THE POET IN THE TEXT: A COURT-POET

The internal evidence which I have been relying on can be pressed further still: in all of his poems the voice of the poet seems to come from the inside of an aristocratic household. As has often been remarked, *Sir Gawain and the Green Knight* shows the most intimate knowledge of the court and its pastimes: the feast, the hunt, or the indoor games. It is quite possible that the scene with which the story of *Gawain* opens, that of a court at Christmas waiting to be entertained, was the kind of occasion for which the *Gawain*-poet wrote his Arthurian romance, supplying, as it were, the demand for a tale of adventure which in the poem itself sets the adventures going. *Sir Gawain and the Green Knight* may well have been recited to an audience similarly assembled in the hall for a seasonal celebration. In his poem the *Gawain*-poet at any rate speaks as a public entertainer, calling on his audience for good-will and attention:

> If ȝe wyl lysten þis laye bot on littel quile,
> I schal telle hit as-tit, as I in toun herde ...
>
> (30–1)

> (If you will listen to this lay for a little while, I shall tell it promptly, as I heard it told ...)

One can readily see that formulas of this kind could have been intended for a reading audience as well; their literary effect is to create a sense of occasion, to which even a solitary reader can be susceptible. And readers certainly seem to be catered for by the surviving manuscript. In Cotton Nero A.x. the text of all four poems is illustrated with twelve manuscript illuminations, and carefully laid out by means of coloured initial capitals, implying an audience that met the text with the eye as well as the ear. However the division of *Gawain* into fitts of about equal length, marked in the manuscript by large capital letters, also indicates that the text is organized so as to make a public recitation in several instalments at least a possibility (Turville-Petre 1977, 39).

The fact the *Gawain*-poet was at home in the court is shown by far more than his convincing portrayals of life at a noble household in *Gawain* and *Cleanness*. For even when the scene of action is nowhere near a court, the *Gawain*-poet cannot actually get away from it: if it is not the place where the action is, it is still the vantage point which the poet looks out from. Thus the forest in *Gawain* is defined, for both good and bad, as the opposite of the court, as an anti-court, where, for instance, the knight does *not* feast:

> Oft leudlez alone he lengez on nyȝtez
> Þer he fonde noȝt hym before þe fare þat he lyked.
>
> (693–4)

> (Often he spends his nights there completely alone, without finding the food that he liked.)

In *Cleanness*, too, the court forms the poet's frame of reference, and it is clearly within this frame that the poet conceives of moral issues and characters. No one who knows the New Testament could call Christ a courtier, but *Cleanness* portrays him as setting the highest standards of courtliness:

> And 3if clanly he þenne com, ful cortays þerafter,
> Þat alle þat longed to luþer ful lodly he hated;
> By nobleye of his norture he nolde neuer towche
> O3t þat wat3 vngoderly oþer ordure wat3 inne.
>
> (1089–92)

(And just as he came into the world immaculate, he was very courteous thereafter, so that he hated everything vile with great loathing. Because of the nobility of his upbringing he would never touch anything that was bad or inwardly filthy.)

Christ's 'courtesy' is of course not of the ordinary kind, as the poet frequently reminds us. Thus Christ can break his bread in two clean pieces without needing expensive cutlery, 'toles of Tolowse' (1108). But the world of understanding that Christ transcends is, as this example suggests, precisely the world of the court, the place where people *do* carve with imported knives.

The obvious explanation of why the *Gawain*-poet's vocabulary falls back so often on cognates of 'court' when he talks about God or about right and wrong is that he identified himself with an audience for whom these words instantly evoked a familiar *locus* of shared experience and values, a place from which they could orientate themselves when forced out into unfamiliar territory. In *Pearl* this unfamiliar territory is heaven, and again the court functions as the *Gawain*-poet's home ground, the place which is always assumed to be present in the audience's mind as a point of contrast or comparison. Like many other works, *Pearl* likens heaven to a court but, unusually, the implications of this metaphor are pursued so insistently that the court becomes almost an instrument of thought, the possibilities and limitations of which define quite precisely what can and cannot be understood about heaven. Below is an example:

> 'The *court* of þe kyngdom of God alyue
> Hat3 a property in hytself beyng:
> Alle þat may þerinne aryue
> Of alle þe reme is quen oþer kyng,
> And neuer oþer 3et schal depryue,
> Bot vchon fayn of oþere3 hafyng … '
>
> (445–50)

('The court of God's kingdom has this inherent quality: all those who enter
in it are queens or kings of the whole realm, and yet no one will deprive
another, but everyone will be glad with what the other has ... ')

As in *Cleanness*, the poet invites his audience to think about the unfamiliar by using the court both as a place of similitude and dissimilitude: like
heaven, the court is the place to be, but whereas at the king's court it is
each man for himself, in the court of heaven all are kings and queens,
each pleased with the favour found by the others. In an important essay
on the *Gawain*-poet, Derek Brewer observed that the words 'court',
'cortaysye', and 'cortays' occur so often in the works of the *Gawain*-poet
that they could be considered as the *Gawain*-poet's personal signature
(Brewer 1966). The significance of this kind of vocabulary, however,
goes beyond the level of style. It is not a literary mannerism: it is an
idiom that comes naturally to the poet, and which he uses (and expects
his audience to use) as a conceptual base camp from which understanding departs and to which it always returns.

Evidently, the *Gawain*-poet knew the court and spoke its language,
and it would seem reasonable to conclude that he was attached to and
writing for a nobleman's household. This is not to say that the *Gawain*-
poet's works were written for an exclusive aristocratic circle. The 'you'
which the *Gawain*-poet addresses is a remarkably open-ended group of
listeners or readers, whose precise social status the poet nowhere specifies or prescribes. The different kinds of sociolects that intermingle in his
work suggest that the poet's social appeal could have been as broad then
as it is today: *Sir Gawain and the Green Knight* may be about knights and
ladies, but some of its vocabulary is legal and mercantile; *Patience* is
famous for a passage full of nautical jargon; *Pearl* takes us to the court in
heaven but equally to the world of the craftsman, the jeweller in search
of his pearl; *Cleanness* opens with a brief exhortation on the state of
priests. But this social diversity was not alien to a sizeable medieval
household, which, like the poet's works, brought people from many different backgrounds together: craftsmen who fashioned the luxury goods;
lawyers retained for professional advice; priests and chapel clerks for religious service; bureaucrats and officials who acted as secretaries and
administrators, and so on. All these groups formed part of the court in its
wider sense.

No internal evidence can help us recover in whose service or in what
capacity the *Gawain*-poet was employed, but there is at least some
indirect evidence for the presence of a lord and patron in the *Gawain*-
poet's life. One small clue is the poet's reference in the prologue of

Patience to 'my liege lord', a term used by household retainers for their personal lord, and employed in this strict sense in the *Gawain*-poet's other works (*Gawain*, 545; *Cleanness*, 94, 1368). The passage in which this reference is made is not without its problems, and should be read in its context:

> ȝif me be dyȝt a destyne due to haue,
> What dowes me þe dedayn oþer dispit make?
> Oþer ȝif my *lege lorde* lyst on lyue me to bidde
> Oþer to ryde oþer to renne to Rome in his ernde,
>
> What grayþed me þe grychchyng bot grame more seche?
> Much ȝif he ne me made, maugref my chekes,
> And þenne þrat most I þole and vnþonk to mede,
> Þe had bowed to his bode, bongre my hyure.
>
> Did not Jonah in Jude suche jape sum-whyle?
> To sette hym to sewrte, vnsounde he hym feches.
>
> (49–58)

(If an appointed task were ordained for me, what good would it do me to be indignant or defiant? Or if it pleased my liege lord to command me to ride or run to Rome on his errand, what would grumbling do but invite more trouble? I would be lucky if he did not force me to go, despite my objections, receiving threats and displeasure as my reward, when having done his bidding I might have earned his thanks. Did not Jonah do such a foolish deed once? In an attempt to get himself to safety, he brought distress upon himself.)[13]

The difficulty with the passage is that the impulse behind the poet's personal reflections is not straightforwardly autobiographical. The story which the *Gawain*-poet is about to tell is that of the rebellious prophet Jonah, who refuses God's order to travel to Nineveh but fetches up there despite his protests. The pragmatic moral which the poet draws from the story is that servants had better do as they are told, and the poet's alleged employment in the service of a lord makes him see the wisdom of that moral sharply. Like Jonah, he might be asked to go to Rome on his lord's mission and, like Jonah, he would sooner or later discover that there is no point in grumbling.

The personal aside thus takes the form of a hypothesis, and one could argue that the poet invented the entire situation to illustrate the point of the Book of Jonah. But two objections to this can be put forward. The

---

13. In my translation I follow Burrow (1989), who reads 'bongre' as a noun meaning 'gratitude' rather than a preposition 'in accordance with'.

first is that not *all* the personal information contained in the poet's imagined situation—'If my liege lord were to order me to go to Rome'—is
presented as hypothetical: the big *if* pertains to the question of whether
or not the poet's lord will give his order, not to the question of whether
the poet has a lord or not. His existence in the life of the poet is stated as
a fact rather than a possibility. The second objection is that, even when
the scenario of being sent to Rome was invented for the sake of the
argument, this scenario must have been *credible* for the argument to
work. No doubt, the poet's contemporary audience would have
regarded it as such. Rome was where the pope traditionally had his
abode, and thus Rome is where many English clerics were sent to secure
papal permission for their lord's plans to, for instance, appoint a servant
to an ecclesiastical benefice, or marry off a son or daughter to a distant or
not so distant cousin. 'Rome-running' was so common in later-medieval
England that it acquired proverbial status as an odious task. This has
again persuaded some readers that the poet's hypothesis is too conventional to be of autobiographical value, but let us not put the cart before
the horse. The reason why many Middle English documents speak of
going to Rome as a dangerous undertaking is not that this was conven-
tionally said, but that this was habitually experienced. The correspondence
of an early-fifteenth-century English clerk at the papal curia, William
Swan, frequently mentions the 'dangerous obstacles and fearful perils'
faced by the hundreds of English clerics who made the journey to or
from Rome,[14] and his letters remind us that going to Rome was not for
most people a figure of speech but a fact of life. When, therefore, the
Gawain-poet speculates that he might be dispatched to Rome, he is not
speaking rhetorically: he is talking about something that could *plausibly*
happen to him. This plausibility ensures the success of the poet's attempt
to show the relevance of the Bible to his own mundane circumstances.
His lord's order to go to Rome is all it would take to turn the poet into a
potential Jonah, and the realism of this prospect explains why the poet
should find the story of Jonah so instructive.[15]

---

14. Quoted from Swan's correspondence, edited and discussed in Jacob (1968), an
    illuminating study of English missions to and from Rome. Andrew (1982) concen-
    trates on the phrase 'Rome-running' in Middle English literature.
15. For the record, let me emphasize again that the servant who has a 'liege lord', and
    who might plausibly be asked to 'renne to Rome in his ernde' is the poet inside his
    text. But while this poet is probably slightly stylized, he remains the poet that he
    wished his audience to imagine and that he thought his intended audience could
    accept without requiring too great a suspension of disbelief.

A patron, probably a nobleman of some means, finally seems to stand behind the manuscript of the *Gawain*-poet's works. The original of this manuscript has not survived, and all that can be known about it must be reconstructed from our single surviving copy Cotton Nero A.x. This manuscript has one unusual feature which I briefly mentioned earlier: it contains a number of large manuscript illuminations. The pictures in Cotton Nero A.x. would have been too amateurish to impress anyone, yet the amazing thing, and the thing that needs explaining, is that they are there at all. They make Cotton Nero A.x. the first illuminated manuscript in Middle English (Lee 1977). There are earlier illuminated manuscripts in French, and slightly later ones of Gower and Chaucer, which can without exception be traced to the circles of the higher aristocracy who could afford the considerable expense involved in the production of illustrated manuscript books. Since the scribal errors show that Cotton Nero A.x. was not the original, it may well be a clumsy copy of an original *de luxe* manuscript with illuminations, either a presentation copy or 'a repertory book commissioned by a magnate of wealth' (Mathew 1968, 117).

DIALECT AND METRE: THE *GAWAIN*-POET'S 'REMOTENESS'

We have come some way towards pinning down the elusive *Gawain*-poet: his reading shows a clerical background; his outlook and self-portrait suggest that he was a minor cleric, in the service of a 'lege lorde', for whose household some of the poems of Cotton Nero A.x. may well have been written. But in a way the real problem only begins here: the poet's dialect might encourage us to think of an aristocratic household in or around Cheshire, but historical research tells us we would be looking in the wrong place:

> Sparsely populated and economically under-developed, the Northwest could boast no important seignorial households and few large monastic establishments, nor a sizeable commercial sector to stimulate large-scale demesne farming.
>
> (Bennett 1983, 68)

Noble families did have some holdings in the area, but these were considered 'too poor and remote' to serve as residences (Bennett 1983, 75). For a courtly audience, which the *Gawain*-poet's works imply, it is necessary to look elsewhere.

These facts have not sufficiently deterred literary historians; remoteness has its own romantic appeal, and the idea of an entrenched provincial household has attracted scholars who find the characteristics of regionalism and primitivism in the *Gawain*-poet's own works: in his 'archaic' dialect, and in the choice of alliteration over rhyme. Historical evidence from the *Gawain*-poet's own day and age will show that alliterative poetry in regional dialects could find appreciative audiences all over England, but before turning to this evidence, it is worth asking why the impression of remoteness given by the *Gawain*-poet has lasted for modern readers. One answer is that, as an *impression*, it rings true, since the course of linguistic and literary history from the fifteenth century up to the rediscovery of the *Gawain*-poet has indeed managed to push his works into cultural isolation. The mistake lies in assuming that this isolation was an internal necessity, that, from the very beginning, the poet's dialect and the alliterative metre did not have the possibilities which future developments of the English language and its literature were to close off.

Since these developments are part of our history, our first impressions of the *Gawain*-poet's language and style are not innocent: the English most of us speak and write is descended from the London dialect that Chaucer spoke, which established itself as the 'official' form of English in the middle of the fifteenth century.[16] Judged by that linguistic standard, the *Gawain*-poet's dialect seems marginal compared with Chaucer's; but in the fourteenth century, no standard English had as yet emerged, and the degree of linguistic tolerance, especially in the city of London, was high. This is reflected in the range of dialects found in single manuscript collections, which until the second quarter of the fifteenth century happily combine texts in southern or east Midland dialects with works from the *Gawain*-poet's native area, without apparently discriminating against Cheshire dialects (Lawton 1989).

The linguistic development of English is not alone in giving us the impression that the *Gawain*-poet is more remote than his contemporary Chaucer. As the 'father of English poetry', Chaucer stands at the beginning of a literary tradition which has profoundly affected our view of what kind of verse or metre is natural and mainstream. That view, if I can generalize, is that lines of poetry first *rhyme* at the end, and secondly have a regular number of syllables with a regular stress pattern. The best-known member of this family of 'syllabic-accentual verse' (so called

---

16. On the rise of 'standard' English see Fisher (1977).

because it depends both on the number of syllables and on the pattern of accents or stresses) is the iambic pentameter, which Chaucer can be said to have discovered for English poetry. In *Troilus and Criseyde*, for example, the lines of verse do not only have a set number of syllables (ten; or eleven in the case of feminine rhyme) but also an alternating stress pattern. Thus the following end-rhymed lines from *Troilus* can be broken down into rhythmic units with the same stress pattern: one unstressed syllable followed by a stressed one:

> And whan that he bythought on that folie,
> A thousand fold his wo gan multiplie.
>
> (I, 545–6)

Chaucer's innovative choice of metre today seems self-explanatory because the rhymed iambic pentameter established itself as the standard medium of English poetry (Woods 1985). While this development retroactively turned Chaucer into our 'father', it has also had the unfortunate consequence of making alliterative metre, which is a very different metrical system, seem strange. The distinct principles on which alliterative metre operates can be illustrated with a stanza from *Patience*:

> 'Éwrus and Áquiloun þat on éste síttes,
> Blówes bóþe at my bóde vpon bló wátteres.'
> Þenne watȝ no tóm þer bytwéne his tále and her déde,
> So báyn wer þay bóþe two his bóne for-to wýrk.
>
> (133–6)

('Eurus and Aquilon, who are in the east, blow on the blue waters at my commandment, both of you.' Then there was no delay between his speech and their action, so eager were they to do his request.)

Unlike Chaucerian verse, the alliterative lines have no end-rhyme. The formal feature that makes them lines of poetry rather than prose is alliteration, the repetition of the same sound at the beginning of stressed syllables. In the quotation the accents show where the stress (or accent) falls. As the example illustrates, vowels can alliterate with any other vowel (or with an *h*): 'Ewrus and Aquilon þat on est sittes'. Consonants alliterate only with identical consonants, as in the final line of the passage: 'So *b*ayn wer þay *b*oþe two his *b*one for-to wyrk'. As the difference in length between lines 133 and 135 highlights, the total number of syllables per line can vary substantially; only the number of stressed syllables is regular: there are *four* in each line, of which only the first three normally alliterate. Occasionally a line has four alliterating syllables, as in line 134: '*Blowes* b*oþe* at my b*ode* vpon b*lo* watteres'. Because the metre is accentual (dependent on stress) and the lines vary in the number and distribution of unstressed syllables, the alliterative line cannot be read according to the conventions of syllabic pairing. The way to approach it is to listen for the *stressed* syllables only, and to determine which of these alliterate. Using the conventional symbols of *a* for an alliterating stressed syllable and *x* for any syllable that is stressed but does not alliterate, a formal analysis of the four lines from *Patience* would give us:

aaax
aaaax
aaax
aaax

The notation could be further refined (see Duggan 1986), but the patterns 'aaax' and 'aaaax' sum up the elementary 'laws' of alliterative metre, as the poet practised it in *Patience, Cleanness,* and *Gawain*.[17] Of course, the *Gawain*-poet did so without scanning his verse as we have just done, but, lacking his instinct, we can benefit from the way a formal analysis brings out the acoustic and rhythmic regularities of alliterative metre, which are easily missed by readers used to rhyme and syllabic verse.

Alliterative metre as I have described it had a long and distinguished history.[18] It was the metre of Old English poetry. It survived into the twelfth and thirteenth centuries in a looser form, and was often used in conjunction with rhyme. Alliterative metre re-established itself firmly as a popular medium for longer narratives (e.g. *William of Palerne*) and political and satirical verse (e.g. *Winner and Waster*) in the middle of the fourteenth century. This period heralds the beginning of the alliterative revival, to which the works by the *Gawain*-poet belong. After the first decades of the fifteenth century, alliterative poetry was edged out by accentual-syllabic rhymed verse, although it lingered on in some isolated pockets in the north, and held its own in Scotland. By the sixteenth century it had become possible to disregard alliterative verse altogether. George Gascoine, an early 'literary theorist', simply defined poetry as

---

17. Largely written in unrhymed alliterative lines, *Gawain* also uses rhyme in the 'bob and wheel', the five short lines at the end of each stanza. *Pearl* is not written in alliterative metre: its main characteristics are a strict rhyme scheme and stanza form, sometimes combined with heavy alliteration (see below pp. 147–8).
18. Turville-Petre (1977) describes this history in detail.

rhymed verse in feet (iambic whenever possible), the discovery of which he credited to his 'father' Chaucer. Gascoine also quotes Chaucer's comic allusion to alliterative poetry in the *Parson's Prologue*—'I am a Southren man, / I kan not geeste "rum, ram, ruf," by lettre' (42–4)—but the strange context in which Gascoine uses it implies that he no longer recognized it as a reference to alliterative verse at all:

> It is not enough to roll in pleasant wordes, nor yet to thunder in 'Rym, Ram, Ruff by letter' (quoth my master Chaucer).[19]

The differences between what Chaucer said and what Gascoine thought Chaucer had said are symptomatic of the demise of alliterative poetry. For Chaucer, or his Parson, alliterative verse was a 'northern' thing—and even then, the fact that Chaucer had heard it and occasionally used alliteration in his own poetry, suggests that its influence extended beyond the west Midlands, where the revival of alliterative verse originated. For Gascoine, however, 'rum, ram, ruf' is no longer recognizable as a different type of verse at all: it has become nothing more than a stylistic infelicity, pointless 'thundering'.

Only the establishment of a Chaucerian verse tradition could have made this disregard for alliterative metre possible. However, to imagine the place of fourteenth-century alliterative verse in its proper context, it is necessary to see it in fourteenth-century terms, when alliterative metre may have looked no more unfamiliar than rhyme does today. Talking about Langland, another alliterative poet whose poetry is far from provincial, Anne Middleton exposes the blind spot inherent in the assumption that alliteration was *a priori* the outsider's choice:

> It is reasonable to suppose that in the 1360s, when Langland's fundamental choice of mode and verse form was made, and no Chaucer or Gower yet existed on the literary scene, the alliterative long line might well have seemed as likely as any other in English use for sustained narration to command a wide readership …
>
> (Middleton 1982, 119)[20]

---

19. George Gascoine, 'Certain Notes of Instruction Concerning the Making of Verse', in *Elizabethan Critical Essays*, 2 vols (Oxford: Oxford University Press, 1904), 47.
20. The 1360s is the date usually given for the A-text of *Piers Plowman*, which has traditionally been dated earlier than the B-text (probably composed in the late 1370s). However, as Jill Mann (1994a) has argued, the B-text may well be the first version of *Piers Plowman* we have. While this does not alter Middleton's basic point, it means that the situation she sketches for alliterative verse need not be tied to the 1360s.

Just as the London dialect had not yet established itself as the linguistic standard, accentual-syllabic verse had not yet emerged as the literary one. Octosyllabic couplets or tail-rhyme were established alternatives to alliteration, but they were nothing more than that. When the *Gawain*-poet's works were written, around 1390, Chaucer had only just abandoned the octosyllabic couplet in favour of something close to an iambic pentameter, and only a prophet could have predicted that, a century later, the alternative alliterative line was to look decidedly *passé*.

The increasing isolation of north west alliterative verse from the middle of the fifteenth century onwards deserves more detailed attention than I have given it. My main point here has been to suggest that our sense of the *Gawain*-poet's marginality with respect to Chaucer may at least partly be explained as an effect of history rather than a quality inherent in the work or its author.

A HISTORICAL CONTEXT FOR ALLITERATIVE POETRY FROM THE NORTH WEST MIDLANDS

The fact remains, of course, that the *Gawain*-poet did not, for a long time, achieve a large readership. Possibly his works were known to a few other alliterative poets. Some critics believe that they influenced the alliterative *Wars of Alexander* and the *Awntyrs of Arthur*. The formal demands of alliterative metre, however, tend to force the same words into association in otherwise unrelated poems, and in deciding whether one alliterative poet borrowed from another it is hard to tell whether parallels of phraseology are echoes or simply established collocations. There is one later poem that definitely recycles the story of *Sir Gawain and the Green Knight*, namely the ballad known as *The Green Knight* from the seventeenth-century Percy Folio. Yet one is bound to say that where quantity and, in the case of *The Green Knight*, quality are concerned, the *Gawain*-poet deserved a better literary offspring.

The absence of direct literary affiliations makes it difficult to recover the textual community in which the *Gawain*-poet's works might originally have been read. The problem is compounded by the chance survival of his works in a single manuscript, the earliest history of which remains shrouded in mystery. The poet's dialectal area is Cheshire, but as has been mentioned, no sizeable secular or ecclesiastical household in the area is known to us. Yet despite the dearth of patrons in the north west Midlands, a surprising number of contemporary poems in alliterative metre from this region survive, many in the same dialect as the works by the *Gawain*-poet. These poems provide a meaningful context for the *Gawain*-poet, and I should like to say something about the milieux in which they were read and composed.

Two facts emerge clearly from an investigation into the audience of other alliterative poetry: one is that alliterative poetry often reached audiences outside its dialect area, another that the movements of alliterative poets were not limited to this area either. Manuscript evidence clearly shows that alliterative poetry was a national rather than a local phenomenon in the fourteenth and early fifteenth centuries, and actually enjoyed some popularity in London. *Piers Plowman* is a case in point. Its author Langland hailed from near the south west Midlands—along with Cheshire/Lancashire an epicentre of the alliterative revival. But as Langland tells us in the C-version of *Piers Plowman* (V, 1–5), he had gravitated towards the capital, and ended up living at Cornhill in London. The use of alliterative metre did not inhibit the poem's circulation, and the distribution of the numerous manuscripts shows that Langland possessed a readership well beyond that of his compatriots in the Malvern Hills (Doyle 1982, 90). And William Langland is no isolated case. The poems in the '*Piers Plowman* Tradition'—*Piers the Plowman's Creed, Richard the Redeless, Mum and the Sothsegger*, and the *Crowned King*—are all in alliterative metre, yet their topical social and religious satire shows that their writers had a first-hand knowledge of London.

Piers Plowman and the poems in its tradition suggest that the sounds of alliteration—'rum, ram, ruf'—cannot have been as strange to Chaucer's ears as he pretended. Otherwise, their value as a context for *Sir Gawain and the Green Knight* is limited. Dialectally they belong to the south west Midlands, and as such they are both linguistically and geographically closer to Chaucer than the *Gawain*-poet. However, the literary sources from the *Gawain*-poet's own area, the north west Midlands, point to a similarly diverse audience, and hence to the possibility of poetic patronage from many possible quarters. The *Siege of Jerusalem*, of about the same date and in the same dialect as the works by the *Gawain*-poet, is a good example. Its seven manuscripts, the earliest two from the late fourteenth century, and the last one copied around 1450, tell an interesting story, in that none of them was apparently copied in the north west Midlands where the poet originated.[21] Two manuscripts were copied

---

21. Turville-Petre (1989, 158–9) lists the manuscripts and their provenance. Some additional information about the manuscript and its scribes is given in Doyle (1982).

in—or by scribes from—Yorkshire (Princeton U.L., R.H. Taylor Collection, Petre MS, and the Thornton manuscript, BL Additional 31042); one manuscript was copied in the south east Midlands (BL Cotton Caligula A.ii.); another in Oxfordshire (Bodley Laud misc. 656). The remaining three manuscripts all have links with the book trade in London. Cambridge U.L., Mm.V.14 was copied by the London scribe Richard Frampton in the early fifteenth century. The scribe of the roughly contemporary copy of the *Siege* in Huntington Library HM 128 was from Warwickshire, but the manuscript contains a copy of *Piers Plowman* that was acquired from a commercial scriptorium in London. The Essex scribe of London, Lambeth Palace 491, which also contains the *Siege*, was almost certainly 'a habitual paid copyist, either as a free-lance or a regular employee within the book-trade: if the latter, possibly in London' (Doyle 1982, 94). This same professional scribe was also responsible for Huntington Library HM 114, which contains two more late-fourteenth-century alliterative works from the north west Midlands: The *Pistill of Susan* and the *Awntyrs of Arthur*, both of which must have been deemed marketable by the entrepreneur who employed the scribe. A second copy of the *Awntyrs* (Oxford, Bodleian Library, Douce 324) has the name of a London layman in it, and also originally formed part of a set of booklets such as might be obtained at a London bookshop.

A different late-fourteenth-century romance, *Alexander and Dindimus*, probably composed by a poet who came from somewhere south of Cheshire (Shropshire or Staffordshire), may also have owed its partial survival to its being available in a London scriptorium. The surviving lines of this romance were copied into a richly illuminated copy of the *Roman d'Alexandre*, prepared in France. On its arrival in England an early-fifteenth-century scribe noticed some gaps in the manuscript, which he filled with an extract from the English alliterative poem. The manuscript (Oxford, Bodleian Library, Douce 264) was owned by Lord Rivers in London in 1466 (Turville-Petre 1977, 43).

These works cannot have turned up in London by chance, for a num-ber of alliterative works from the north west Midlands were demonstrably *composed* in the capital, or at least composed with a London audience in mind: *St Erkenwald*, often attributed to the *Gawain*-poet in the past, is set in London, and takes as its subject an episode from the life of St Erkenwald, the first London saint, whose shrine at St Paul's cathedral became a focal point of civic pride following the rebuilding of St Paul's in 1386. Finally, a clerk to the Chapter of St Paul's, probably John Tickhill, scribbled forty-one lines of perfect alliterative verse (with northern features) on the back of an account roll (Kennedy 1987). The wide dissemination of alliterative poetry from the north west, and its popularity in the capital city of London, remind us that the search for a poet's milieu should not be restricted to his native area. This is especially true for the *Gawain*-poet, since the inhabitants of late-fourteenth-century Cheshire, among whom he numbers, showed a remarkable degree of mobility. Cheshire may have been under-developed, but this gave its people all the more reason for looking outside the boundaries of their county for opportunities to participate in national affairs. One such opportunity came in the form of commerce; another was political.

Thanks to its location, some major trade routes converged in Cheshire: merchants and seamen trading with Ireland embarked and disembarked in the port of Chester. For trade with north Wales and Cumbria, Cheshire was a natural stopping point. Salt and cattle from Cheshire were imported as far south as London. Cheshire thus had commercial connections with most parts of the kingdom, a fact which might explain the wide dissemination of its most distinguished export article: alliterative poetry (Salter 1966–7). The traffic between Cheshire and the rest of the kingdom involved people as well as products. Cheshiremen established themselves in all important English towns, and it is possible to document a large-scale migration to London in the decades around 1400 (Bennett 1983, 125).

The enthusiasm with which many Cheshiremen took to London was enhanced by Richard II's choice of Cheshire as the catchment area for the recruitment of a private standing army with which he surrounded himself in the last fifteen years of his reign.[22] Richard II showered privileges on the region, culminating in his elevation of the earldom of Chester to an independent principality within the realm. The extent of Richard's fondness for Cheshire (reciprocated by Cheshire's loyalty to the Crown) may be said to have stood in inverse relation to the king's popularity in Westminster and London. In the 1380s a series of Parliaments attempted to curb the extravagance of Richard II's court, and to rid it of Richard II's personal advisers, who were accused of lining their pockets with tax-money raised for the defence of the realm. In 1386, key figures in Richard II's council were removed, and a group of

---

22. For more historical detail see Davies (1971) and Gillespie (1975).

baronial opponents was appointed to oversee a reform in government. Richard II looked for support further afield. In Lancashire, and in Cheshire especially, he recruited a personal bodyguard of three hundred men, under the command of local Cheshire knights who were soon appointed to high office in Richard II's household. Apart from a permanent bodyguard, Richard recruited a large retinue of soldiers, who could be called upon to add force to the king's word, as they did in 1397, when two thousand Cheshire archers marched to Westminster, to remind Parliament which way it should vote. Richard II's policies, which brought Cheshire into unprecedented political prominence, coincide strikingly with the flowering of alliterative poetry from this region, and it is not unlikely that the same circumstances that thrust the north west Midlands upon the national scene in the drama of Richard II's final years contributed to the confident cosmopolitanism of alliterative poetry from the area, and to its evident vogue in later-fourteenth-century London (Bennett 1979).

This sketch of the historical situation of Cheshire and its poets in the later fourteenth century does not, unfortunately, reduce the number of possible answers to the question of where the *Gawain*-poet may have worked and lived, or who his liege lord might have been. It serves, however, to restore some of the authentic complexity to the picture of the cultural environment in which the *Gawain*-poet moved. An oversimple view of regional society can unduly constrict one's conception of the sophistication and breadth which the *Gawain*-poet's works are capable of attaining. The *Gawain*-poet and his fellow poets from Cheshire were no parochial bards. Even if they had tried, it would have been difficult for them to remain unaffected by the political upheavals in which their principality was plunged at the close of the fourteenth century, or to remain insulated from the traffic in people and products that bound the north west Midlands to the rest of England. If the *Gawain*-poet was at all like other Cheshiremen and poets of his time and kind, he would have travelled; he could have counted on an audience for his work outside his native area; and he may even have settled in London, where the concentration of Cheshire knights in Richard II's household could have lured him with chances of patronage which the north west Midlands denied him.

While yielding a picture of a cosmopolitan and mobile 'school' of poets, neither the poetry from the north west Midlands, nor the manuscripts in which it is preserved, allow us to forget about the provinces altogether. Michael Bennett (1983, 16–17) has shown that the immigrants from Cheshire and Lancashire kept in close contact in London, preserving their sense of being from a different part of the country, while profiting from the advantages of not being there any longer. The poetry from the north west shows similar signs of loyalty to the region. *St Erkenwald* may be a London poem that praises the capital as the 'metropol & þe mayster-toun' (l. 26),[23] but by referring to it as 'London in Englond' (1) the poet also speaks of England as about a different country: a reminder that Cheshire had its own corporate identity, and was an independent palatinate with its own chancery and exchequer (Burrow 1993). *Winner and Waster* similarly faces two ways: its poet writes with commitment about Edward III's domestic affairs; and both his knowledge of the royal household and the 'Londonisms' in his dialect suggest a mobile poet (Trigg 1990, xxi–xxii); but this poet also speaks of the difficult old age of parents who see their children disappear south and never come back:

> Dare neuer no western wy while this werlde lasteth
> Send his sone southewarde to see ne to here
> That he ne shall holden byhynde when he hore eldes.
>
> (7–9)[24]

(While this world lasts, no western man dares send his son southward to look or to listen, lest the son should stay behind when he grows old and grey.)

The poet of *Sir Gawain and the Green Knight* may well have travelled to London, or even composed his poems there, but the lands of the Wirral loom large in his romance. From the south of England, Gawain travels haphazardly in quest of the Green Chapel, and where should he end up but in Cheshire, where the poet appears to have set Castle Hautdesert and the Green Chapel.

The poets of *Winner and Waster*, *St Erkenwald* and *Sir Gawain* cannot be accused of trying to hide their origins: the dialect and the alliterative metre must both have sounded distinctly northern to Londoners, and together with such 'memories of home' as their poems contain, they assert their poets' regional background with pride. This background is confirmed when we look at where alliterative poetry was read at the very end of the Middle Ages. We have seen that, before 1450, alliterative works were copied and read in London and other parts of the country. But at the turn of the fifteenth century, it had retreated to the

---

23. *St Erkenwald*, ed. Ruth Morse (Cambridge: Brewer, 1975).
24. *Wynnere and Wastoure*, ed. Stephanie Trigg, EETS 297 (Oxford: Oxford University Press, 1990).

north west Midlands, where an interest in alliterative poetry was kept alive after it had died out in the capital. Thus the only copy of *The Destruction of Troy* (Glasgow University Library, Hunterian 388), probably composed in the fourteenth century by 'John Clerk', is preserved thanks to the labour of Thomas Chetham of Nuthurst in Lancashire, who as late as 1540 copied out this alliterative romance (Luttrell 1958). Thomas Chetham was a bailiff to the important Stanley family, who by the end of the Middle Ages were lords and masters of Cheshire and Lancashire. The unique manuscript of the 'London poem' *St Erkenwald* was owned in the early sixteenth century by Thomas Bowker, a priest in Eccles in Lancashire. A note in the margin also contains the name of Elizabeth Booth of Dunham Massey 'in the comytye of Chester' (Luttrell 1958, 39). The neighbours of the Booths, a respectable Cheshire family of landowners and church dignitaries, were the Newtons, one of whom, the wealthy Humfrey Newton (d. 1536), produced some poems in the same alliterative style and diction as *Sir Gawain and the Green Knight* (Robbins 1943). Another very late poem in the alliterative tradition, *Scottish Field* (c. 1515), was composed by a local Cheshire squire in celebration of the English victory over the Scots at Flodden, and a good deal of space is devoted to praising the courage and prowess of the Stanley clan. The poem survives, with another alliterative poem, *Death and Life*, in the Percy Folio, which was copied by a scribe from Cheshire or Lancashire, and contains several other poems—*Lady Bessy*, the heavily alliterative *Bosworth Field* and *Flodden Field*—glorifying the deeds of the Stanleys and the bravery of local fighting men (Lawton 1978).

These examples bear out the narrowness of the audience that still preserved a taste for alliterative poetry in the early sixteenth century: a few families in Cheshire and Lancashire, under the political and cultural hegemony of the Stanley family who dominated local politics from the Wars of the Roses onwards. In this milieu fourteenth-century alliterative poetry continued to be read. It is relevant to us because it would appear that the alliterative reading matter of the local gentry included the works by the *Gawain*-poet. The Percy Folio, with its Stanley encomia, also contains the *Green Knight*, the ballad version of *Sir Gawain and the Green Knight*. Nor is this the *Gawain*-poet's only link with the Stanley family. At the end of the sixteenth century, John Stowe borrowed from 'Henry Savyll', the first known owner of Cotton Nero A.x., or his father, a copy of the Stanley poem *Bosworth Field*, also found in the Percy Folio (Lawton 1978, 52). Edward Wilson suggested that *Sir Gawain and the*

Green Knight could have been composed for the Stanley family, whose founder was a forester of the Wirral. The likelihood of Henry Savile's joint ownership of Stanley literature and the *Gawain*-poet's works, and the connections of *Gawain* with the Percy Folio lend some support to Wilson's speculations (Wilson 1979).

But about one thing we should be clear: by the sixteenth century the prospects of the region and those of the Stanley family were not what they had been. The qualitative differences between the crudely chauvinistic Stanley poems and earlier alliterative poetry reflect all too clearly the narrowing of horizons of opportunity for people of the region. After the death of Richard II, no new monarch emerged to act as a patron to the north west Midlands. Instead, the region regrouped itself around the leadership of the local Stanleys, and became increasingly dependent on their influence and brokerage for access to the capital or the court. In the fourteenth century, on the other hand, the avenues to the court and the capital were still open. It is indicative of the mobility of Cheshiremen in the later fourteenth century that the first lord of Stanley, Sir John Stanley (d. 1414) was merely one Cheshire careerist among many others.[25]

If *Gawain* was a Stanley poem, it is this John Stanley who may have been the *Gawain*-poet's patron, and we should appreciate that, unlike later family-members whose fortunes he made, his involvements were not in local politics, nor indeed in the north west Midlands at all. For John Stanley left his native area to pursue a career in the service of Richard II. After some years at the fringes of the royal court, he was appointed Deputy to the Lieutenant of Ireland, Robert de Vere, and soon afterwards Lieutenant in his own right; in the 1390s John Stanley presided over Richard II's recruitment of his Cheshire bodyguard, becoming Controller of the Wardrobe in 1397.

Admittedly, the best evidence for any association between the Stanleys and the *Gawain*-poet is late and circumstantial: both the *Green Knight*, and the Percy Folio in which it has survived, have Stanley connections, and an early owner of Cotton Nero A.x., Sir Henry Savile, was in possession of Stanley literature. The case for linking the *Gawain*-poet with Sir John Stanley, a knight of Richard II's chamber, therefore depends on whether or not the Stanleys' interest in alliterative poetry and the story of the Green Knight can be extrapolated back across more than a

---

25. For the historical information about the Stanley family I am indebted to Coward (1983) and Bennett (1981a).

century of change. If we do so extrapolate it, however, we end up rather intriguingly not in a remote provincial household, but in London with Sir John Stanley, within the ambit of the royal court.[26]

Perhaps the group of royal household servants from the north west would offer the sort of milieu most consistent with the characteristics of the *Gawain*-poet's work and his imagined audience: cosmopolitan, but not oblivious to regional identity; sophisticated and courtly, but no more socially exclusive than the circle of Cheshire courtiers at Richard II's court. To this tight network belonged not only knights like Sir John Stanley or Sir Richard Craddock, to whom Richard II entrusted his presentation copy of Jean Froissart's poems, but also clerics of the chancery and the privy seal like John Clitheroe and John Macclesfield, and the goldsmith Christopher Tildesley, clerk of the royal works (Bennett 1983, 127, 134).

This milieu would, finally, explain the poet's knowledge of Italian literature, which was available in London, and the tantalizing appearance of a text entitled 'the Green Knight' in the library of Sir John Paston II, attached to the household of Edward IV.[27] It used to be thought that the 'Green Knight'—mentioned in Paston's inventory as one of several pieces in a 'black book'—was the ballad version of *Sir Gawain and the Green Knight* (Madden 1839, 352). However, John Paston's 'Green Knight' must have been written before 1479 when John Paston died. The ballad *The Green Knight*, however, survives only in the seventeenth-century Percy Folio. No doubt it is older than that, but a date much before 1500 is unlikely. Nor is the ballad a plausible candidate for inclusion in the courtly miscellany in which 'the Green Knight' is listed. Among such texts as Chaucer's *Legend of Good Women*, and Lydgate's *Temple of Glass*, *Sir Gawain and the Green Knight* makes a more congenial manuscript companion than the crude ballad version. In either case, however, the mention of 'the Green Knight' in Paston's book suggests that *Sir Gawain and the Green Knight* or a version of it was around in London, where John Paston II lived and collected his books.

Inevitably, when there are no hard facts, little scraps of evidence, such

---

26. For an attempt to link *Pearl* more closely to the royal court and to Richard II's politics see Bowers (1995).
27. *Paston Letters and Papers of the Fifteenth Century*, 2 vols, ed. Norman Davis (Oxford: Oxford University Press, 1976), I, 516–18. The inventory of Paston's library is damaged. The third item in the fragmentary list reads: '*Item*, a blak bok wyth the Legende off Lad< ... >saunce Mercye, þe Parlement of Byr< ... >Glassse, Palaytse and Scitacus, The Med< ... >the Greene Knyght, valet< ... >'.

as a mention in a damaged inventory, are asked to bear an enormous weight of speculation, increasing in proportion to the amount of detail that we seek in a reconstruction of the poet. I admit, therefore, to ever-diminishing degrees of conclusiveness as I restate the *Gawain*-poet's profile that has emerged in this opening chapter: he was almost certainly a cleric from the north west Midlands—probably a relatively unimportant cleric; perhaps in the service of a nobleman; and, arguably, his patron belonged to the circle of prominent Cheshire courtiers at the royal household in London.

Chapter 2

Sir Gawain and the Green Knight

INTRODUCTION

Sir Gawain and the Green Knight is the most immediately attractive work by the *Gawain*-poet. The substantial body of criticism which the poem has inspired reveals something about its richness. In a single chapter I cannot fully cover the poem, and I have not attempted to do so. Instead I shall begin with some factual observations about the poem's genre, its sources and literary affinities, its relation to contemporary texts, and its thematic interests. These preliminary observations will serve to highlight two distinctive qualities of *Sir Gawain and the Green Knight*. The first is its curious blend of realism and moral seriousness on the one hand, and marvel and fantasy on the other; the second its irresistible momentum towards the ending of the hero's ordeal at the Green Chapel, which is deceptively presented as the climax of the story, but which, in the end, unexpectedly reduces itself to a statement about an earlier episode in the poem. The following two sections explore these two distinctive qualities of the poem in depth. The sustained argument developed in these sections cannot pretend to comprehensiveness in the way a line-by-line analysis of the poem might, but since the sections focus on aspects that are unique and central to the poem, they can perhaps more consistently address the question of what makes reading *Gawain* a different and more engrossing experience than reading any other medieval romance.

  Sir Gawain and the Green Knight belongs to the genre of Arthurian romance, which, by the time *Gawain* was composed (c. 1390), was the most popular literature of entertainment for the higher strata of society. The libraries of those English men and women who could afford manu-script-books were well stocked with romances about Arthur and his Round Table knights in Old French (Strohm 1986). The interest in Arthurian literature was not, however, simply bookish. English craftsmen, for example, carved scenes from French Arthurian romances on the woodwork of parish churches (Whitaker 1990, 97–8), and episodes from Arthurian romance were performed by knights in court-spectacles and tournaments, in Britain and on the continent (Loomis 1959). Most relevant to *Gawain* is a 'Round Table' feast held by Edward III at Windsor. A contemporary chronicler has this account:

> On Thursday [22 January 1344], following after the jousts of the young gentlemen, the Lord King held a great feast at which he inaugurated his Round Table, and received the oaths of certain earls, barons, and knights, who wished to be of the said Round Table in the same place on the following Pentecost and thereafter ...
>
> (Murimuth, *Continuatio Chronicarum*, quoted in Boulton 1987, 104–5)

Edward III had already given orders for a giant Round Table to be built in Windsor Castle 'of the same manner and standing as that which the Lord Arthur, formerly King of England, had relinquished'. The revival of a fellowship of the Round Table was, in the end, abandoned, but Edward III's idea of a chivalric order bore fruit in the Order of the Garter, founded by Edward in 1348. The device of the Order, which was to be worn by all Knights of the Garter on public occasions, was a blue garter. It carried the inscription: *hony soyt quy mal y pense* ('shame be to him who thinks evil of this'). With this very motto, the *Gawain*-poet (or possibly a scribe) rounds off his romance, hinting perhaps at a resemblance between Edward's Order of the Garter and the poet's Round Table, which at the end of the poem adopts as its chivalric badge not a blue garter but a green girdle. The Arthurian history and associations of the garter, which the *Gawain*-poet may be alluding to, are a reminder that Arthurian literature existed not merely on the parchment of dusty manuscripts, but in the minds of many English people. At feasts and tournaments, kings and noblemen are known to have acted the parts of famous Arthurian knights, not for the sake of comedy, but as if they had discovered in Arthur and his knights some important truth about themselves. Although their lively engagement with Arthur—too often dismissed as a symptom of the decadence or vanity of medieval chivalry —does not concern us directly, it does suggest that they read Arthurian literature not as fiction but as a mirror of reality (Stanesco 1988). However naïve this way of reading Arthurian romance may strike us initially, I hope to show that as an approach to *Sir Gawain and the Green Knight* it has much to recommend itself.

As we have seen, Arthurian literature was well known, and the

Gawain-poet could therefore have assumed his audience's familiarity with the postulates of the genre when he announced his intention to tell an Arthurian tale:

> For-þi an aunter in erde I attle to schawe
> Þat a selly in siȝt summe men hit holden,
> And an outtrage awenture of Arþurez wonderez.
>
> (27–9)

(Therefore I intend to show you an adventure on earth, which some men consider a plain marvel, and an extraordinary adventure among the wonders of Arthur.)

From the rich store of 'Arþurez wonderez' the poet promises a story of 'outtrage awenture'.

The *Gawain*-poet's romance is more original and idiosyncratic than his simple statement of intent might suggest, but we may be clearer about the kinds of innovations he brought to the genre if we accept his invitation to read his work against the background of other Arthurian romances. The *Gawain*-poet himself hints at the basic quality it shares with this tradition, namely the element of marvel and the narrative impulse offered by the abrupt arrival of an adventure (*aunter* or *awenture*). As Arthur and his knights celebrate the Christmas season, a Green Knight, carrying a huge axe in one hand and a branch of holly in the other, rides in and offers a Beheading Game on the following terms: to any knight brave enough to give him a blow with his axe, the Green Knight will forfeit his weapon, on condition that this knight will present himself at the Green Chapel in a year's time to receive, without defending himself, a blow of the axe in return. Arthur is the first to respond to the Green Knight's bizarre game, but as he makes ready to give the Green Knight his blow, Gawain politely steps into the fray to relieve Arthur of the undertaking. With one well-placed stroke, Gawain lops off the Green Knight's head. Then, to everyone's amazement, the Green Knight picks up the head, and reminds Gawain of his obligation to seek out the Green Chapel, where he must submit himself to the Green Knight's return blow.

The promised 'outtrage awenture' has arrived, and it is a classic of its kind. The Green Knight's magic represents the sudden irruption of the supernatural and the irrational into the realm of the ordinary. Moreover, as in other Arthurian romances, the inexplicable magic of adventure forms part of a more fundamental evasion of meaning that is typical of romances, which tend to withhold from both hero and reader the sense and purpose of the adventure until it is well and truly over (Shippey 1971). Neither the Green Knight nor the *Gawain*-poet explains the bearing which this adventure has on the life of Gawain, who finally undertakes it: why him? why anyone? The rationale of the Beheading Game is never explained, and the Green Knight who offers it not only arrives from nowhere, without any apparent ulterior motives, but also rides off into the realm of the unknown from whence he came:

> To quat kyth he becom knwe non þere,
> Neuer more þen þay wyste fram queþen he watz wonnen.
> What þenne?
>
> (460–2)

(No one there knew to what land he went, no more than they knew from whence he had come. What then?)

Mysterious in both its causes and its effects, the Green Knight's Beheading Game is the perfect example of an *adventure*: something about which, at least initially, nothing more can sensibly be said than that it happens, which is no more and no less than what the word *adventure* (from Old French *avenir*: to arrive, or occur) means. Above all, it is this tantalizing silence to the question 'why?' which characterizes romance, and the silence effectively propels both hero and reader forward in the mutual anticipation of an eventual answer.

The pursuit of adventure is thus simultaneously the pursuit of meaning (Kelly 1992, 115–21). *Sir Gawain and the Green Knight* has this in common with earlier Arthurian romances (Mann 1994b). Indeed, source studies of the poem have shown that the *Gawain*-poet borrowed the motif of the Beheading Game itself from a French Arthurian romance, known as the *First Continuation* of Chrétien de Troyes's *Perceval*.[1] In one episode from this romance, which I shall briefly summarize, Arthur's call for an adventure is swiftly answered when a knight arrives at court and offers an exchange of blows. Carados, son of King Caradus—or so he thinks—takes up the challenge, and strikes off the knight's head. The

---

1. Larry D. Benson has argued that the closest analogue to *Gawain* is a lost metrical version of the *First Continuation* that can now only be reconstructed from a late prose redaction, *Le tresplaisante et recreative histoire du Perceval le galloys*, printed in Paris in 1530. For a different view see Luttrell (1979). Relevant passages from the prose redaction are edited in an appendix to Benson (1965b). It is translated in the useful anthology *Sir Gawain and the Green Knight: Sources and Analogues*, ed. Elisabeth Brewer (Woodbridge: Boydell and Brewer, 1992). For a complete modern edition of the *First Continuation*, see vols I–III of *The Continuations of the Old French Perceval of Chrétien de Troyes*, ed. William Roach (Philadelphia: University of Pennsylvania Press, 1949–83).

stranger, however, simply puts his head back on and warns Carados that he will be back in a year's time to give Carados the return blow. A year later, Carados bravely turns up at Arthur's court for his own beheading. The stranger raises his sword to land the blow, but fortunately only taps Carados with the flat of the sword: Carados is safe. At this point, the stranger unveils the significance of the Beheading Game, explaining that he did not kill Carados because Carados is in fact his son, begotten by him on Carados's mother in a secret extra-marital affair. Only now is the meaning of the adventure clear. By pursuing it, Carados has discovered his true identity. And if initially there seemed no good reason why *he* of all knights should have taken on the adventure, the ending shows that he was somehow destined for it. The plot of the romance thus describes a movement whereby what appeared to be arbitrary and extraneous turns out to be a meaningful and integral stage in the knight's career.

Gawain shares with previous romances this forward momentum towards retrospective coherence, but it exemplifies the romance principle that the extraneous and the peripheral shall become central and integral in an utterly original way. The originality lies in the *Gawain*-poet's combination of the Beheading Game with another plot-motif: the temptation scenes and the Exchange of Winnings, to which Gawain is subjected when he takes lodging at Castle Hautdesert on his way to the Green Chapel. While Gawain enjoys a brief moment of respite before meeting the Green Knight on his home ground, the host proposes that Gawain and he should liven up Gawain's stay by playing a game in which they will exchange the day's winnings. In the mornings, when the host is out hunting, Gawain is cornered in his bedroom by the Lady of the Castle, who tries to seduce him. Gawain accepts from her first one kiss (his winnings for the first morning), then two kisses (his winnings for the second morning), which he duly exchanges for the venison and the boar's head which the host has gained in his hunting expeditions. On the third day, however, the Lady presses on Gawain not only three kisses but also a magic green girdle, which will protect the wearer from all physical harm. Thinking of the beheading which he faces the next day, Gawain gratefully accepts the girdle, and fails to hand it over in exchange for the fox's skin which the host has won in the hunt.

After an enjoyable stay at the Castle, Gawain must resume his journey to the Green Chapel. Armed with the green girdle, he arrives at a kind of cave where the Green Knight is already waiting for him, and sharpening a giant axe. Twice the Green Knight lifts the axe as if to strike Gawain, but twice the axe stops in mid-air. The third time the Green Knight hits

Gawain so gently that he only grazes Gawain's neck. Gawain jumps up ready to fight with his enemy, but the Green Knight simply laughs, and when he next addresses Gawain we know that the moment of retrospective illumination has come.

However, the Green Knight's moment of revelation is of a very different kind from that in the *First Continuation*. In the *First Continuation*, the adventure that we thought mattered (the Beheading Game) is duly endowed with symbolic significance. When, by contrast, the Green Knight discloses his identity as Bertilac de Hautdesert, Gawain's host at the Castle, and reveals that the nick in the neck is Gawain's punishment for having retained a girdle that should have been returned to him under the rules of the Exchange of Winnings, his explanation of the Beheading Game denies it any intrinsic significance. In fact, Bertilac makes it clear that the Beheading Game has *no* significance other than as a reflection of Gawain's performance in a parlour game which he had earlier played at Castle Hautdesert. It was there, in the Exchange of Winnings, that the crucial testing of Gawain's honesty took place. If we experience this explanation as an anti-climax, it is because we, like Gawain, come to realize too late that what we thought of as the main adventure, the Beheading Game, is only a verdict on Gawain's apparently minor 'adventures' in Castle Hautdesert, where Gawain slightly failed a test in complete ignorance of the fact that he was actually being tested. Like other romances, such as the *First Continuation*, the pursuit of adventure leads to the uncovering of a secret which gives retrospective significance to the mysterious happenings that have gone before; but *Sir Gawain and the Green Knight* is unique in placing the burden of meaning not on the adventure we expected would carry it (the Beheading Game) but on a social game which we thought was insignificant. In a startling reversal of expectation, the *Gawain*-poet reduces the Beheading Game to an adventure of secondary importance, while elevating an apparently minor digression at Castle Hautdesert to the pivotal scene. Tests and adventures, as the *Gawain*-poet implies, may take place when you least expect them: when, for instance, you are entertained by a genial host, are asked to play an innocent-looking game, and have your mind on what you think are more urgent matters.

Gawain's crucial test, then, takes place in mundane circumstances, circumstances so utterly unportentous that their importance is never properly recognized by Gawain or the reader until after the fact. These preliminary remarks point to two directions in which the *Gawain*-poet took Arthurian romance, and which I want to pursue further in this chapter. The first involves the *Gawain*-poet's brilliantly deceptive handling of the plot: the way he manages to trick us into believing that Gawain's stay at Castle Hautdesert is a mere interlude before the final showdown at the Green Chapel. The second involves the *Gawain*-poet's use of a tale of 'outtrage awenture' for quite serious purposes: the adventure set in motion by the appearance of a Green Knight at Arthur's court develops into a story about the virtue of *trawþe* (truthfulness, faithfulness), and the sudden significance which the plot confers on Gawain's small moment of weakness—his retention of the girdle in the Exchange of Winnings—suggests just how total the imperatives of *trawþe* are in *Sir Gawain and the Green Knight*.

This deep moral concern with *trawþe* is not in itself exceptional. It occupied many of the *Gawain*-poet's contemporaries. Chaucer explored it in, for example, the *Franklin's Tale* and *Troilus and Criseyde*; Langland did so in *Piers Plowman*; and Gower wrote in his *Confessio Amantis* that:

> Among the vertues on is chief,
> And that is trouthe ...
> (VII, 1723–4)[2]

This literary interest in the theme of *trawþe* may in turn be understood historically. One may predict that the need for *trawþe*, for an enduring commitment to social bonds, will be felt most strongly in a society where the stability of these bonds can no longer be taken for granted. In late-fourteenth-century England this was indeed the case. The traditional understanding of society as a divinely sanctioned hierarchy with knights and clerics at the top and peasants at the bottom had been shaken by the Peasants' Revolt in 1381. The Peasants' Revolt and the unprecedented degree of social mobility in the late-fourteenth-century 'Age of Ambition' (Du Boulay 1970) prompted a heightened awareness that society might be conceived of not only as god-given, but as the realization of dynamic and potentially volatile relations between human beings in pursuit of self-interest. On a more theoretical level, the rediscovery of Aristotle's *Politics* in the thirteenth century similarly challenged the view of society as a preordained hierarchy by making available to later medieval thinkers an alternative model of the state as the natural product of rules and agreements established by human beings for their own well-being (Strohm 1989, 144–51). This increased awareness that

---

2. *The English Works of John Gower*, ed. G.C. Macauley, 2 vols, EETS ES 81, 82 (London: Oxford University Press, 1900–1901).

social relations were man-made might go some way towards explaining why so many Ricardian poets, the *Gawain*-poet among them, put *trawþe* high on their poetic agenda. For the need for *trawþe*—whether it means keeping promises or honouring the rules of a contract—becomes especially pressing for a society which has lost confidence in its immutability, and which is discovering that, without human truthfulness, social relations are as volatile as the changeable human needs and desires that bring these relations into being.

If Chaucer, Langland, or the *Gawain*-poet have anything new to say about the transition to a contractual society, it is their recognition that consensual transactions bring with them sacrifices as well as liberties. When human beings create society by freely entering into contracts, agreements, or any other social relations, the continued existence of these social relations becomes a human responsibility as well. The more a society is seen to be made by human beings, the clearer it becomes that only their *trawþe* can give it permanence.

However, while Chaucer, Langland, and Gower provide analogues for the *Gawain*-poet's interest in *trawþe*, they seem to have had little faith in the potential of Arthurian romance to convey serious thought. The *Gawain*-poet, I think, proved them wrong. Reserving the discussion of the poet's handling of the plot for later, I want to turn first to his motives for combining 'outtrage awenture' with moral seriousness, and more generally for combining the marvellous elements from the world of Arthurian romance with social and descriptive realism.

ROMANCE AND REALISM

I

The story-matter of *Sir Gawain and the Green Knight* strikes a discordant note when compared with that of his other poems. *Patience* and *Cleanness* are retellings of Old Testament stories and take as their theme the Christian virtues of patience and cleanness. *Pearl* is a vision of heaven, in which the Dreamer meets, for a fleeting moment, the daughter he has lost. *Sir Gawain and the Green Knight* instead conjures up a world in which Morgan le Fay waves her magic wand as Merlin has taught her. I put this somewhat flippantly in order to suggest that *Gawain* poses an interpretative challenge which none of the *Gawain*-poet's other works raises: how can we take it seriously?

This question has always been central in *Gawain*-criticism, but I think it might have pressed itself on the *Gawain*-poet's contemporary audience as well. True, they would not have doubted the existence of an historical Arthur. Geoffrey of Monmouth's *Historia regum Britanniae* (*History of the Kings of Britain*, c. 1150)[3] was largely responsible for inventing King Arthur, and for bringing him to the attention of numerous medieval English readers and writers, who almost unanimously accepted Geoffrey of Monmouth's account of Arthur's reign as historical truth (Dean 1987, 3–31). The *Gawain*-poet's first twenty-six lines give a rapid summary of the 'historical facts' which most medieval Englishmen would have known: Aeneas's flight from Troy, the foundation of Britain by Brutus, and the pre-eminence of Arthur:

> Bot of alle þat here bult, of Bretaygne kynges,
> Ay watz Arthur þe hendest, as I haf herde telle ...
>
> (25–6)

(But of all the people that settled here, kings of Britain, Arthur was always the noblest, as I have heard tell.)

So far, this would have been 'history' for the *Gawain*-poet's audience. But when the *Gawain*-poet next promises 'an outtrage awenture of Arþurez wonderez', he transports his audience from the world of Geoffrey of Monmouth's 'history' to the enchanted world of Arthurian romance. The earliest Arthurian romances by Chrétien de Troyes (fl. 1160–80) were already blatantly fictitious works, in which knights fight giants, and rescue supremely beautiful and marriageable ladies. Two centuries later, Arthurian romances seemed to many of the *Gawain*-poet's contemporaries to be far removed from the concerns of their time. Chaucer's Wife of Bath speaks of the 'old days' of Arthur only as an imaginary time before the cynical present:

> In th'olde dayes of Kyng Arthour,
> Of which that Britons speken greet honour,
> Al was this land fulfild of fayerye.
> The elf-queene, with hir joly compaignye,
> Daunced ful ofte in many a grene mede.
> This was the olde opinion, as I rede;
> I speke of manye hundred yeres ago.

---

3. Geoffrey of Monmouth's *Historia* was soon translated into French by Wace in his *Roman de Brut*. It is presumably to Wace's *Brut*, or to any of the later prose redactions of Wace's *Brut*, that the *Gawain*-poet refers in line 2523: 'þe Brutus bokeȝ þer-of beres wytnesse'.

But now kan no man se none elves mo,
For now the grete charitee and prayeres
Of lymytours and other hooly freres,
That serchen every lond and every streem,
As thikke as motes in the sonne-beem,
Blessynge halles, chambres, kichenes, boures,
Citees, burghes, castels, hye toures,
Thropes, bernes, shipnes, dayeryes—
This maketh that ther ben no fayeryes.
                                    (III, 857–72)

> *lymytours*: friars; *motes*: specks of dust; *boures*: bedrooms; *burghes*:
> boroughs; *thropes*: villages; *shipnes*: stables

In the Wife of Bath's nostalgic words, the world of Arthurian romance
already appears as 'modern culture's construction of a symbolic form
prior to itself' (Duncan 1992, 10–11), as a 'passing fancy' displaced by
the onset of cynicism, disenchantment, and strict truth (Fradenburg
1986). Add to this Chaucer's other occasional references to Arthurian
heroes—'Gawain, with his olde curteisye, / Though he were comen
ayeyn of Fairye' (V, 95–6) or 'This storie is al-so trewe, I undertake, /
As is the tale of Launcelot de Lake' (VII, 3212–13)—and it is clear that
in Chaucer's mind Arthurian romance had little more to offer than
entertainment value.

Chaucer's view, in which Arthurian romance and reality are each
other's opposites, is perhaps hard to get away from, but anyone who
attributes to romance what he or she denies to reality—fictitiousness,
wonder, playfulness—will be ill-equipped to deal with *Gawain*'s para-
doxical blend of the verisimilar and the marvellous. The *Gawain*-poet's
descriptions of castles, of manners, of feasts, of human emotions and
interaction, are so detailed and so probable that readers often fancy
themselves to be in the real world of the fourteenth century; but equally
it is in this plausible world that Gawain, a perfectly sensible knight,
spends much of his time questing for a knight who is green all over and
who can put his own head back on.

This blend of the real and the unreal is the subject of this section. I
shall not, however, approach it on the Wife of Bath's assumption that
romance and realism stand in an antithetical relation to one another.
This assumption runs very deep in *Gawain*-criticism, and it produces
partial readings that tend to segregate what the poet forces into association: either *Gawain* becomes entirely realistic, in which case the motifs
of romance can be dismissed as self-conscious absurdities, or it becomes a

meta-romance, a romance *about* romance, in which case the realistic detail is reduced to a device that allows the romance to bare its own artifice. That *Gawain* is indeed a self-consciously fictitious romance is evident, but I shall be arguing that in spite of this, or even by virtue of this, it sets out to reveal something elementary about the way things are, or how, from a certain angle, they might be seen to be. The potential for romance to function as an imaginative commentary on ordinary life (Gradon 1971, 212–72) may give us some answers to the question of why a thoughtful poet—the poet who also wrote *Pearl*, *Cleanness*, and *Patience* —might have wanted to turn his attention to Arthurian romance.

II

Let us now look more closely at some examples of the peculiar mixture of fact and fancy in *Sir Gawain and the Green Knight*. In fitt two, Gawain sets out to find the Green Chapel so that he may keep his part of the bargain in the Beheading Game. Unfortunately, however, the Green Knight has failed to say where the Green Chapel is, so that Gawain rides at hazard:

> Now ridez þis renk þurȝ þe ryalme of Logres,
> Sir Gauen, on Godez halue, þaȝ hym no gomen þoȝt.
> Ofte leudlez alone he lengez on nyȝtez ...
> ... Til þat he neȝed ful neghe into þe Norþe Walez.
> Alle þe iles of Anglesay on lyft half he haldez,
> And farez ouer þe fordez by þe forlondez,
> Ouer at þe Holy Hede, til he hade eft bonk
> In þe wyldrenesse of Wyrale; wonde þer bot lyte
> Þat auþer God oþer gome wyth goud hert louied.
> And ay he frayned, as he ferde, at frekez þat he met,
> If þay hade herde any karp of a knyȝt grene,
> In any grounde þeraboute, of þe grene chapel;
> And al nykked hym wyth nay, þat neuer in her lyue
> Þay seȝe neuer no segge þat watz of suche hwez
> of grene.
>
> (691–709)

(Now the man rides through the realm of Logres, Sir Gawain, for God's sake, though he thought it no game. Often alone and without companions he rests at night ... until he got very close to North Wales. All the isles of Anglesey he keeps on his left, and crosses the fords near the forelands, and passes over at the Holy Head, until he again reached dry land in the wilderness of the Wirral. There only few people lived who loved God or man with a good heart. And as he went, he always asked strangers that he met whether they had heard talk of a green knight in any place nearby, or of the green chapel. And everyone said no to him, that never in their lives had they ever seen a man that had that colour of green.')

Readers of romance will recognize in this passage the motif of the quest, in the course of which knights tend to stumble, by chance, on the object of their search. Knights in romance are knights *errant*; they wander or 'err' into the unknown, just as Gawain does himself. His goal is the Green Chapel, but it is not a goal to which Gawain can direct himself purposefully: he has, after all, no idea of where this chapel might be. It is his destination only in the strict sense that he is destined to find it (Mann 1994b, 111). The land through which he travels is thus appropriately called the 'ryalme of Logres' (691), the mythical realm of adventure in which Arthurian knights wander in hope of adventures. The Old French prose *Lancelot* describes Logres as follows:

[Perceval] brought an end to the adventures of the Dangerous Adventurous Kingdom (Reiaume Perilleus Adventureus), known as the Realm of Logres.[4]

Yet as we read the passage from *Gawain* I quoted we cannot imagine ourselves in the *Reiaume Perilleus Aventureus* of Arthurian romance for long, because it goes on to list, with remarkable precision, the various places Gawain passes. He rides into 'Norþe Walez'; keeps the 'iles of Anglesay' on his left; crosses the fords (probably across the rivers Coswy and Clwyd); traverses the Dee at the 'Holy Hede', and lands in the forest of 'Wyrale'. The itinerary matches in detail the customary route taken by medieval people travelling from the south of England to Cheshire or making the crossing to Ireland (Bennett 1981b, 76). The *Gawain*-poet expected his audience to bring their topographical knowledge to bear on this passage, as his insistent use of the definite article suggests: *þe* iles of Anglesay, *þe* fordez, *þe* forlondez.

Gawain seems to have strayed from the imaginary realm of Logres back on to the beaten tracks of fourteenth-century England. It is not surprising that, back there, he asks the country yokels of the Wirral in vain whether they have ever set eyes on a 'kny3t grene' belonging to a 'grene chapel'. The *Gawain*-poet only reports their response indirectly, but in their multiple negations ('Al *nykked* hym wyth *nay*, þat *neuer* in her lyue / þay se3e *neuer no* segge') and in the unexpected stress which

4. Translated from the early-thirteenth-century *Lancelot do Lac*, ed. Elspeth Kennedy (Oxford: Oxford University Press, 1980), 33.

the alliterative metre forces on the word *such* (þay seȝe neuer no segge þat watz of suche hwez') we may nevertheless hear their incomprehension: no, they have certainly not heard of a *green* knight. Now, we cannot be sure exactly how they understand Gawain's question 'If þay hade herde any karp of a knyȝt grene', since it is posed in a way that allows them to take the *grene* in the phrase *knyȝt grene* to refer simply to the colour of the knight's arms. This is what references to colour mean when Malory speaks of a Green Knight, a Black Knight, or a Red Knight. But the possibility that they take it in this way, or that Gawain's host takes it in this way when later on Gawain asks him, too, about a knight 'of colour of grene' (1959), only increases one's sense of the absurdity of what Gawain knows to be the case: that somewhere in England there dwells a knight who is green all over.

Such moments where the *Gawain*-poet strains our belief in the existence of green knights, even on the assumptions of his own romance, must be balanced, however, against those where Gawain's question about the whereabouts of the Green Knight meets with an entirely straightforward answer. Gawain's host in the Castle serenely replies to Gawain: 'Mon schal yow sette in waye, / Hit is not two myle henne' (1077–8). Like Gawain, we may on the one hand be reassured that the object of the quest has been found, and on the other hand be slightly perturbed by the implication that a green monster, who should be confined to the realm of the imaginary, should literally live within a two-mile radius of Castle Hautdesert.

This unsettling use of a literalism of reference for the blatantly imaginary marks the entirety of the romance, which manages to confer an extraordinary degree of 'realness' on the unreal. The landscapes through which Gawain travels, for example, possess all the solidity they have in real life. We might contrast them with the predominantly shadowy settings of the thirteenth-century Arthurian prose cycles (Ruberg 1965), which Malory adapted into English, and which would have shaped the horizon of expectation of the *Gawain*-poet's audience. Malory's romances (with the possible exception of the final two books in which Malory's own historical moment begins to penetrate his idealized world) evoke a symbolic outside world Whitaker 1984, 99). Consisting largely of forests, glades, castles, and hermitages, the setting possesses none of the contents that would persuade a reader it could exist anywhere else but inside Malory's fiction. *Gawain*, by comparison, describes the landscape in such convincing detail that he seems to draw not on conventions of literature but on his own experience (Eliott 1984). Here is an example of how vividly the *Gawain*-poet renders the wilderness in which Gawain wanders in fitt two:

> Bi a mounte on þe morne meryly he rydes
> Into a forest ful dep, þat ferly watz wylde,
> Hiȝe hillez on vche a halue, and holtwodez vnder
> Of hore okez ful hoge a hundreth togeder;
> Þe hasel and þe haȝþorne were harled al samen,
> With roȝe raged mosse rayled aywhere,
> With mony bryddez vnblythe vpon bare twyges,
> Þat pitosly þar piped for pyne of þe colde.
>
> (740–7)

(Near a hill he rides handsomely one morning into a very deep forest, which was wondrously wild, with high hills on both sides, and, below, forests of grey and huge oaks, a hundred together. The hazel and the hawthorn were tangled together, with rough and ragged moss growing everywhere, with many unhappy birds on bare branches that piped piteously there, for pain of the cold.)

Reading this one can almost feel the cold, hear the birds, see the wildness of nature. And yet, however vividly the realities of nature are portrayed in *Gawain*, they sometimes have a way of changing aspect rather too quickly to be only realistic (Markus 1971). Once inside the protecting walls of Castle Hautdesert, where Gawain rests on his way to the Green Chapel, the weather suddenly improves. The sun puts the clouds to flight, and the forest looks beautiful in the morning frost:

> Ferly fayre watz þe folde, for þe forst clenged;
> In rede rudede vpon rak rises þe sunne,
> And ful clere costez þe clowdes of þe welkyn.
>
> (1694–6)

(Marvellously beautiful was the earth, since the frost still clung to the ground. In fiery red the sun rises above the clouds, and brightly it chases the clouds from the sky.)

But gone is the fair weather when Gawain lies in his bed, the night before the dreaded encounter with the Green Knight:

> Bot wylde wederez of þe worlde wakned þeroute,
> Clowdes kesten kenly þe colde to þe erþe,
> Wyth nyȝe innoghe of the norþe, þe naked to tene ...
>
> (2000–2)

(But wild storms of the world arose outside; clouds keenly threw the cold to the earth, with much bitterness from the north, to harass the naked.)

The weather in *Gawain* often seems to obey psychological rather than natural laws: it is hostile when Gawain travels on his quest, crisp and clear when Gawain is safe in the castle, while a storm *awakens* ('wakned') when Gawain lies *awake* in bed, anxious about what tomorrow will bring.

These correspondences between inner and outer worlds seem too close to be simply coincidental. Despite its solidity, the natural world in *Gawain* often loses its pure 'objectivity' to make contact with the mysterious world of romance where the outer world is more systematically subordinated to the hero's mind (Mullally 1988, 138). One may think, for instance, of scenes from romance in which savage lions or seductive ladies vanish into thin air once the hero has made up his mind to obey his conscience, or castles appear from nowhere once the knight has said his prayers, as in the following passage from *The Didot-Perceval*:

> And after Perceval had left, he rode all day without finding an adventure. Evening approached, and he prayed our Lord to send him a hostel where he could spend the night, because he had only poor lodging the night before. And then he looked ahead, and in the midst of the dense forest the top of a beautiful and a big tower loomed up.[5]

In just this way, the desolate landscape of *Gawain*, described so realistically that it seems utterly true to life, makes way for a vision of a majestic castle when Gawain crosses himself:

> Nade he sayned hymself, segge, bot þrye,
> Er he watz war in þe wod of a won in a mote,
> Abof a launde, on a lawe, loken vnder boȝez
> Of mony borelych bole aboute bi þe diches:
> A castel þe comlokest þat euer knyȝt aȝte,
> Pyched on a prayere, a park al aboute,
> Wyth a pyked palays pyned ful þik,
> Þat vmbeteȝe mony tre mo þen two myle.
>
> (763–70)

> (No sooner had the man crossed himself three times than he became aware in the forest of a fortress surrounded by a moat, above a field, on a mound, enclosed by the branches of many massive trees that stood near the ditches: the most beautiful castle owned by any knight, set on a meadow, with a hunting ground all around it, and securely hedged in by a fence of sharp pales, which surrounded many a tree for more than two miles.)

5. Translated from *The Didot-Perceval*, ed. William Roach (Philadelphia: University of Pennsylvania Press, 1941), 165–6.

The seemingly miraculous apparition of the castle, and its superlative beauty ('þe comlokest þat euer knyʒt aʒte'), betray the making of romance, but as always the *Gawain*-poet never allows his audience to settle in either the real world or the world of romance definitively. Whereas in *The Didot-Perceval* the shadowy description of the setting makes it easy to accept it as a mysterious emanation from a different order of reality, the castle in *Gawain* visibly hardens and solidifies when Gawain gets up closer, until it is too concrete to be a mere shadow:

> Þe burde bode on blonk, þat on bonk houed
> Of þe depe double dich þat drof to þe place;
> Þe walle wod in þe water wonderly depe,
> And eft a ful huge heʒt hit haled vpon lofte
> Of harde hewen ston vp to þe tablez,
> Embaned vnder þe abataylment in þe beste lawe;
> And syþen garytez ful gaye gered bitwene,
> Wyth mony luflych loupe þat louked ful clene:
> A better barbican þat burne blusched vpon neuer.
> And innermore he behelde þat halle ful hyʒe,
> Towres telded bytwene, trochet ful þik,
> Fayre fylyolez þat fyʒed, and ferlyly long,
> With coruon coprounes craftyly sleʒe.
> Chalkwyt chymnees þer ches he innoʒe
> Vpon bastel rouez, þat blenked ful quyte;
> So many pynakle payntet watz poudred ayquere,
> Among þe castel carnelez clambred so þik,
> Þat pared out of papure purely hit semed.
> (785–802)

(The man paused on his horse, which tarried on the bank of the deep double moat that encircled the site. The wall went into the water wondrously deep, and it rose up again to an enormous height, made of hard hewn stone up to the cornice-mouldings, with steps underneath the battlements done in the best way; and turrets were handsomely fashioned in between, with many lovely loopholes that could be shut completely. The knight had never set eyes on a better outer fortification, and within he beheld the high hall, the towers erected at intervals, provided with much ornamental masonry, with fair and well-fitted pinnacles that were marvellously long, with carved tops expertly made. Chalk-white chimneys he saw there in plenty, on the roofs of towers which shone brightly. So many painted pinnacles were scattered everywhere and clustered so thickly among the embrasures of the castle, that it simply seemed to be cut out of paper.)

Two qualities make this description extremely persuasive. First, the greater precision in the description is made dependent on Gawain's closer proximity to the castle (Benson 1965b). After seeing the castle from a distance 'loken under boȝes', framed by the trees in the forest from which he emerges, Gawain rides up to the gate, and can now make out the intricate masonry on the roof. Secondly, all the details that Gawain notices—the palisade, the pinnacles, the ornamental turrets, the numerous chimneys—correspond to the latest fashions in fourteenth-century castle design (Coldstream 1981, 190, 201). The density of reference places us in the natural world, or, more precisely, the world of the high nobility of later-fourteenth-century England.

The castle which Gawain sees is not a castle in the air, we might conclude. Or is it? As if to keep us guessing, the final line of the description ends by loosening the castle's moorings to the real world: 'pared out of papure purely hit semed'. The allusion is to the miniature paper castles used in the period to decorate platters of food. The *Gawain*-poet himself describes them in his retelling of Belshazzar's feast in *Cleanness*:

> Burnes berande þe bredes vpon brode skeles,
> Þat were of sylveren syȝt, and seves þerwyth;
> Lyfte logges þerouer and on lofte coruen
> Pared out of paper and poynted of golde ...
>
> (1405–8)

(Men bore the meat on broad plates, which looked like silver, and stews to go with it; they bore artificial houses as covers that were carved on top, cut out of paper and painted over with gold ...)

As Belshazzar's feast is shown up as an empty pageant where outward appearances of silver, gold, or castles substitute for the things themselves, so the materiality of the castle threatens to evaporate when it is compared to a paper cut-out.

The *Gawain*-poet thus teases us with the question of whether his world is verisimilar or fabulous, real or artificial; and as the examples may have begun to suggest, he seems to want it both ways. In *Gawain*, the real world and the world of romance with its different set of rules coexist. So far from ruling one another out, as they should if, like the Wife of Bath, we take the worlds of Arthurian romance and reality to be polar opposites, the two run parallel to one another, and we are shuttled back and forth between the two as if they were only different ways of talking about, or different ways of experiencing, the same thing.

This movement back and forth between reality and romance needs to be emphasized, because much criticism of the poem comes down heavily on the side of the real. This, for instance, was W.P. Ker's influential view of the *Gawain*-poet:

> The author might almost have been a modern novelist with a contempt for romance, trying, by way of experiment, to work out a supernatural plot with the full strength of his reason, merely accepting the fabulous story, and trying how it will go with accessories from real life, and with modern manners and conversation.
>
> (Ker 1955, 102–3)

This remains perceptive in that it puts its finger on the *Gawain*-poet's distinctive blend of the real and the supernatural. But according to Ker we are always secure in our grasp of reality: we never see a miraculous apparition of a castle 'pared out of papure', and are never in the 'ryalme of Logres', but always in the actual world, from where the supernatural and the fabulous can be dismissed with 'contempt'. Modern reincarnations of this view run along similar lines: the realism of *Sir Gawain and the Green Knight* 'undercuts' or 'parodies' the conventions of romance; or it allows the poet to draw attention to the fictitiousness of romance motifs like the 'land of adventure' or the 'fairy castle'. On this view, the poet infused Arthurian romance with realism to highlight the incommensurability of the two.

Yet one of the effects of the many transitions between the 'real world' and the world of romance is to produce moments where it becomes nearly impossible to decide in which of the two worlds we might be. The rich confusion can be demonstrated by looking at the vocabulary which the *Gawain*-poet uses to describe the marvellous. When first used in the poem, the words *ferly* (marvel), *selly* (wonder), *mervayle* or *wonder* evoke the supernatural world of 'outtrage awenture', but they soon slide across into different contexts where the realness of objects or events is not at issue. Recall, for example, the lines from the description of Castle Hautdesert, certainly not built out of thin air:

Þe walle wod in þe water *wonderly* depe …

Fayre fylyolez þat fyʒed, and *ferlyly* long …

Intriguingly, the same adverbs that previously described the Green Knight's magic now appear in a description of a realistic castle, at which Gawain marvels, just as he marvelled at the spectacle of the Green Knight. Putting a different gloss on the words *wonderly* and *ferlyly* could of course prevent the sense of wonder from spilling over into these lines, but this would be to miss the point that for Gawain the vision of the castle *is* a magic moment. By describing it as such the *Gawain*-poet seems to suggest not that romance and reality are incompatible, but that, in experience, they can at times be virtually indistinguishable.

Romance, to paraphrase Bertilac on the location of the Green Chapel, is 'not two miles hence', and the *Gawain*-poet tends to be unusually clear about the points where romance and reality intersect. As he implies, the realm of Logres, the knight errant, or the sudden apparition of a castle are all translatable into common experiences. If, like Gawain, we travel in parts of England where we do not quite know the way, we are like the adventurous knights in romance; if, in these circumstances, we are unsure whether we will arrive at the point that we set out for, we *wander*; and should it happen that chance throws the perfect bed and breakfast on our path, it is *as if* our wishes had been miraculously granted. The motifs of Arthurian romance used by the *Gawain*-poet are unreal only to the extent that they magnify these ordinary experiences so as to bring their strangeness into view.

III

This colouring of reality is also the function of what is surely the most bizarre plot-motif in *Sir Gawain and the Green Knight*, the Beheading Game. Both stages of the Beheading Game, the first at Arthur's court, the second at the Green Chapel, repay close attention because they exemplify beautifully the poet's tendency to conflate the fantastic with the verisimilar. The first stage opens when the Green Knight storms into the hall, just as Arthur stands waiting for the arrival of an adventure. In the hearing of all, the Green Knight offers a 'Crystemas gomen' (283): would a knight please strike him, with the understanding that, in a year's time, he can return the favour? As has already been mentioned, the source for this bizarre adventure is the *First Continuation* of Chrétien's *Perceval*, and in order to show how the *Gawain*-poet reworked his source, I will quote the beginning of the adventure in the *First Continuation*:

> While they talked together there, it was announced that a knight who rode in very great haste had come through the door. And he came singing a song very sweetly, and had on his hat a circlet from which hung a wreath of flowers, and he was dressed in green satin furred with ermine. He was girded with a sword with which later his head was cut off, and he had fringes to the belt of fine silk embroidered with gold and thick with pearls scattered on top. When he came before the king he very humbly greeted him in this manner:

'Sir,' he said, 'I greet you as the best and noblest king who reigns on this earth at the present time. Know that I come to ask you a boon, if it may please you to grant it to me.' 'Friend,' said the king, 'I grant it to you ... '[6]

The changes and additions which the poet made to his source-material are various, but I think they fall into place when we observe that whereas the stranger fails to make much of an impression on his onlookers in the *First Continuation*, the Green Knight's dramatic entry in *Gawain* produces bafflement and fascination. From the moment that Arthur and his knights first set eyes on him, they are thrown into confusion:

> For wonder of his hwe men hade,
> Set in his semblaunt sene;
> He ferde as freke were fade,
> And overal enker-grene.
> (147–50)

(Men had great wonder at his hue, which was clear to see in his appearance. He acted as an elf-like man, and everywhere he was bright green.)

And their amazement in turn arouses ours, for if Arthur's knights, who are after all used to strange adventures, are taken aback by the Green Knight, then something extraordinary must indeed be at hand.

There is, however, a danger of misunderstanding the sense of *wonder* which the poet provokes if we think the *Gawain*-poet arouses it only by making his Green Knight more outlandish than the challenger in the *Perceval-Continuation*. True, the *Gawain*-poet's knight is green all over, and does not simply wear a green tunic, like his counterpart in the source. Yet while a green knight is obviously altogether weirder, this weirdness is compounded by the fact that, in almost any other respect, this green knight is entirely normal. The clothes he wears—and the *Gawain*-poet describes them appreciatively and precisely—are simply those befitting a fashionable courtier. Descriptions of Gawain later in the poem show him dressed in very similar garb. Compare, for example, some lines from the *Gawain*-poet's description of the Green Knight with Gawain's outfit in fitt two:

> And al grayþed in grene þis gome and his wedes:
> A strayte cot ful streȝt, þat stek on his sides,
> A meré mantile abof, mensked withinne
> With pelure pured apert, þe pane ful clene

---

6. I am quoting the translation of the prose version of the *First Continuation* by Elisabeth Brewer, op. cit., 130.

Wyth blyþe blaunner ful bryȝt, and his hod boþe,
Þat was laȝt fro his lokkez and layde on his schulderes ...
(151–6)

(And all arrayed in green were the man and his clothes: he wore a tight and straight surcoat that fitted closely to his sides, a fine mantle on top, adorned within with neatly trimmed fur, lined very elegantly with beautiful and bright ermine, just as was his hood, which hung back from his locks and rested on his shoulders ...)

And þenne a meré mantyle watz on þat mon cast
Of a broun bleeaunt, enbrauded ful ryche
And fayre furred wythinne with fellez of þe best,
Alle of ermyn in erde, his hode of þe same ...
(878–81)

(And then a fine mantle was cast on the man, of bright and rich material, embroidered very finely, and fairly furred on the inside with the best skins, all of true ermine, just like his hood ...)

The only difference between Gawain and the Green Knight's clothes consists in the Green Knight's marked preference for the colour green. Other than that, neither the Green Knight's elegant garb, nor, for that matter, the trappings of his horse, give much cause for surprise, and the realistic details in the poet's descriptions of the horse and its rider only serve to underline that point. But the *Gawain*-poet is equally clear that, despite the sheer plausibility of their accoutrements—the horse's expensive breast-harness or saddle-skirts, the Green Knight's well-fitting hose, and so on—they are all green. For the narrator this is clearly a fact that bears repeating: there are references to the colour green about every five lines in the lengthy description. But it also *needs* repeating, for the simple reason that without his colour (and his size) the knight would sink into utter normality. The *Gawain*-poet has created *wonder* not by lifting the Green Knight over the threshold of credibility, but more precisely by giving an elegant knight with a stylish sense of dress a different colour. Seeing the Green Knight is like looking at the ordinary world through green-coloured spectacles.

This combination of familiarity and strangeness which the Green Knight embodies gives rise to what the *Gawain*-poet calls *mervayle* or *wonder*:

Ther watz lokyng on lenþe þe lude to beholde,
For vch mon had meruayle quat hit mene myȝt
Þat a haþel and a horse myȝt suche a hwe lach,

As growe grene as þe gres and grener hit semed,
Þen grene aumayl on golde glowande bryȝter.
Al studied þat þer stod, and stalked hym nerre
Wyth al þe wonder of the worlde what he worch schulde.

(232–8)

(For a long time they gazed to see the man, for each man had wonder what it might mean that a man and a horse should take such a colour, as to grow green as the grass and still greener it seemed, glowing brighter than green enamel on gold. All watched intently, and stalked closer to him, with all the wonder of the world as to what he might do next.)

It might have been easier for Arthur's court to place the Green Knight if he were some ugly fiend; but as it is, they cannot quite make up their minds whether he is a *trompe l'oeil*, some supernatural monster, or a natural phenomenon. And so they wonder and marvel, in the strongest sense of that word. The words *wonder* or *marvel* have through long use lost the force which they have in the passage I have just quoted, but it needs only a brief glance at a comparable scene in medieval literature, where courtiers likewise marvel at the strange spectacle before them, to recapture their original flavour. This scene is from Chaucer's *Squire's Tale*, which begins when a number of exotic gifts are presented to Cambuskyan. As the Green Knight does in *Gawain*, the presents, in particular the gift of a brass horse that can fly, arouse both curiosity—'Greet was the prees that swarmeth to and fro / To gauren on his hors that stondeth so' (V, 189–90)—and wonder:

Swich wondryng was ther on this hors of bras
That syn the grete sege of Troie was,
Theras men wondreden on an horse also,
Ne was ther swich a wondryng as was tho.

(V, 305–8)

syn: since; *theras*: when

Now, it might be thought that Cambuskyan's courtiers wonder because they know that the horse *is* supernatural, but in fact they reach no unanimous agreement on this issue: the flying horse could, so they think, be the latest thing in engineering, black magic, or a trick of the senses. Like the Round Table, the court wonders because the nature of the horse, like that of the Green Knight, resists classification. As Todorov remarks on the subject of the fantastic, *wonder* does not spring from the realization that the object under observation is supernatural, but rather from the *hesitation* about exactly which laws, natural or supernatural, are in operation (Todorov 1970, 30).

The problem with the Green Knight is that he seems to obey both laws. He is green all over (and therefore unreal), but fashionably dressed (and therefore life-like). His indeterminacy is summed up by his size. He is almost a giant, but not quite as tall as that:

> Half etayn in erde I hope þat he were,
> Bot mon most I algate mynn hym to bene ...
>
> (140–1)

> (I thought he might have been a half-giant on earth, but I nevertheless declare him to be the biggest man ...)

In that in-betweenness he remains suspended, neither comfortably identifiable as one of those giants that inhabit the world of Arthurian romances, nor as one of those tall men that occasionally walk past in the street.

As the Green Knight's over-the-top performance at Arthur's court shows, he clearly relishes his unresolvable ambiguity. His words for the outrageous challenge he offers, a harmless 'Christmas game' to honour the season, and his comic impatience when Arthur's courtiers do not respond immediately, radiate a complete confidence in his own normality, while at the same time the madness of his proposition, his colour, and his excessive body-language ensure that this confidence convinces no one but himself:

> If he hem stowned vpon fyrst, stiller were þanne
> Alle þe heredmen in halle, þe hyȝ and þe loȝe.
> Þe renk on his rouncé hym ruched in his sadel,
> And runischly his rede yȝen he reled aboute,
> Bende his bresed broȝez, blycande grene,
> Wayued his berde for to wayte quo-so wolde ryse.
>
> (301–6)

> (If he astounded them at first, they were even more silent then, all the warriors in the hall, the high and the low. The man on his horse turned in his saddle, and fiercely rolled his red eyes around, knitted his bristly brows, shining green, and waved his beard, waiting to see who would get up.)

Waving his beard, rolling his eyes, and turning and twisting in his saddle, he startles Arthur's court with a histrionic act that both dramatizes his strangeness and teases his spectators with the possibility that this strangeness could, after all, simply be reduced to theatrical make-believe. By so clearly acting a part, the Green Knight again sharply raises the insoluble question which he had already set the court in his meticulously groomed, but green, appearance: 'Am I for real?'

The world of *Gawain* teases the reader with the same question, incorporating as it does a similar mixture of the implausible and the probable. That probability reaches its summit when characters *within* the poem experience difficulty in believing the story they are in. In the *First Continuation*, by contrast, no one at Arthur's court bats an eyelid at the arrival of a challenger who wants to play a beheading game. The strangeness of it does not enter their consciousness. In other Arthurian romances, too, characters have usually thoroughly internalized the postulates of the genre. When, for example, in Malory's *Tale of Sir Gareth* the hero decapitates a knight, he shows no surprise when he sees how a damsel glues his head back on with some magic ointment:

> And forthwithall com dame Lyonett and toke up the hede in the syght of them all, and anoynted hit with an oyntemente thereas it was smytten off, and in the same wyse she ded to the othir parte theras the hede stake. And then she sette hit togydirs, and hit stake as faste as ever hit ded. And the knyght arose lyghtly up and the damesell Lyonett put hym in hir chambir. All this saw ... sir Gareth, and well he aspyed that hit was dame Lyonett that rode with hym thorow the perelouse passages.[7]

Malory's characters accept the magical laws that rule their world. What astonishes Gareth is not therefore the fact that heads can come off and on again, but the fact that of all people 'dame Lyonett', whom Gareth counted among his friends, should have wanted to bring his opponent back to life. In *Gawain*, on the other hand, characters find the postulates of romance harder to swallow. Arthur and Gawain may act as if they are unruffled by the Green Knight's survival of decapitation—

> Þaȝ Arþer þe hende kyng at hert hade wonder,
> He let no semblaunt be sene ...
>
> (467–8)

(Although Arthur the courteous king felt wonder at heart, he let no sign be seen ...)

but the effort that goes into pretending, for the benefit of all, that nothing out of the ordinary has actually occurred shows how uneasily they

---

7. *Sir Thomas Malory: Works*, ed. Eugène Vinaver and P.J.C. Field, 3rd edn, 3 vols (Oxford: Clarendon Press, 1990), I, 334.20–8.

adjust from watching a romance-marvel to resuming the festive business of the day.

The *Gawain*-poet's assumption of ordinary attitudes and expectations means that the line that separates reality from romance no longer falls between the world inside the text and the world outside it, but becomes a division internal to the text itself. Thus Arthur's knights in *Gawain*, whom one might have imagined (as Chaucer did) to belong to the land of 'Fairye' themselves, decide on the basis of their experience of adventure that the Green Knight cannot possibly be a natural phenomenon but must be from fairyland:

> For fele sellyez had þay sen, bot such neuer are;
> Forþi for fantoum and fayryӡe þe folk þere hit demed.
>
> (239–40)

(For many wonders had they seen, but never before one like this; therefore the people there put it down to illusion and magic.)

More bewilderingly still, in fitt three, Gawain, a famous romance hero with a long literary tradition, comes face to face with a hostess who believes he is not acting as romance heroes should, since the 'tyxt of her werkkes' (the text about their deeds) specifies that knights should bring bliss into the bedrooms of women. When Gawain refuses to speak about chivalric romances to her, refuses to 'discuss the themes of the text and tales of chivalry' ('towche þe temez of tyxt and talez of armez'), one might almost forget that Gawain is *himself* a literary character who owes his existence and his fame to the 'tyxt and talez of armez' that he dismisses as irrelevant to his own situation.

The assumptions that the *Gawain*-poet's Arthurian characters have about the world they inhabit are at times disturbingly close to our own. Green monsters are dismissed as 'fantoum and fayryӡe'; ladies are reminded that they are not in a romance where knights fall in love with beautiful women in castles. But, paradoxically, the firmer their grasp on reality, the weaker ours becomes. For, ultimately, the more the *Gawain*-poet populates his romance with sensible and sceptical people like ourselves, the more he authenticates their imaginary world as an accurate copy of our own. Like the Green Knight, who spellbinds his onlookers by reflecting back to them a differently coloured image of themselves, the fascination of *Sir Gawain and the Green Knight* lies in the slightly distorted image which it gives of reality, an image whose unlikelihood never entirely obscures a recognizable likeness.

Even when the plot is at its most outrageous, the reality it distorts still remains visible. To see this we must follow the way the Beheading Game unfolds. Up to the point where Gawain steps forward to take up the axe, and exposes himself to the risk of a return blow in the event of the Green Knight's survival, the 'Christmas game' is, not surprisingly, dismissed as sheer folly: 'þyn askyng is nys' (323), as Arthur says. But this foolish game, apparently unworthy of serious attention, acquires a definite note of gravity when the Green Knight asks Gawain to rehearse the rules of the game in the following manner:

'Refourme we oure forwardes, er we fyrre passe.
Fyrst I eþe þe, haþel, how þat þou hattes
Þat þou me telle truly, as I tryst may.'
'In god fayth', quoþ þe goode kny3t, 'Gawan I hatte,
Þat bede þe þis buffet, quat-so bifallez after,
And at þis tyme twelmonyth take at þe an oþer
Wyth what weppen so þou wylt, and wyth no wy3 ellez
        on lyue.'

...

'Bigog', quoþ þe grene kny3t, 'Sir Gawan, me lykez
Þat I schal fange at þy fust þat I haf frayst here.
And þou hatz redily rehersed, bi resoun ful trwe,
Clanly al þe couenaunt þat I þe kyng asked,
Saf þat þou schal siker me, segge, bi þi trawþe,
Þat þou schal seche me þiself, wher-so þou hopes
I may be funde vpon folde, and foch þe such wages
As þou deles me to-day bifore þis douþe ryche.'
                              (378–97)

('Let us repeat the conditions, before we pass further in this matter. First I ask you, man, what your name is, that you tell me this truly, so that I can trust it.' 'In good faith', said the good knight, 'I am called Gawain, who offer you the blow, whatever may happen afterwards, and at the same time, twelve months from now, shall take from you the other blow with whatever weapon you want, and from no other man alive.' [...] 'By God', said the Green Knight, 'I am pleased that I shall receive from your hand, Sir Gawain, what I have asked for. And now you have obediently and completely rehearsed, in true words, the entire contract that I requested from the king, except that you must assure me, on your truth, that you will seek me yourself, wherever you think that I may be found in the land, and receive the same wages that you deal me today before this illustrious company.')

The romance motif of the Beheading Game is discussed by the two players in a language drawn from two familiar spheres of life: law and commerce (Blanch and Wasserman 1984). Like the Exchange of Winnings later in the poem, the 'exchange' of blows is described as a consensual transaction, in which Gawain pays *wages* that will be repaid to him in a year's time. In order that Gawain may be held accountable to this contract (*couenaunt*), he must declare his name, and confirm that he has fully understood the conditions (*forwardes*) of the deal. On the face of it, the conditions are such that Gawain cannot lose. Since the first blow is Gawain's, there will no longer be anyone to keep *couenaunt* with if he succeeds in beheading his opponent. Of course, we suspect a catch, and Gawain does too. Being someone who takes his *trawþe* seriously, he does not enter into the agreement rashly, but goes through the contract point by point, even making sure there is not a snag in the small print: he will receive the return blow from the Green Knight, and not from any of his executors ('wyth no wyȝ ellez'). On that understanding, Gawain pledges his truth that he will abide by the rules of the game 'quat-so bifallez after'.

The language of law and commerce thus sets the ludicrous romance-motif of the Beheading Game in a close relation to ordinary life, as if playing the Beheading Game were somehow similar to sealing contracts. To appreciate how that curious relationship between the two can exist we might compare it to the special relationship that holds between games and reality. On the one hand, the fact that the poet calls the Beheading Game a game ('gomen') distances it from reality: games, after all, take place in imaginary play-worlds with their own distinct and artificial sets of rules. Yet on the other hand, human playing, as Hans-Georg Gadamer writes, 'is always a playing *of* something' (Gadamer 1975, 96; my italics), and as the *Gawain*-poet's language suggests, the 'game' that is about to engage Gawain is a play of entering into contracts, and of pledging one's *trawþe* to abide by the rules.

In the most dramatic way imaginable, the Beheading Game brings out exactly what is involved in such a promise or pledge of *trawþe*. Gawain duly strikes the Green Knight with his axe, and sends his head rolling on the floor. But to everyone's shock and horror, the Green Knight leaps forward to retrieve his head. Held by its hair, the head begins to speak:

> And hit lyfte vp þe yȝe-lyddez and loked ful brode,
> And meled þus much with his muthe, as ȝe may now here:
> 'Loke, Gawan, þou be grayþe to go as þou hettez,
> And layte as lelly til þou me, lude, fynde,
> As þou hatz hette in þis halle, herande þise knyȝtes ... '
>
> (446–50)

(And it lifted up its eyelids and stared with wide-open eyes and mouthed the following words, as you may now hear: 'Look to it, Gawain, that you are ready to go as you promised, and search faithfully until you find me, man, as you have promised in this hall, in the hearing of these knights ... ')

The catch concealed in the contract which Gawain and the Green Knight have sealed is graphically exposed: the Green Knight lives. What Gawain could not possibly have anticipated has happened, and the 'couenaunt' which Gawain thought he could not lose now sentences him to a suicidal journey to the Green Chapel.

Of course, the *Gawain*-poet knew as well as we do that the Green Knight's magical trick is fantastical. However, by means of it, he magnifies the kind of predicament that his contemporaries might have recognized. His pact with the Green Knight is a 'couenaunt', the technical legal term for a written or verbal agreement, and, in the idiom of contemporary English common law, any person who makes a 'couenaunt' is bound to 'make it good' regardless of the supervention of any 'sudden adventure' which he or she could not foresee.[8] Gawain's situation is extraordinary because he confronts this 'sudden adventure' and its consequences in their most extreme form: the Green Knight can put his head back on, and Gawain's promise now forces him to put his own head on the line.

Who would not here have turned to the Green Knight and said: 'I've changed my mind about this agreement of ours'? But before dismissing Gawain's situation as factitious, we should recognize that, when Gawain makes no such excuses, he is acting absurdly only in so far as he takes his 'trawþe' to the *couenaunt* with deadly seriousness. *Trawþe* or faithfulness is a commitment to an agreement beyond the moment it was made, which is why truth exacts its demands irrespective of any reversal in the original circumstances in which it was pledged: it binds 'for better or worse' or, as Gawain put it, 'quat-so bifallez after'. The Green Knight's magical trick actualizes the unthinkable for Gawain, and by virtue of its unrealness it brings into focus the remorselessly unconditional nature of truth,

8. The phrases quoted are taken from the records of actual cases (one from 1366) brought before the common law court, and discussed by Simpson (1975), 31–3. It may be relevant to note that *Gawain*'s date of composition coincides with a revolutionary development in common law. The Ordinance and the Statute of Labourers of 1349 and 1351 had made it a punishable offence for labourers to withdraw their service from their present lord or master and to seek more lucrative employment elsewhere. This set a legal precedent for the enforcement of *unwritten* agreements, breaches of which had not previously been punishable by common law (McGovern 1971).

the way it binds without bending itself to a change of circumstance or a change of mind. While real life fortunately spares us beheading games in which opponents put their heads back on, the *Gawain*-poet reminds us that it does have contracts (*couenaunts*) with rules (*forwardes*) which human beings solemnly vow fidelity to. And each time they do so, they commit themselves to actions in a future which may no longer be the one they envisaged when the promise was made. As the *Gawain*-poet's legal and commercial vocabulary insists, even the fantastical events in fitt one—in which the impossible occurs when the Green Knight picks up his head and calls upon Gawain to keep his 'trawþe'—find an equivalent in the day-to-day business of making agreements and contracts, whose fulfilment depends on the co-operation of a multitude of imponderable factors which even the most prudent person cannot predict. Making a promise or signing a contract always involves a bet on an incalculable future, and this abandonment to unpredictable forces, which any *couenant* presumes, lets all of us become adventurers like Gawain.[9]

Rather than treating the fabulous plot of a Beheading Game with contempt, the *Gawain*-poet seems to exploit its distance from reality to bring the nature of truth into sharper focus. This potential of romance is again illustrated by the second stage of the Beheading Game. Gawain's adventure at the Green Chapel has, in more than one sense, a double agenda. The fact that Gawain turns up at the Green Chapel, willing to lay down his life, first of all establishes the extent of the hero's commitment to *trawþe*. When the Green Knight first sees Gawain in fitt four, he gives due recognition to Gawain's punctilious observance of the terms of the Beheading Game, referring to it, once again, as a *couenaunt*:

> Þat oþer sayde, 'Now, sir swete,
> Of steuen mon may þe trowe.'
>
> 'Gawain,' quoþ þat grene gome, 'God þe mot loke!
> Iwysse þou art welcom, wyȝe, to my place,
> And þou hatz tymed þi trauayl as truee mon schulde,
> And þou knowez þe couenauntez kest vus bytwene ... '
>
> (2237–42)

9. In formulating this idea I am indebted to the stimulating essay 'The Adventure' by the sociologist Georg Simmel (1960), who, like the *Gawain*-poet, appreciated the immanence of adventure in everyday existence. I quote from the essay: 'The sliding of our existence over a scale on which every point is simultaneously determined by the effect of our strength *and* our abandonment to impenetrable things and powers ... lets all of us become adventurers. Within the dimensions into which our station in life with its tasks, our aims, and our means places us, none of us could live one day if we did not treat that which is really incalculable as if it were calculable ... '(257).

(The other man said, 'Now, dear sir, you can be trusted to keep your promise.' 'Gawain', the green man said, 'you are very welcome to my dwelling, and you have timed your travel as a true man should, and you know the contracts made between us.')

But the Beheading Game, to which Gawain truthfully submits himself, soon turns out to have another side to it: unexpectedly, it reveals itself to be merely a curious kind of shadow-boxing. Of course, this does not detract from its importance as a test and a touchstone of Gawain's truth. Gawain, after all, believes that the Beheading Game is for real, and since he acts in that belief, the courage and honesty that he displays when he turns up for his own beheading are not in the least diminished when this beheading fails to materialize.

By showing us that the Beheading Game is not for real, the *Gawain*-poet seems to admit unashamedly that this particular adventure was indeed contrived and unreal. In the final dénouement of his story, the Green Knight reveals that he is after all not a monster from whom knights can only deliver themselves with a magical talisman, but Bertilac de Hautdesert, Gawain's amicable host at the castle, where Gawain's truth was tested in a parlour game. The moment when Gawain has to deal with his devilish opponent, which the poem has been building up to in fearful anticipation, turns out to be something of an anti-climax. The real adventure, the Exchange of Winnings in which Gawain kept the girdle, has already taken place, and all the Green Knight does with his terrifying axe is to pronounce his verdict on Gawain's behaviour at Castle Hautdesert. The Green Knight's revelations suddenly lift the curtain, and the actors stand exposed in their true light: the Green Knight is a country gentleman; Morgan le Fay, who has put him up to all this mischief, is Gawain's old aunt, who hides her wrinkles behind kerchiefs; the magic talisman, the green girdle, is only a piece of cloth.

The way the *Gawain*-poet confronts us with our suspension of disbelief in the supernatural says much about his understanding of romance as a matter of make-believe, but it also illustrates how the make-believe world of romance allows something that is real and serious enough to find expression. The terror of the Green Knight may prove in the end harmless enough, but this is only because Gawain has, unbeknown to himself, already passed a test which could have had lethal consequences if he had not performed as well as he did. The 'play' at the Green Chapel which the Green Knight directs is again a play *of* something—in this case, a *replay* of earlier events. Three times Gawain's loyalty was tested in the bedroom and the Exchange of Winnings, and accordingly the Green Knight swings his axe three times. As Bertilac explains to Gawain, each of the blows corresponds to Gawain's earlier performance at Caste Hautdesert:

> 'Fyrst I mansed þe muryly with a mynt one,
> And roue þe wyth no rof-sore, with ryȝt I þe profered
> For þe forwarde þat we fest in þe fyrst nyȝt,
> And þou trystyly þe trawþe and trwly me haldez,
> Al þe gayne þow me gef, as god mon schulde.
> Þat oþer munt for þe morne, mon, I þe profered,
> Þou kyssedes my clere wyf—þe cossez me raȝtez.
> For boþe two here I þe bede bot two bare myntes
>   boute scaþe.
> Trwe mon trwe restore,
> Þenne þar mon drede no waþe.
> At þe þrid þou fayled þore,
> And þerfore þat tappe ta þe.'
>
>   (2345–57)

('First I threatened you cheerfully with one feint, and cut you with no wound, and properly I offered you this in view of the covenant we made fast on the first night, and you trustworthily and truly kept your truth to me. All the winnings you gave to me, as a good man should. The second swing of the axe I gave you for the next day; you kissed my wife—and gave the kisses to me. For both two I offered you only two feints without harm. Truth must pay back truth, then need a man fear no danger. On the third day you failed in this regard; take the tap for that.')

The first two feints of the axe mirror Gawain's impeccable honesty in the first two Exchanges of Winnings; the third blow which grazes Gawain's neck mirrors his slip on the third day of the test, when he accepted and retained the girdle that he should have handed back to his host. Under the guise of a monster wielding a huge axe, the Green Knight stages Gawain's adventures at Castle Hautdesert once more, but this time in a dramatic form that renders the dangers involved in the innocuous games at Castle Hautdesert fully apparent. That the fabulous plot of a monster who is out to behead our hero is not finally for real matters perhaps less than what that plot tells us about the invisible dangers that may surround even the most trivial of social games.

IV

The most mundane actions in *Sir Gawain and the Green Knight* have their counterparts in the world of romance, and the further that world takes us from reality, the purer is the perspective on reality which this distance affords. The *Gawain*-poet understood and appreciated the possibilities of romance too well to supplant it with realism. His resistance to realism appears, I think, from his final decision not to explain away the supernatural elements in his poem, even when that option was evidently open to him. His Green Knight could have revealed, for instance, that he survived Gawain's blow because he was wearing a false head. The *Gawain*-poet had probably seen tricks with false heads in medieval popular drama, where they were not uncommon,[10] and it would surprise me if this way of rationalizing the story had not occurred to him. Arthur himself tries to make sense of the Green Knight's re-heading by appealing to play-acting—'layking of enterludez' (472)—and the poet's description of the Green Knight's size—'Herre þen ani in þe hous *by þe hed and more*' (333)—flirts with the possibility that the Green Knight's magic may be no more than a theatrical trick. Yet rather than disenchanting his world, the *Gawain*-poet chose an alternative explanation that draws on all the standard characters of Arthurian romance. The miracle is conveniently accredited to the 'myȝt of Morgne la Faye' (2446), whose role in earlier romances as the student of Merlin and as Arthur's enemy had made her name a byword for anything malicious or magical (cf. Kennedy 1986, 287). Protected by Morgan's magic, Bertilac had been sent to orchestrate his own decapitation in order to scare Guinevere:

'Ho wayned me þis wonder your wyttez to reue,
For to haf greued Gaynour and gart hir to dyȝe
With glopnyng of þat ilke gome þat gostlych speked
With his hede in his honde bifore þe hyȝe table.'
(2459–62)

10. Quite a few medieval plays require a false head. In the *Robin Hood* play (c. 1475), Robin cuts off Sir Guy's head and carries it in his hood (Axton 1977, 6–7). John Redford's early-Tudor *Wyt and Science* contains the following stage direction: 'Heere Wyt cum'th in and bryng'th in the hed upon his swoorde ... ' (l. 961); ed. David Bevington, in *Medieval Drama* (Boston: Houghton Mifflin, 1975). False heads are also referred to in the account books for the Chester mystery cycles. See *Chester*, Records of Early English Drama, ed. Lawrence M. Clopper (Toronto: University of Toronto Press, 1979), 176, 179, 183. I am grateful to Richard Axton for supplying me with these references. On the relationship between *Gawain* and contemporary interludes see Weiss (1991).

('She arranged for me this wonder to rob you of your wits, and to harm Guinevere and to cause her death for dismay at the man that spoke like a phantom with his head in his hand before the high table.')

How does Gawain's adventure fit into this 'explanation'? Well, it does not. Poor Gawain has somehow managed to get himself caught up in a feud between Morgan and Guinevere, to which his own tribulations are entirely incidental. If that were not baffling enough, the *Gawain*-poet then sends Bertilac riding off beyond the horizon of the narrative:

Gawayn on blonk ful bene
To þe kyngez burȝ buskez bolde,
And þe knyȝt in þe enker-grene
Whiderwarde-so-euer he wolde.
(2475–8)

(Gawain on his fair horse hastens straight to the king's castle, and the knight in bright green rode wherever his fancy took him.)

Why not dispatch the Green Knight to Castle Hautdesert, where by now we all know he lives? Why not explain his stunt as a trick with a false head? And why not accommodate Gawain's harrowing experiences into a more meaningful design that is proportionate to the significance that Gawain sees in them? The answer is, quite simply, that the *Gawain*-poet did not want to end his romance realistically. And I think that a rational ending would have been as undesirable as to have Gawain accept Bertilac's invitation to return with him to Castle Hautdesert and shake hands with the Lady of the Castle and Morgan le Fay. The disenchantment that this would have produced is too awful to contemplate. The mystery must remain unsolved (Spearing 1970, 236), and so the *Gawain*-poet wisely steered his story back into the realm of romance. He does so humorously, but also with a real affection for the different model of comprehending the world that romance admits. Faithful to that model, he finishes his romance by substituting marvel for rationality, haphazardness for purpose.

In *Sir Gawain* the play of these substitutions is more visible than in any other Arthurian romance, since *Gawain* is in many other ways a very realistic work. But, as I have argued, the *Gawain*-poet does not have a mind that treats the motifs of Arthurian romance with contempt or makes them the object of parody. Romance motifs are in his work stylizations of reality that capture, if not the way things are literally, then the way they sometimes seem imaginatively.

To put it more strongly, the poet did not dismiss the conventions of romance as eccentricities on the conviction that these eccentricities are in fact immanent in ordinary life. In the cycles of nature and the history of peoples there lurks, in the *Gawain*-poet's view, the potential for romance, and the reader of the poet's fine descriptions of the passing seasons and the foundations of kingdoms will discover it there. Both are places where one would least expect it. The yearly cycle of nature, which an audience might have imagined as an orderly progression of seasons, yields in *Gawain* not regularity or certainty, but surprise and contingency:

> A ȝere ȝernes ful ȝerne, and ȝeldez neuer lyke,
> Þe forme to þe fynisment foldez ful selden.
>
>> (498–9)

(A year runs by quickly, and yields never the same, the beginning rarely corresponds to the end.)

And in history, where a medieval audience would have looked for purposeful progress or the unfolding of God's design, the *Gawain*-poet detects *wonder* and arbitrariness (Bonjour 1951):

> And fer ouer þe French flod Felix Brutus
> On mony bonkkes ful brode Bretayn he settez
>> wyth wynne,
> Where werre and wrake and wonder
> Bi syþez hatz wont þerinne,
> And oft boþe blysse and blunder
> Ful skete hatz skyfted synne.
>
>> (13–19)

(And far over the Channel, Felix Brutus on many broad hills founds Britain in prosperity, where war and distress and wonder have dwelt at different times. And often both bliss and blunder have quickly alternated.)

Unpredictability and *wonder* thus inhere in the coming and going of seasons or kingdoms. The reason why the *Gawain*-poet did not place romance and realism in an antithetical relation to one another appears here in its clearest form: life, according to the *Gawain*-poet, is too much like romance. And that, finally, is a statement not only about the veracity of romance, but about the fictitiousness of life, which, in its blithe imperviousness to human reason and foresight, can seem as unreal and fantastic as the genre of romance itself.

PLOT-TELLING AND THE MANIPULATION OF MEMORY

I

The importance of the poet's belief that the meanings and the repercussions of actions may only be partially intelligible to human beings can hardly be overestimated, for, as the poet absorbs his readers in a story that hides its true significance until the end, the sense of partial control is built into the very experience of reading, or hearing, *Gawain* for the first time. The surprising plot and the *Gawain*-poet's philosophy of life are inseparable. What human beings anticipate and what they get is rarely the same thing: 'þe forme to þe fynisment foldez ful selden'; and the poet's deceptive telling of the plot makes sure that we all fall victims to his gnomic wisdom. The 'fynisment' of the story is indeed not the one which we had been led to expect.

Gawain, whose point of view we are made to share in the romance, had assumed that his adventure would culminate in his encounter with the Green Knight, and his view of the situation only changes when the Green Knight reveals he is in fact the Lord of the Castle, pronouncing his judgment on the test that had taken place at Castle Hautdesert. It takes only a short while for the implications of this news to sink in. Then Gawain is understandably overwhelmed by anger and shame:

> Þat oþer stif mon in study stod a gret whyle,
> So agreued for greme he gryed withinne;
> Alle þe blod of his brest blende in his face,
> Þat al he schrank for schome þat þe schalk talked.
>
> (2369–73)

(The other bold man stood in thought for a long time, so aggrieved by anguish that he shuddered inside; all the blood from his heart rushed into his face, so that he shrank for shame at the man's words.)

For a year Gawain has had to live, quite unnecessarily, with the awful prospect of being beheaded at the Green Chapel. Then his only relief as he made the journey to the Chapel, his stay at Castle Hautdesert, suddenly stands revealed as a test in which he has failed. And as Gawain has reason to be aggrieved, he naturally feels shame, for it has become clear that his every move in Castle Hautdesert has been carefully monitored by his host. In what Gawain believed was a secret pact with the Lady of the Castle, he accepted the green girdle, which Gawain and the Lady agreed would remain hidden from the host:

þe leude hym acordez
Þat neuer wyȝe schulde hit wyt, iwysse, bot þay twayne
   for noȝte ...

                (1863–5)

(The man agrees that no man should ever know about it, for sure, apart from
the two of them, for nothing in the world.)

But, as it turns out, the secret coalition was never between Gawain and
the Lady but between the Lady and her husband, and nothing, not even
Gawain's one moment of stealth, has escaped Bertilac's watchful eye.
The knowledge that Gawain stands before Bertilac totally exposed
makes his blood rush to his face.

One of the painful morals in all of the *Gawain*-poet's work is that
there is no hiding from the judge.[11] In *Cleanness* or *Patience* that judge is
God; in *Gawain* it is Bertilac de Hautdesert, who teaches Gawain that
secrecy cannot fool someone who knows all. But since the reader, too, is
duped by the plot, Gawain is hardly alone in having to face up to the
fact of omniscience. For like Bertilac, the poet knew all along that
Gawain's stay at Castle Hautdesert was the real test, and the Beheading
Game only the pretext. And as Bertilac carefully screens this knowledge
from Gawain, so the poet keeps the 'fynisment' of the story from his
readers, who for most of the poem know as much (or as little) about
what is really going on in Castle Hautdesert as Gawain himself. Forced
by Bertilac's revelation to revise our interpretation of the relation
between the plot-motifs—the temptation scenes, the Exchange of
Winnings, and the Beheading Game—we finally and belatedly reach the
point of full understanding from which the poet started out.

All this makes the poet sound more unreliable than his voice in the
text. Where he addresses the reader directly, it is usually in the voice of
the simple story-teller, who is merely relating a tale as he heard it recited:

If ȝe wyl lysten þis laye bot on littel quile,
I schal telle hit as-tit, as I in toun herde,
   with tonge ...

              (30–2)

(If you care to listen to this lay for a little while, I will tell it anon, as I heard
it amongst men, told by tongue.)

At other places, he takes up the position of the observer, ignorant of the

---

11. See below, pp. 199–200.

precise intentions of his characters. When, for example, the Lady of the Castle tempts Gawain, he comments:

> Þus hym frayned þat fre, and fondet hym ofte,
> For to haf wonnen hym to woȝe, what-so scho þoȝt ellez.
>
> (1549–50)

(Thus that noble lady questioned him and tempted him often, in order to entice him to wooing, whatever else she had in mind.)

He does not know (or so he says) whether the Lady has a hidden agenda. The throw-away remark 'what-so scho þoȝt ellez' even suggests to readers that it is pointless to look for one. But these professions of simplicity or ignorance are belied by the unexpected ending, in which the *Gawain*-poet surprises us by telling us for the first time how the story 'really' worked, and exactly what the Lady had in mind when she visited Gawain in the bedroom.

The belated disclosure of information that has been deliberately concealed from Gawain and the reader shows the *Gawain*-poet's complete control over his story and his readers. Anyone who tries to tell the plot without giving the game away from the start will appreciate how this seemingly simple task implicates him or her in a careful economy with the truth. The sophistication of this economy in *Gawain* is best illustrated if we compare the *Gawain*-poet's handling of the story with that of the poet of the ballad version of *Sir Gawain and the Green Knight*. The ballad version, known as *The Grene Knight*, has been dated to the sixteenth century, and it claims our interest as the earliest surviving retelling of the story of *Sir Gawain and the Green Knight*. Some of the details have changed in the ballad version. The Green Knight, for instance, is called Sir Bredbeddle rather than Bertilac, and after he enlightens Gawain at the Green Chapel, he returns with Gawain to Arthur's court. But for our purposes, its most striking difference from *Gawain* is that the balladeer recounts Gawain's adventures in a way that gives the audience the full benefit of his omniscience. Loose-lipped, the poet of *The Grene Knight* lays all his cards on the table. When recounting Gawain's arrival at the Castle, for instance, he spells out that Gawain's host and the Green Knight are one and the same person:

> for that was the greene Knight
> that hee was lodged with that night,
> and harbarrowes in his hold.
>
> (p. 156)[12]

12. *The Grene Knight*, ed. Elisabeth Brewer, *Sir Gawain and the Green Knight: Sources and Analogues* (Woodbridge: Boydell and Brewer, 1992).

Similarly, the poet pre-empts the *Gawain*-poet's revelation that Gawain's retention of the girdle is morally significant by ticking Gawain off the moment he fails to return the girdle to the host:

> ever privily he held the lace:
> that was all the villanye that ever was
> proved by Sir Gawaine the gay.
>
> (p. 162)

The balladeer's openness has the advantage of clarifying the logic of the plot from the start, but the price he pays is that the tale loses all the suspense and forward momentum of its source. Because the poet of *The Grene Knight* has not mastered the art of guarding secrets he totally spoils the surprise that awaits us in *Sir Gawain and the Green Knight*, which rarely tells us more than Gawain knows himself.

I want to suggest, however, that there is more to the *Gawain*-poet's art of secrecy than merely withholding information. Part of the joke which the *Gawain*-poet plays on us is that he reveals things which, to some extent, we might always have known: that the green girdle is a piece of cloth, for example, and that Gawain should have returned it to his host. Bertilac's account of what really happened at Castle Hautdesert makes instant sense of the story we have been reading, which is why it catches us and Gawain in the horrible realization that we have been tricked. The sensation that Bertilac's revelation produces is one of 'things suddenly falling into place', and this expression usefully directs us to the issue that we need to examine: why have we not been able to 'place' things properly before this point? Focusing on Gawain's stay at Castle Hautdesert, I should like to explore how the text invites us to misinterpret details that only later fall into their proper place.

II

Let me begin by making the general observation that in the process of making sense of a story, readers or listeners constantly make informed guesses about what facts they believe are going to be especially significant for the outcome of the plot. According to a constantly evolving hypothesis about where the story is tending, and about the kind of story we are in, events or objects may either be retained in the reader's consciousness as organic elements of the story-line, or (if they do not seem to contribute meaningfully to the progression of the story) drop from working memory to passive memory.[13]

13. On the essential role of memory and forgetting in the process of reading see the suggestive comments in Beer (1989, 12–15).

The distinction between these two different ways of remembering—also known as primary memory (or retention) versus secondary memory—can be illuminated by looking at the passage which describes Gawain's battles en route to the Green Chapel in fitt two:

> So mony meruayl bi mount þer þe mon fyndez,
> Hit were to tore for to telle of þe tenþe dole.
> Sumwhyle wyth wormez he werrez, and with wolues als,
> Sumwhyle wyth wodwos, þat woned in þe knarrez,
> Boþe wyth bullez and berez and borez oþerquyle,
> And etaynez, þat hym anelede of þe heȝe felle;
> Nade he ben duȝty and dryȝe, and Dryhten had serued,
> Douteles he hade ben ded and dreped ful ofte.
> For werre wrathed hym not so much þat wynter nas wors …
>
> (718–26)

(So many marvels on the hills the man found there that it would be too hard to tell you even the tenth part. Sometimes he fights with dragons, and also with wolves, sometimes with wild men that lived in the rocks, both with bulls and bears, and at other times with boars and giants, that pursued him from the high fells. If he had not been doughty and fearless, and had not served God, doubtless he would have been dead and killed often. But combat hurt him not so much that the weather was not still worse …)

In contrast with the rest of the poem, where action is subordinated to reflection, and where warfare is verbal or psychological, this passage introduces all the standard ingredients of romance. Numerous wild men, dragons, and giants are successfully dispatched by the hero. Only when the *Gawain*-poet declares that the trouble they cause is nothing in comparison with the weather, do we shift back from the realm of hyperbole to the realistic observation of nature. The lines provide ample evidence of Gawain's qualities as a fighting man, but, as we will recall, the Green Knight has summoned Gawain on a mission that depends not primarily on prowess but on Gawain's passive surrender to the Green Knight's axe. Whatever interest the list of Gawain's battles may have in its own right, it comes as a digression to what the story has told us is Gawain's main adventure, the Beheading Game, and it could be deleted from the story without interrupting its flow. Consequently, we do not need to remember the episode in the same way we need to remember that Gawain has a promise to keep at the Green Chapel. Loosely adapting the distinction between working memory, which *retains* past experiences that continue to be relevant for the psychological present, and secondary memory, which stores details that do not need to be maintained in consciousness, we can say that while Gawain's fights against dragons and giants may not be entirely forgotten (we have, after all, read about them) they are not likely to be *retained* by the reader as the story progresses. Instead they will drop into secondary memory, from where they can regain their life only if the text prompts their resuscitation.[14]

One of the pleasures of reading Arthurian romances is that on the whole they do not severely tax the reader's working memory. In the long French prose cycles of Lancelot or Tristan, popular with fourteenth-century English readers, and adapted by Malory, a single plot-motif such as the quest may connect any number of discrete adventures which can be irresponsibly forgotten as soon as they are read, without losing the sense of where the story is going. Arthurian romances are characterized by their 'tolerance of bad memory' (Edwards 1990), and to this tolerance they no doubt owe their long-standing reputation as 'light reading', which stretches back all the way to the Middle Ages (Bumke 1986, II, 141–4).

The most ingenious way in which the *Gawain*-poet exploits the reader's familiarity with Arthurian romances of this kind is his presentation of Gawain's stay at Castle Hautdesert as precisely a 'forgettable episode', an episode which, because of its apparently tangential relation to the Beheading Game which it interrupts, we are actively dissuaded from retaining, or from keeping in working memory once the episode is over. I do not mean to say that Gawain's stay at Hautdesert is presented as being without significance—the sheer length of the episode seems to be sending different signals. But while the poet indicates its importance (at line 1768 he plainly talks of Gawain's great danger in his bedroom), he avoids any suggestion that the episode has any bearing on the Beheading Game. And since the text encourages us to work with the hypothesis that

---

14. The distinction between 'primary memory' and 'secondary memory' was made by the psychologist William James, and developed by Edmund Husserl (Casey 1987, 49–52). Husserl's term for primary memory, 'retention', has the advantage of suggesting that the role of primary memory is not to recall experiences that are no longer in perception but to carry forward, or prolong in the mind, those events in the past which give meaning and purpose to the task at hand. The task of reading for the plot depends precisely on *retaining* events that give a sense of unity of action. Husserl's recognition that events which are not retained are not necessarily wholly lost, but drop from consciousness into secondary memory, can explain how it can be that narratives like detective stories provide dénouements that are both unexpected—because the reader has been tricked into retaining red herrings—and painfully obvious, since the dénouement recalls from secondary memory details which the reader realizes he or she has failed to retain. As we shall see, the dénouement of *Gawain* confronts the reader and the hero with precisely this kind of misremembering.

the Beheading Game is Gawain's main task, any intervening incidents inevitably appear slightly off track, however great their intrinsic interest.

The question of which elements of the story we retain and which we leave behind depends primarily on our hypothesis on where the plot is going. In *Gawain*, this hypothesis is strongly influenced by the way the poet time and again places the termination point at the Green Chapel at the centre of our attention. No sooner has the Green Knight put in his appearance at Arthur's court than the poem starts to look forward to a grim finale at the Green Chapel, so that, like Gawain, the reader cannot help regarding anything that happens along the way as a diversion. The anticipation of a dreadful 'fynisment' is first planted in our minds in the description of the Green Knight:

> Hit semed as no mon myȝt
> Vnder his dynttez dryȝe.
>
> > (201–2)

(It seemed that no man could survive under his blows.)

After Gawain has taken on the Green Knight's adventure, the narrator himself asserts that we should not be surprised if 'þe ende were heuy'. The sense of foreboding gathers momentum as the day of Gawain's appointment with the Green Knight approaches. After Gawain takes his leave from the Round Table, the courtiers join in the swelling chorus of voices predicting a tragic ending:

> 'Bi kryst, hit is scaþe
> Þat þou, leude, schal be lost, þat art of lyf noble!'
>
> > (674–5)

('By Christ, it is a disaster that you, man, should be lost, who are so noble of life.')

Although Gawain puts on a brave face when he says goodbye to his friends, he fears the worst as well. His apprehension, interestingly, never finds a public outlet, and it is a testimony to his exquisite courtesy that he never unburdens himself of his terrible secret at Castle Hautdesert. Even when he tells his host that he has set out to find the Green Knight, he heroically keeps the reason why to himself:

> 'Þer watz stabled bi statut a steuen vus bytwene
> To mete þat mon at þat mere, ȝif I myȝt last ... '
>
> > (1060–1)

('By our solemn agreement an appointment was made between us, that I would meet that man at the agreed place, if I should live to see the day.')

In an almost superhuman effort to be sociable, as the festive occasion at Castle Hautdesert requires, Gawain nobly suppresses the fate that hangs over his head. Gawain is not one to spoil his hosts' fun by bothering them with his own problems.

But the reader, who has access to Gawain's private world, is occasionally reminded of the terrible knowledge that Gawain tactfully spares his fellows. While Gawain does not permit them to cast a shadow over the festive atmosphere, and even banishes them from his consciousness, his dark thoughts about a gruesome death subsist in his dreams:

> In dreȝ drouping of dreme draueled þat noble,
> As mon þat watz in mornyng of mony þro þoȝtes,
> How þat destiné schulde þat day dele hym his wyrde
> At þe grene chapel, when he þe gome metes,
> And bihoues his buffet abide withoute debate more ...   (1750–4)

(In heavy slumber of a dream the noble man muttered, as a man that was troubled with many oppressive thoughts, about how destiny should that day deal him his fate at the Green Chapel, when he meets the man, and must suffer his blow without any defence.)

As will be clear from these examples, the text holds Gawain's impending 'destiné' ominously before our eyes, with the consequence that the intervening adventures at Castle Hautdesert disappear into the margins of our vision.

The hypothesis, offered by the poem itself, that Gawain's meeting at the Green Chapel is to be all-important carries such conviction that even on a second or third reading one finds oneself submitting to its force. Indeed, there are passages in *Gawain* that will only make sense in the context of this hypothesis. Take, for example, the Lady of the Castle's sense of frustration after her first failed attempt to seduce her guest, when she seems to realize that Gawain's preoccupation with his impending doom makes him totally unreceptive to her charms:

> 'Þaȝ I were burde bryȝtest', þe burde in mynde hade,
> 'Þe lasse luf in his lode for lur þat he soȝt
>   boute hone,
> Þe dunte þat schulde hym deue,
> And nedez hit most be done.'
> Þe lady þenn spek of leue,
> He granted hir ful sone.   (1283–9)

('Though I were the most beautiful woman', the Lady thought, 'he would bring little love with him because of the disaster he sought without delay, because of the blow that was to strike him down, and yet this had to be done.' The Lady then asked permission to go, and he granted it quickly.)

In quoting this passage I depart from the standard Tolkien and Gordon edition, and I should therefore draw attention to the disagreement among scholars about where the Lady's internal monologue ends and where the narrator takes over. The placement of the punctuation marks, and especially the inverted commas, thus becomes crucial.

It needs to be remembered that quotation marks (like so many modern forms of punctuation) were not used in the Middle Ages,[15] and that they have disadvantages as well as advantages. Quotation marks provide unambiguous visual cues about whether we are in the mind of a character or in the mind of the story-teller, without allowing for the possibility that there may be no clear-cut demarcation between the two. The above passage from *Gawain* confronts us with precisely this kind of grey area, where the requirements of modern punctuation unfortunately force editors (myself included) to misrepresent the fluidity of the transition between the voice of a character and that of the narrator. Evidently, the subclause at the beginning of the passage 'þaȝ I were burde bryȝtest' takes us into the mind of the Lady, but it is not so easy to determine precisely where we are taken out of her mind. The beginning of the next sentence—'þe lady þenn spek of leue'—is the only unambiguous signal that a transition from internal monologue to reported speech has taken place. Before that point, the lines form a continuous syntactical unit, in which each idea grows naturally out of the preceding one, and in which every clause requires the other to complete the sense and the grammar of the sentence. Yet while the thread of the argument continues seamlessly, the shift from the subjunctive ('þaȝ I *were* burde bryȝtest') to past tense ('for lur þat he *soȝt*')—suggests a change from direct to indirect 'thought'. And by the time we reach the final line of the sentence—'And nedez hit most be done'—we seem to have shifted almost imperceptibly from the Lady's thoughts to the narrator's (or Gawain's) consciousness of the harsh call of duty.

Where, then, should an editor close the inverted commas to mark the end of the Lady's internal monologue? The problem is that while the person who does the thinking seems to change, the train of thought on which the Lady embarks develops without any interruption. Closing the

15. Quotation marks, as we understand that term today, are an eighteenth-century innovation (Parkes 1992, 59).

quotation marks after this train of thought has come to a halt, as I have done, is not problem-free, but it avoids giving the false impression that there is any clear indication about which reflections are still attributable to the Lady and which are not. Tolkien and Gordon have firmer views on this than the poet, and they close the inverted commas after the very first clause:

'Þaȝ I were burde bryȝtest', þe burde in mynd hade.
Þe lasse luf in his lode for lur þat he soȝt
            boute hone.

(1283–5)

Yet this way of punctuating the lines creates awkward syntax. The Lady never concludes the concessive subclause which she introduces by 'þaȝ', and the full stop after line 1283 breaks up two lines that are not only related grammatically, but logically as well. 'Even if I were the prettiest lady, he would bring little love in his mission because of the disaster he sought without delay': the thought is coherent, and the chiasmus 'burde bryȝtest'-'lasse luf' expresses the problem that she perceives beautifully. More plausibly, Cawley and Anderson (1976) close the inverted commas after 'in his lode', but this too creates a pause where in the poet's syntax there is none.

Editors have based their decision to end the Lady's thought at the first possible opportunity on the conviction that the Lady *cannot think* the thought that Gawain is headed for trouble. Since no one in the Castle has ever been told that Gawain has set out on a suicidal quest, the Lady would seem to know more than she should know. Tolkien and Gordon call this a 'serious flaw in the *Gawain*-poet's handling of the plot' (p. 110), and, at the expense of garbled syntax, their punctuation disallows a possibility which the passage from *Gawain* itself permits. The absence of any clear sign by the poet about where the Lady's thought ends shows that the *Gawain*-poet did not share his editors' concern about what his readers should and should not assume about the Lady's knowledge—and for good reasons. For we should note that, rather than giving the game away, and rather than raising our suspicion about the Lady's role in the Beheading Game, the assumption that the Lady *does* know that Gawain is to be struck down has the effect of making Gawain's beheading at the Green Chapel seem inevitable, out of her control. This is why, on a second reading, when we know the Lady is 'in' on the Green Knight's plot, her thoughts become not more but less 'thinkable'. They demand, even from the reader who has discovered that

Gawain's destiny is in the Lady's hands, a submission to the fiction that Gawain's beheading is a fact which the Lady is unable to alter. The scholarly debate about whether the Lady's thoughts are thinkable or not becomes irrelevant once their function is perceived: they are intended to strengthen the hypothesis of a climactic ending to the Beheading Game with which the *Gawain*-poet wants us to work, and by doing so, to trick us into sharing the Lady's thought that, in view of that ending, her own designs on Gawain can lead nowhere. Her attempted seductions of Gawain are thus made to appear beside the point.

III

I have so far dwelt on one fact that prevents the reader from seeing the centrality of the hospitality episode. Since the *Gawain*-poet focuses our minds on how the Beheading Game will end, Gawain's hospitality sticks out amidst the rest of the story like a long parenthetical clause in the middle of a sentence that still awaits completion. As the mind cannot fully attend to a parenthetical remark when it remains in anticipation of how the interrupted sentence will conclude, so the mounting suspense about how the unfinished Beheading Game will end veers attention away from the intervening incidents at the Castle.

But there is another deceptive facet in the *Gawain*-poet's presentation of Gawain's hospitality in fitts two and three. The *Gawain*-poet sets Gawain's testing in a hectic atmosphere of fun and games that lures both Gawain and the reader into a false sense of security, and never gives them an occasion to pause and take stock of the situation. In the forest where Gawain travelled the dangers were obvious: giants pursued him, wild beasts attacked him, but Gawain had no difficulty in defending himself. In Castle Hautdesert on the other hand, the dangers are all the more insidious for not being readily apparent. The appearance of the host who comes to welcome Gawain perhaps raises some suspicion:

> Gawayn glyȝt on þe gome þat godly hym gret,
> And þuȝt hit a bolde burne þat þe burȝ aȝte,
> A hoge haþel for þe nonez, and of hyghe eldee;
> Brode, bryȝt, watz his berde, and al beuer-hwed,
> Sturne, stif on þe stryþþe on stalworth schonkez,
> Felle face as þe fyre, and fre of hys speche;
> And wel hym semed, for soþe, as þe segge þuȝt,
> To lede a lortschyp in lee of leudez ful gode.
>
> (842–9)

(Gawain glanced on the man that kindly greeted him, and he thought that the man who owned the castle was a bold man, a huge man indeed, and of mature age. Broad and bright was his beard, and reddish brown; he was strong, and firm in his stride on stalwart legs, his face as intense as fire, and he was outgoing in his speech; and, in truth, he certainly seemed the right man to be in command of many good men in his castle.)

Like the Green Knight, Gawain's host (who remains unnamed until fitt four) is immensely tall, outspoken, has a big beard, and walks around briskly on stout legs. The last detail recalls the gait of the Green Knight as he runs after his head that is rolling on the floor—'Bot styþly he start forth vpon styf schonkes' (431)—and it looks forward to the Green Knight's acrobatics when he meets Gawain at the Green Chapel:

When he wan to þe watter, þer he wade nolde,
He hypped ouer on hys axe and orpedly strydez ...
(2231–2)

(And when he got to the water, which he did not want to wade through, he hopped over with his axe and strode boldly.)

But Gawain leads the way in allaying this initial suspicion. His host strikes him as a fine lord of a provincial household. Immediately afterwards, the *Gawain*-poet follows suit when he shows the host's surprise on hearing that the guest is none other than the famous Gawain:

When þe lorde hade lerned þat he þe leude hade,
Loude laȝed he þerat, so lef hit hym þoȝt ...
(908–9)

(When the lord had been told that he had that man with him, he laughed loudly about it, so delightful it seemed to him ...)

In the notes to these lines, the Tolkien and Gordon edition needlessly finds fault with this:

[The lord of the castle] must have recognized Gawain when he arrived (835); but if suspense is to be maintained by his behaving as if he had not met him before, his satisfaction should be public and assumed, not private and apparently surprised.

(p. 101)

Yet suspense is the last thing that the *Gawain*-poet wants us to feel at this point. As J.A. Burrow writes, the lines are designed to reassure us that the host is merely 'a genial host, delighted at the prospect of a distinguished and interesting guest' (Burrow 1965, 59). His apparently genuine surprise when he is informed that his guest is Gawain effectively dissolves any hypothesis about a connection between Gawain's host and the Green Knight, which their physical resemblance might for a moment have supported. As the *Gawain*-poet deviously suggests, we can 'forget' about their likeness until, of course, the dénouement confirms our initial suspicion.

After being disarmed, Gawain finds the household in party mood and joins in the celebrations without reserve. The *Gawain*-poet knew that 'Men ben mery in mynde quen þay han mayn drynk', and Gawain's spirits rise with the generous supply of wine:

> Þat mon much merþe con make,
> For wyn in his hed þat wende.
> (899–900)

(That man made much mirth, as the wine went to his head.)

The numerous references to servings of wine (see 980, 1025, 1112, 1403, 1409, 1668, 1684, 1935) suggest that Gawain spends most of his time in the castle slightly intoxicated, enjoying the little pleasures of life while he still can. No stern moralist, the *Gawain*-poet no doubt knew from personal experience that drink is not conducive to vigilance, but Gawain's hosts seem to like their drink as well, and let themselves go in a way that makes aloofness seem quite simply unbecoming. Only occasionally does the poet hint that their behaviour is not spontaneous. He frequently refers to them as 'making' joy (910) or 'making' mirth:

> and chefly þay asken
> Spycez, þat vnsparely men speded hom to bryng,
> And þe wynnelych wyne þerwith vche tyme.
> Þe lorde luflych aloft lepez ful ofte,
> Mynned merþe to be made vpon mony syþez,
> Hent heȝly of his hode, and on a spere henged,
> And wayned hom to wynne þe worchip þerof,
> Þat most myrþe myȝt meue þat Crystenmas whyle—
> 'And I schal fonde, bi my fayth, to fylter wyth þe best
> Er me wont þe wede, with help of my frendez.'
> (978–87)

(And especially they ask for spiced cakes, that they be brought to them unsparingly and quickly, and the pleasant wine to accompany it each time. The lord amiably jumped up many a time, ordered mirth to be made on every occasion. Gaily he took off his hood, and hung it on a spear, and encouraged them to win the honour of it, whoever could arouse the highest joy at that Christmas time. 'And I shall try, by my faith, to compete with the best before I lose this garment, with the help of my friends.')

If joy can be made on command, there might be more to the festivities than meets the eye after all. Yet the possibility that the 'making' of joy, or the lord's generosity with the 'wynnelych wyne', is calculated to catch Gawain off guard is deflected by the impression that the inhabitants of Castle Hautdesert are even more carried away by the occasion than Gawain himself. Moreover, cheerfulness is clearly 'in season', and knowing this Gawain readily obeys his host's order that 'merþe … be made'. Conviviality, as the word suggests, depends on the contribution of all, which is why Gawain never lets on that his head hangs in the balance. The creation of joy is so successful and contagious that it soon becomes a psychological reality for the merry-makers. Jumping up and down 'ful ofte' and stirring up joyfulness 'vpon mony syþez', the master of ceremonies is soon himself swept up by the escalation of excitement he seeks to encourage. Can this be a man scheming to ensnare his guest?

Gawain's warm reception at the castle leaves no room for suspicion. What is more, it does not give us much time for it either. We follow Gawain on his frenzied daily round from bedroom to mass, from the chapel to the hall, from dinner to evening entertainments, and after much drinking and carousing, back to bed for Gawain's well-deserved sleep. The *Gawain*-poet's own words best convey the haste with which one event follows another:

Much dut watz þer dryuen þat day and þat oþer,
And þe þryd as þro þronge in þerafter …
                    (1020–1)

(Much joy was made there that day and the next, and the third day, equally packed, pushed its way in thereafter.)

As each day is driven by joy, the following day is so eager to begin that it seems to start the relay race even before the previous day has fully run its course.

The merry-go-round turns at great speed at Castle Hautdesert and Gawain never has a chance to get off. The partying continues until the early hours of the morning, and when Gawain is finally allowed to sleep in, his rest is always cut short by the Lady of the Castle, who interrupts his sleep on her early visits to his bedroom:

Þe lady noȝt forȝate,
Com to hym to salue;

Ful erly ho watz hym ate
His mode for to remwe.
(1472–5)

(The Lady did not forget to come to greet him. Very early she was at him, to alter his frame of mind.)

The reader, too, is deprived of opportunities for rest. After bedtime, when Castle Hautdesert is quiet, the poet either leaps straight to the next day (1411), or condenses the night into a short bob and wheel:

Þus wyth laȝande lotez þe lorde hit tayt makez,
For to glade Sir Gawayn with gomnez in halle
þat nyȝt,
Til þat hit watz tyme
Þe lorde commaundet lyȝt;
Sir Gawen his leue con nyme
And to his bed hym diȝt.
(988–94; cf. 1121, and 1472–5)

(With noise of laughter the lord makes things merry, so as to amuse Gawain with games in the hall that night; until the time was come that the lord asked for light. Sir Gawain took his leave, and made his way to bed.)

The swift and bouncy lines of the bob and wheel give little respite before the next busy day is announced by the first words of the next stanza: 'On þe morne'. And, as always, the Lord of the Castle rises early. While Gawain is allowed (in theory) to sleep in, the *Gawain*-poet occupies the reader with descriptions of the lord and his men, who are raring to go before sunrise:

Bi þat þe coke hade crowen and cakled bot þryse,
Þe lorde watz lopen of his bedde ...
(1412–13; cf. 1126)

(By the time that the cock had crowed and cackled only three times, the lord had leapt from his bed ...)

The sheer pace of the hospitality scenes makes them hard to keep up with for the reader, let alone for an audience of listeners. Following the movements of the characters in them poses an equally formidable challenge. The lord leaps, runs, and jumps around like a madman. As the lines quoted above also show, haste is the host's middle name:

Þe leue lorde of þe londe watz not þe last
Arayed for þe rydyng, with renkkez ful mony;

Ete a sop hastyly, when he hade herde masse,
With bugle to bent-felde he buskez bylyue.

(1133–6)

(The dear lord was not the last to be dressed for going out riding with many men. He ate a bite hastily, and when he had heard mass, he hurries quickly to the hunting-field with his bugle.)

As Marie Borroff remarks, verbs in *Gawain*, especially those describing surges of energy, 'seem to work overtime' (Borroff 1962, 17–18), and with a man as indefatigable as the Lord of the Castle one can see why they should.

As disorientating as the pace of the hospitality scenes is the profusion of detail in which they are described. Like the verbs expressing rapid movement, a delight in superabundant detail is a conventional feature of alliterative poetry (Turville-Petre 1977, 6, 70–1), but the poet cleverly uses it to frustrate the reader's capacity to take everything in (Ganim 1976, 383). Many details of course do not need to be taken in. For instance, the lengthy itemization of the Castle's interior decoration or Gawain's Christmas dinner serves only as a stylistic equivalent to the lavishness of Gawain's reception. But other details—such as the Lord of the Castle's physical appearance, or the green and gold colours of the Lady's girdle, to which I shall return later—are accorded retrospective significance by the dénouement of the story. However, singling out such details for retention as they race past for the first time is no mean achievement, for where, in the haystack of insignificant trivia, does one begin to look?

It is not surprising, then, that Gawain, who is caught up in the midst of this swirl of events and objects, cannot see things clearly when the Lord finally makes his move and proposes to play another game. To catch up with his sleep, Gawain can stay in bed (where on three consecutive mornings he will be joined by the seductive Lady), and so as to liven up the evenings the host persuades Gawain to exchange winnings with him, without of course adding that the game will test his truthfulness. Retrospectively, the moment that the Lord proffers his 'game' can justly be identified as the one where Gawain's troubles begin, but the *Gawain*-poet represents it so subtly that it slips by almost unnoticed.

Here the *Gawain*-poet's supreme sense of timing makes a critical contribution. The Lord of the Castle does not spring his 'game' on Gawain on his arrival. That *would* be suspicious. Instead, the poet has, in truly prodigal style, spent about an entire fitt describing three long and

eventful days that Gawain spends in the lap of luxury. I have perhaps not
given enough attention to the first three dizzying days of entertainments,
considering that they take up 450 lines in *Gawain*, but from the point of
view of narrative economy, one can only call these lines wasteful. They
do not throw up a single event that determines the outcome of the plot.
Yet their effectiveness lies for a large part in exhausting Gawain and the
reader's vigilance, by occupying them with food and drink, with refined
manners, and interestingly enough, with many innocent games. Thus,
when the host at the end of a very long fitt, and at the end, therefore, of
his audience's natural attention span, proposes another game, the
Exchange of Winnings, the moment does not obtrude itself upon the
attention.

On the day itself, the Lord's first step is likewise timed to catch
Gawain off guard. It comes late in the evening, just when Gawain has
told his host that he must be off early next morning to keep his appointment at the Green Chapel. The host reassures him that the Green
Chapel is only two miles away, and prevails on Gawain to stay with him
a little while longer. The information about the whereabouts of the
Green Chapel comes as welcome news to Gawain. His resolve to keep
his part of the bargain with the Green Knight is such that it relieves his
mind to know, for the first time, that he will be in a position to do so:

'Now I þonk yow þryuandely þurȝ alle oþer þynge,
Now acheued is my chaunce, I schal at your wylle
Dowelle, and ellez do quat ȝe demen.'

(1080–2)

('Now I thank you heartily for this, beyond all other things. Now that my
adventure has been achieved, I shall stay on according to your will, and in
other things I shall do as you decide.')

Prematurely, Gawain concludes that his only active part in the
Beheading Game has been achieved. He can turn up at the Green
Chapel; there he can do nothing else but hope, and wait for the Green
Knight to do his worst. Just now, when Gawain is still heaving sighs of
relief, and when the poem reminds us once more that Gawain's stay
interrupts an as yet unfinished adventure, the Lord proposes that Gawain
should stay in bed and play the Exchange of Winnings.

Gawain suspects nothing, and the text seems to prove him right. Not
only does the Lord time his moment beautifully, but, on the face of it,
his idea wears the mask of common sense. Gawain has been staying up
drinking with the Lord into the early hours, and could do with some

sleep. Since most of the other guests who kept Gawain entertained are off the next morning (1127–32), a little diversion would not be unwelcome either. Gawain has had games in plenty from his host, and all have managed to create an uncomplicated sense of togetherness by transporting complete strangers—in the way only games can—into a temporary world of shared rules and common purposes. Moreover, Gawain is not alone in giving in to the demands of the situation. As usual, Bertilac appears beside himself. Excited at the prospect of Gawain's extended stay, he acts 'as wyȝe þat wolde of his wyt, ne wyst quat he myȝt' ('as someone gone mad, who did not know what he was doing') (1987). Naturally, Gawain sees no harm in acceding to his request that he spend the mornings with the attractive Lady and play the Exchange of Winnings game that will later seal his fate. More drinks follow and, after rehearsing the rules of the 'bargayn' (1112) which they have struck, Gawain and Bertilac say goodnight:

> To bed ȝet er þay ȝede,
> Recorded couenauntez ofte;
> Þe olde lorde of þat leude
> Cowþe wel halde layk alofte.
>   (1122–5)

> (Yet before they went to bed, they repeated the contracts often. The jolly old lord of that household could well keep a game going.)

Asked jovially to 'sware with trawþe', Gawain consents to the contract that will later oblige him to return the girdle that might save his life.

Here the alarm bells should ring briefly. The words applied to the game—'bargayn', 'trawþe', 'recorded couenauntez', 'forwarde' (1105)—treat the game with the same earnestness as the Beheading Game in the first fitt, in which Gawain and the Green Knight also dutifully 'rehersed þe couenaunt'. Like making a 'couenaunt' or a 'bargayn', entering into games requires from the player a blind submission to the incalculable, for, in the words of Geoffrey Chaucer, 'what man that is entred in a pley, / He nedes moot unto the pley assente' (IV, 10–11). And as Gawain earlier could not foresee the oppressive constraints upon his freedom which his assent to the Beheading Game would force him to bear, his pledge to abide by the rules of the Exchange of Winnings commits him to accept any sacrifice which these rules may demand him to make. Just how exorbitant that sacrifice will be (the sacrifice of a life-saving girdle), neither Gawain nor the reader can as yet foresee.

But there are important differences between the two games as well. In comparison with the Beheading Game, in which the stakes have soared, the Exchange of Winnings appears as an amusing distraction, as some light relief. And whereas the Green Knight's Russian roulette answers Arthur's call for 'sum mayn meruayle' (94), the Exchange of Winnings, by contrast, fails to announce itself as an adventure at all. Had it done so, Gawain would have found it easier to refuse the Lady's gift of a green girdle, or to give it up to his host.

IV

Gawain's acceptance of the girdle is one of the finest scenes in the romance, and I would like to spend some time on the way the *Gawain*-poet again manipulates the focus of our attention so that on a first reading we fail to pick up on its true significance. With the benefit of hindsight it is tempting to prejudge the issue, to import our knowledge of the ending back into fitt three and accuse Gawain of failing an important test of loyalty when he accepts the girdle and promises to hide it from the host. It needs therefore to be emphasized that the *Gawain*-poet's handling of this moment deliberately precludes moral judgements. These come only *after* the Green Knight has revealed his identity, and readers who expect disapprobation of Gawain when he keeps the girdle will look for it in vain before that point. What the text does is altogether different, and altogether more subtle. As we shall see, it actually colludes with Gawain's suppression of the knowledge that the girdle should be returned.

Before giving some examples of that collusion, we should again pause to admire the *Gawain*-poet's sure sense of timing, which contributes so powerfully to catching Gawain and the reader unawares. Like Bertilac's 'spontaneous' proposal of the Exchange of Winnings, the Lady's offer of the girdle comes towards the end of a fitt, just when Gawain has successfully coped with her advances. The peril of her temptations is never in doubt, nor is the fact that Gawain comes close to succumbing to the Lady's seductions on the third day:

> Gret perile bitwene hem stod,
> Nif Maré of hir kny3t mynne.
>   (1768–9)

(Great danger stood between the two, if Mary did not look after her knight.)

But in the end Gawain stands firm, says no to the Lady as delicately as he can, and seems to have averted the 'gret perile' that threatened him. Gawain is no doubt relieved when the Lady finally admits defeat:

'Kysse me now comly, and I schal cach heþen,
I may bot mourne vpon molde, as may þat much louyes.'
Sykande ho sweȝe doun and semly hym kyssed,
And siþen ho seueres hym fro, and says as ho stondes,
'Now, dere, at þis departyng do me þis ese,
Gif me sumquat of þy gifte, þi gloue if hit were,
Þat I may mynne on þe, mon, my mournyng to lassen.'
                                                      (1794–800)

('Now kiss me graciously, and I shall go hence. Only grief remains to me, a
maiden who loves much.' Sighing, she bowed down and kissed him
graciously, and then she moves away from him, and says as she stands: 'Now,
dear man, at this goodbye do this to console me, give me one of your gifts, if
only your glove, by which I may remember you, sir, to lessen my grief.')

The Lady who has caused Gawain so much trouble has almost left the
bedroom, when she turns and asks, as if in an afterthought, for a little
souvenir to remember him by—an innocent question that smoothly and
imperceptibly prepares the ground for her subsequent offer to Gawain of
a present from her. Her timing could not be improved on. The moment
of real crisis again comes just when the 'gret perile' is apparently over. In
this 'slack and unguarded aftermath' (Burrow 1982, 215), the Lady
presses on Gawain a love-gift: first a ring, which Gawain refuses, and
next a girdle 'gered ... with grene sylk and with golde schaped' (1832).
The 'grene' and 'golde' of the girdle—the colours of the Green Knight
—make no impact on Gawain, but the description of the ring that pre-
cedes it—'a riche rynk of red golde werkez' (1817)—cunningly invites
the reader, too, to take the colours of the girdle not as a warning signal
but as another unmemorable descriptive detail.

    The green girdle is initially refused by Gawain, but he changes his
mind when the Lady explains it is a magical talisman. Then Gawain
thinks:

Þen kest þe knyȝt, and hit come to his hert
Hit were a juel for þe jopardé þat hym iugged were:
When he acheued to þe chapel his check for to fech,
Myȝt he haf slypped to be vslayn, þe sleȝt were noble.
Þenne he þulged with her þrepe and þoled hir to speke,
And ho bere on hym þe belt and bede hit hym swyþe—
And he granted and hym gafe with a goud wylle—
And bisoȝt hym, for hir sake, disceuer hit neuer,
Bot to lelly layne fro hir lorde; þe leude hym acordez

Þat neuer wyȝe schulde hit wyt, iwysse, bot þay twayne
for noȝte.

(1855–65)

(Then the knight thought, and it occurred to him that it would be a jewel for the danger that had become his lot. When he reached the chapel to receive his misfortune, it would be a noble stratagem if he could manage to escape without being slain. Then he was patient with her importunity and allowed her to speak. And she pressed the belt on him and insisted he take it—and he granted her this and agreed with good will—and she asked him, for her sake, never to disclose it, but to hide it loyally from her lord; the man promised that, for nothing in the world, would any man ever know of it, for certain, apart from the two of them.)

This passage is a perceptive study of a 'sliding' of the will, as Chaucer described his heroine's betrayal in *Troilus and Criseyde*. Gawain's thought that the girdle might save his life does not, strictly speaking, itself constitute the moment of untruth, but it opens the defensive door wide enough for the Lady to get a foot in. All Gawain does afterwards is to keep the door open: he tolerates her ('þulged with her þrepe'), and does not shut his ears to her suggestions ('þoled hir to speke'). The poet's phrasing—Gawain is *patient* and *endures*—indicates that Gawain's lapse is not a matter of doing wrong actively; he merely allows something to happen. Thus he never actually *takes* the girdle; he only lets the Lady 'bear' it on him. But that relaxation of resistance, which the poet goes as far as presenting as a virtue, suffices. Before Gawain knows it—and before the reader has time to take note—he has accepted the girdle:

And ho bere on hym þe belt and bede hit hym swyþe—
And he granted and hym gafe with a goud wylle—
And bisoȝt hym, for hir sake, disceuer hit neuer ...

I would like to draw attention to the necessary editorial dashes around the line in which Gawain surrenders to the Lady's pressure, in order to make the point that Gawain's slip is matched by a moment of apparent carelessness in the poet's grammar. In the lines preceding and following it, the Lady is the grammatical subject, and the abrupt switch of subject in 'And he granted and hym gafe with a goud wylle' makes the line appear as a casual remark, an insignificant parenthesis that interrupts a sentence in which the Lady's words and actions form the proper focus of semantic attention. Thus, however crucial Gawain's consent to the Lady's suggestions becomes in retrospect, only an unnaturally scrupulous reader, who holds out against the flow of the poet's syntax, would make much of it on a first reading. In just one parenthetical line Gawain becomes the owner of the girdle. After that, the rest simply follows. Since it is a love-gift, Gawain must promise to keep it from his host, and when that promise is made, he can no longer hand the girdle over to his host in the Exchange of Winnings.

Gawain, then, does not decide for or against truth—the facts are simply not phrased in these terms—but allows himself to be thrown in a different direction. The *Gawain*-poet's choice of off-beat moments for the turning points in his plot, the creditable presentation of Gawain's mollification as 'patience', and the cursory mention of Gawain's acceptance of the girdle, all these conspire to throw the reader off course as well. The sheer conventionality of the direction that Gawain believes himself to have taken makes the *Gawain*-poet's task easier. The girdle, Gawain thinks, is not just any old girdle, but a magic girdle, which may save his life when he meets up with his supernatural opponent. This belief accords well with what a reader might expect to happen in romance, in which ladies frequently equip their lovers with magical talismans before they ride out on an adventure (Putter 1995, 142–3). In Chrétien de Troyes's Arthurian romance, *Yvain*, for instance, a lady (Laudine) gives the hero a magical ring, with the assurance that it will protect him from harm:

> Now I will put this ring of mine on your finger, and I lend it to you. And I want to tell you plainly about the nature of its stone: no true and faithful lover will be taken prisoner or will shed blood, and nothing bad can happen to him; but he who wears it, and cherishes it, will remember his beloved, and thereby become tougher than stone ...[16]

The sheer plausibility of this plot-motif in the world of romance strengthens Gawain's hypothesis that he is in the kind of story where knights can legitimately take the love-gifts of ladies along into their subsequent adventures. Of course, Gawain has promised to return the girdle to his host under the rules of the Exchange of Winnings, but what difference can this make to the host when, as far as Gawain and the Lady are concerned, he will never even *know* the difference?

It is the remainder of the third fitt that settles this question for us by refusing to treat the girdle as a moral issue at all, as if it were at every point asking the reader to support Gawain's decision to keep it. Let me

---

16. Translated from Chrétien de Troyes, *Le Chevalier au lion (Yvain)*, ed. Mario Roques, CFMA (Paris: Champion, 1982), ll. 2602–11.

give two examples. The first is Gawain's confession at the Castle, which comes just after Gawain has carefully stashed the girdle away for future use. If there were any opportunity where the narrator might—and perhaps some readers think should—raise the girdle as an unresolved moral dilemma, it is here, but the *Gawain*-poet is poker-faced:

> Syþen cheuely to þe chapel choses he þe waye,
> Preuély aproched to a prest, and prayed hym þere
> Þat he wolde lyste his lyf and lern hym better
> How his sawle schulde be saued when he schuld seye heþen.
> Þere he schrof hym schyrly and schewed his mysdedez,
> Of þe more and þe mynne, and merci besechez,
> And of absolucioun he on þe segge calles;
> And he asoyled hym surely and sette hym so clene
> As domezday schulde haf ben diȝt on þe morn.
>
> (1876–84)

(Then quickly he takes the way to the chapel, privately approached a priest, and prayed him there that he would hear his confession and instruct him better about how his soul should be saved when he must go hence. There he confessed himself cleanly and acknowledged his misdeeds, the smaller and the greater ones, and asks for mercy, and calls on the man for absolution. And the priest absolved him so completely and made him as clean as if doomsday should have been ordained for the next day.)

Gawain, no doubt plagued by a bad conscience and by the thought that the next day might be his last, goes looking for a priest who can put his mind at rest. As the passage states unambiguously, Gawain confesses all his sins and is duly absolved. With a clear conscience Gawain can face the Day of Judgment ('domezday'), which for Gawain is indeed 'diȝt on þe morn' when he is to meet the Green Knight.

So far, a reading of the passage seems plain sailing, but notice how it falls apart if the reader raises the question for which it leaves no room: what about Gawain's moral duty to return the girdle to the Lord of the Castle? Let us consider some possibilities:

1. Gawain's confession includes the fact that he intends to keep the girdle. This hypothesis is refuted by the priest's complete absolution, which the priest could only have given if Gawain had restored the girdle to its rightful owner.
2. Keeping the girdle is a sin, but Gawain omits any mention of it. This is plainly contradicted by the *Gawain*-poet's statement that Gawain confesses *all* his sins, 'þe more and þe mynne'.

As should be clear, the passage simply ceases to make sense if it is approached on the assumption that the green girdle is a moral problem. It becomes readable only if we allow the girdle to slip from our conscience, just as Gawain has done. In his characteristically unreliable way, the poet actively makes us forget the moral implications of Gawain's possession of the girdle and seduces us into embracing the false hypothesis that the girdle is simply a talisman for the adventure to come.

For the remainder of the third fitt, the girdle receives no further mention. When the Lord returns from the hunt with a fox's skin, ready to play the third instalment of the swapping game, Gawain's possession of the girdle remains his and our secret. Gawain does appear more impatient than usual to get the exchange over and done with, but the poet presents it at best as a moment of slight awkwardness. The next mention of the girdle, on the morning Gawain arms himself in fitt four, furnishes the second example of the way the text encourages our obliviousness to the strings that are attached to the girdle:

> ȝet laft he not þe lace, þe ladiez gifte,
> Þat forgat not Gawayn for gode of hymseluen.
> Bi he hade belted þe bronde vpon his balȝe haunchez,
> Þenn dressed he his drurye double hym aboute,
> Swyþe sweþled vmbe his swange swetely þat knyȝt
> Þe gordel of þe grene silke, þat gay wel bisemed,
> Vpon þat ryol red cloþe þat ryche watz to schewe.
> Bot wered not þis ilk wyȝe for wele þis gordel,
> For pryde of þe pendauntez, þaȝ polyst þay were,
> And þaȝ þe glyterande golde glent vpon endez,
> Bot for to sauen hymself, when suffer hym byhoued,
> To byde bale withoute dabate of bronde hym to were
>   oþer knyffe.
>
> (2030–42)

(But he did not leave the Lady's gift. That Gawain did not forget, for his own good. After he had girded the sword on his muscular haunches, he draped his love-gift around himself twice; quickly and sweetly he wound around his waist the girdle of green silk, which suited that fair knight well against the background of the noble red cloth, which was splendid to behold. But the man did not wear the girdle because of its preciousness, for pride of its pendants, though they were nicely polished, and though the glittering gold shone at the ends, but to save his own life when he should have to suffer, and stand and face the blow without recourse to a sword or a dagger to protect himself.)

The girdle, which is uppermost in Gawain's mind, is also foregrounded in the passage itself, most strikingly in the inversion of subject and object in the line 'þat forgat not Gawayn for gode of hymseluen', which forces the girdle into first position. But the foregrounding of the girdle makes it all the more noticeable that the poet does all he can to shrug off the idea that Gawain's possession of the girdle is reprehensible. Gawain, the poet assures us, has *not* taken it for pride, *nor* because he is interested in its value. Having taken the hero in his protection, the poet shows no more embarrassment about the hero's wearing of the girdle than he did when he described Gawain with the pentangle in fitt two:

> Then þay schewed hym þe schelde, þat was of schyr goulez
> Wyth þe pentangel depaynt of pure golde hwez.
> He braydez hit by þe bauderyk, aboute þe hals kestes,
> *Þat bisemed þe segge s emlyly fayre.*
>
> (619–22)

(Then they brought out for him the shield, which was of bright red gules, with the pentangle painted on it with pure gold colours. He lifts it by the baldric, and puts it around his neck: it looked becomingly fair on the man.)

I have emphasized the final line because the same innocent sentiment recurs when the poet exclaims how handsome Gawain looks in the girdle: 'þe gordel of þe grene silke, þat gay wel bisemed'. Anyone with residual doubts about whether Gawain ought to be wearing the girdle should be reassured by the poet's wonderfully untroubled observation. And so, only the reader whose worries persist in defiance of the text can come prepared for the dénouement of the story.

V

Gawain's heartfelt goodbyes to the servants at Castle Hautdesert appear to mark the end of the long hospitality scene in *Sir Gawain and the Green Knight*. As Gawain rides off to the Green Chapel, the poet gives the impression that the adventures of the Castle have now been left behind. The guide who sets Gawain on his way and the girdle that will protect Gawain from harm are the only tangible links that connect the hospitality scene with the adventure ahead, and as the poet moves on, the events at Castle Hautdesert seem to sink into an irrevocable past.

Gawain has at this point all the appearances of the many episodic Arthurian romances in which the knight passes from one discrete episode to another, without the hero or the reader needing to retain the earlier adventure when he or she embarks on the next. A long literary tradition of episodic Arthurian romances thus comes to the poet's aid in manipulating our expectation that his romance has made a clean start. But it soon transpires that, in contrast with episodic romance, Gawain has not moved on to a new and unrelated episode, but to an adventure that revisits the past. For the poet will reveal that the Green Knight is none other than the Lord of the Castle whom Gawain thought he had left behind. What is more, his entire journey to and reception at the Green Chapel slowly resuscitate our memories of his earlier arrival at Castle Hautdesert (Putter 1995, 96). The correspondences between these two strands of the plot are too close for comfort. For example, the comment that Gawain 'ofte chaunged his chere þe chapel to seche' harks back to the description of Gawain on his way to the castle: 'His cher ful oft con chaunge, / þat chapel er he my3t sene' (711–12). Like Castle Hautdesert, situated 'abof a launde on a lawe' (765), the Green Chapel lies 'on a launde, a lawe as hit were' (2171). The lord of the chapel, the Green Knight, welcomes Gawain with grim ceremoniousness: 'Ywisse, þou art welcome, wy3e, to my place' (2246), recalling Gawain's welcome at the Castle. The Green Knight's remark that there is no one around who can interrupt the proceedings—'And we are in þis valay verayly oure one' (2245)—echoes the Lady's words on having trapped Gawain in the bed-room: 'And now 3e are here, iwysse, and we bot our one' (1230). When the Green Knight impugns Gawain's bravery—'þou art not Gawain, quoþ þe gome, þat is so goud halden' (2270)—we may recall the Lady's disappointment on finding Gawain less amorously inclined than the 'Gawayn' whom she had heard so much about: 'Bot þat 3e be Gawen, hit gotz in mynde … So god as Gawayn gaynly is halden' (1293–7). As the narrative finally approaches the moment of truth, it begins to hark back persistently to Gawain's hospitality at the Castle, as if what Gawain were confronting at the Green Chapel is not the present but the dimly remembered past.

Above all, it is with the Green Knight's beheading strokes that the past, which Gawain thought he had escaped, definitively catches up with the hero. For the three strokes of the axe are in fact no more than a reflection of how Gawain fared under the Exchange of Winnings: the two feints stand for Gawain's honesty in the first two exchanges, and the nick in the neck is a punishment for his failure to return the girdle:

'At þe þrid þou fayled þore,
And þerfor þat tappe ta þe.'
(2356–7)

('At the third you failed there; for that take this tap.')

Thus the Green Knight, who turns out to be Gawain's host, interprets the beheading strokes. They constitute his judgment on Gawain's performance in the Exchange of Winnings, which Bertilac has orchestrated as a test of Gawain's 'trawþe'. As the Green Knight forces Gawain to revisit the past by the point of his axe, everything suddenly becomes horribly clear, and Gawain's instantaneous acceptance of guilt suggests the extent to which Bertilac's 'news' merely restores to Gawain's consciousness what deep down he always knew himself: the girdle should have been returned to his host.

But I hope to have explained how it should have come about that we, too, stand before Bertilac's revelation as before something that is both unexpected and entirely obvious. For in the revised interpretation of the story which the dénouement forces us to undertake, all the facts which the poet had encouraged us to forget bounce back into view. The resemblances between the Green Knight and Gawain's host recover their significance when Bertilac tells us that the hospitality scene was a set-up; as do the green and gold colours of the girdle, the 'making' of joy, the generous supply of wine, the legal language that described the Exchange of Winnings, and, last but not least, Gawain's retention of the girdle, which the poem had earlier insisted we should regard as a magical talisman rather than a moral problem. Like Gawain, then, we are taught a lesson by the *Gawain*-poet about what we should have retained, and about how easy it is to allow oneself to forget.

CONCLUSION

As we have seen, when Gawain takes the girdle to save his life he for once disregards his innate sense of right and wrong, and allows the pressures of the moment to overshadow his consciousness of his obligations in the Exchange of Winnings. Gawain's awareness of this fact renders comprehensible his determination to *remember* his moment of obliviousness for the rest of his life. Having said goodbye to Bertilac, he takes back on his journey the girdle, as a permanent reminder of his failure:

> 'Bot in syngne of my surfet I schal se hit ofte
> When I rede in renoun, remorde to myseluen
> Þe faut and þe fayntyse of þe flesch crabbed,
> How tender hit is to entyse teches of fylþe.'   (2433–6)

('As a sign of my fault I will look upon it often when I ride in renown, remembering with remorse the fault and the frailty of the wayward body, which is so prone to defilement by spots of dirt.')

With the girdle wrapped diagonally around his body, he arrives back at Arthur's court, who are overjoyed to see him alive and well.

Back home, Gawain relives his adventures and his shame once again, when he recounts his story to the court, and restates his resolution to wear the girdle until the end of his days:

> [He] biknowes alle þe costez of care þat he hade,
> Þe chaunce of þe chapel, þe chere of þe kny3t,
> Þe luf of þe ladi, þe lace at þe last.
>
> ...
>
> 'Þis is þe token of vntrawþe that I am tan inne,
> And I mot nedez hit were wyle I may last ... '
>
> (2495–510)

(He confessed all the tribulations he had suffered—the adventure of the chapel, the behaviour of the knight, the love of the lady, and the lace at the last ... 'This is the token of the untruth that has been detected in me, and I must needs wear it while I may have life.')

By now, the logic of the plot no longer eludes Gawain. Knowing that the encounter with the Green Knight was not the grand finale it purported to be, Gawain reprocesses his adventures in a sequence that reverses the order in which he has had to live them through. From the 'chaunce of þe chapel' and the 'chere of þe kny3t' he works his way back to the hospitality he received at the Castle, to the 'luf of þe ladi' and 'þe lace at þe last'. Just as the poem made the episode at the Green Chapel an occasion for revisiting the hero's past, Gawain inverts the chronology of events, the beginning and the ending, and spells out for his listeners what he was himself allowed to discover only at the end: his stay at the Castle was not, in terms of significance, the 'forme' of his story, but the 'fynisment'.

However, the fact that Gawain has been misled, that he was not clear that the test that he nobly admits to having failed *was* a test until too late, does not, in his own eyes, attenuate his guilt. The severity with which Gawain regards his failure has irritated many readers, who will find their sentiments confirmed in much-published criticism of the poem, which contends that 'Gawain takes himself too seriously'. Yet seldom do people who take themselves too seriously overestimate their shortcomings, and seldom, too, do they incline to Gawain's view that honesty in all matters counts for more than being alive. By that standard of absolute truthfulness, however, Gawain measures himself, and finds himself wanting.

Certainly, neither Gawain nor the story suggests that Gawain's ethical ideals should be abandoned as hopelessly quixotic and unworkable. Gawain has, after all, been able to live up to them when, for example, he resisted the Lady's advances, or turned up at the Green Chapel ready to lay down his life. And if only he had stood by these same ideals when the Lady offered him the green girdle, he would not now have cause for self-reproach. We are of course entitled to take the view that Gawain's ideal of honesty at any price is impracticable or wrongheaded. As an ethical position this view seems to me perfectly valid, but it is not Gawain's. He does not hold it now, nor—and this is important—did he hold it when he accepted and kept the girdle. If he had kept the girdle out of disillusionment with his former ideals, the best he could have done with Bertilac's suggestion that the girdle should have been returned would have been to disagree politely, and to outline to Bertilac the moral deliberations that compelled him to think otherwise. But, as we have seen, Gawain's failure cannot be said to result from a process of moral deliberation, or from a conscious decision to revise his sense of right or wrong; it is the outcome, rather, of Gawain's brief *suspension* of moral judgement, of a half-willing obliviousness to the moral principles which he has set himself and which he has shown himself, in all other respects, perfectly capable of meeting. Gawain's anger and frustration thus follow not from his espousal of ideals that are incapable of fulfilment, but from the recognition that, on the terms of these firmly-held ideals, which he has in every other way upheld, he has let himself down. He has been untrue, that is, not primarily by someone else's abstract standards but by his own. As Gawain's words to Bertilac indicate, he feels he has been false to his own nature:

> 'For care of þy knokke cowardyse me taȝt
> To acorde me with couetyse, *my kynde* to forsake ... '
> (2379–80)

> ('For fear of your blow, cowardice taught me to reconcile myself with covetousness, and to forsake my true nature.')

Hence, Bertilac's (or the Round Table's) assurance that Gawain has done no harm to anyone—'I halde hit hardily hole, þe harme that I hade' (2390)—does not, as is often assumed, imply that Gawain has nothing to be upset about. If the cause for Gawain's anguish could be reduced to the insubstantial damage he has inflicted on others, it could well be scorned as disproportionate, but, in having been dishonest with Bertilac, Gawain feels, above all else, the shame of *self*-betrayal.

Gawain's friends in the poem (Bertilac and Arthur's court) and readers outside the poem, who are presumably satisfied with lower standards, obviously take a more lighthearted view of Gawain's failure. The *Gawain*-poet has portrayed the hero so favourably and lovingly throughout his romance that we can be sure he did not want us to condemn Gawain on the terms of his own self-indictment. For if he were indeed guilty of 'cowardyse', he would not have rescued Arthur from danger by taking up the Beheading Game, let alone turned up at the Green Chapel; and if he were guilty of covetousness he could have pocketed the Lady's rich red ring as well as the girdle. Gawain's self-incriminations seem altogether too crude and extreme to accommodate the nuances of his case.

But it should nevertheless be possible, even for readers who (like me) would personally find Gawain's ideal of self-obliterating 'trawþe' intolerable in practice, to admire Gawain's near-perfect embodiment of that ideal, and to respect his mortification at having slightly missed the mark. A remarkable fact, which, according to the philosopher F.P. Strawson, 'partly explains the enormous charm of reading novels, biographies, histories', is

> the readiness, which a great many people have, to identify themselves imaginatively at different times with different and conflicting visions of the ends of life, even though these visions may receive the scantiest expression in their actual behaviour and would call for the most upsetting personal revolution if they received more ... When some ideal image or form of life is given striking expression in the words or actions of some person, its expression may evoke a response of the liveliest sympathy from those whose own patterns of life are as remote as possible from conformity to the image expressed.
>
> (Strawson 1974, 27)

Whatever faults readers may find in Gawain's anguish, the members of the Round Table are filled with admiration for Gawain, and jovially welcome him back into their midst:

> Þe kyng comfortez þe kny3t, and alle þe court als,
> La3en loude þerat, and luflyly acorden
> Þat lordes and ladis þat longed to þe Table,
> Vche burne of þe broþerhede, a bauderyk schulde haue,
> A bende abelef hym aboute, of a bry3t grene,
> And þat, for sake of þat segge, in swete to were.

For þat watz acorded þe renoun of þe Rounde Table,
And he honoured þat hit hade euermore after,
As hit is breued in þe best boke of romaunce.

(2513–21)

(The king comforts the knight and the court does the same; they laughed
loudly at that, and lovingly agreed that lords and ladies that belonged to the
Table, each man of the brotherhood, should have a baldric, a band cross-wise
around him, and, for the sake of that man, to wear it likewise. For it was
agreed to stand for the renown of the Round Table, and it would honour the
man that was wearing it for evermore, as it is written in the best book of
romance.)

For Gawain's sake, the green girdle, which Gawain saw as the sign of his
failure, becomes a communal symbol of the 'renoun' of the Round
Table; and by all wearing it, they publicly pay homage to Gawain, in
whose honour they adopt it as their chivalric device. While they cannot
alter Gawain's private belief that he has discredited himself, they do what
is possible, as Bertilac had done before them, to convince Gawain that
this private belief has no objective reality. Gawain will no doubt continue to look on his green girdle with vexation, but his painful
reconciliation with the outside world and with himself falls outside the
scope of the poet's 'best boke of romaunce'.

Chapter 3

Patience

INTRODUCTION

Much of the meaning we see in a poem will depend on the expectations we bring to it. Responses to *Patience* have largely been guided by the understanding that it is a sermon, or a homiletic poem.[1] The assumption might seem unproblematic. Like *Cleanness*, *Patience* takes as its subject one of the virtues of the beatitudes, and contains the didactic impulse we would expect from a homily. Like a sermon, it opens with the theme on which it will enlarge: 'Pacience is a poynt, þaȝ hit displese ofte' (1). Although the theme is not taken from the Bible, as was customary, it is given scriptural authority by the poet's paraphrase of the eight beatitudes (Matthew 5: 3–10). After a brief exposition of the beatitudes and the relation between the first and the last blessing, a verse adaptation of the Book of Jonah from the Old Testament follows. The story fulfils the same role as the *exemplum* in a sermon, though it is far longer than the brief and pithy stories typically used by medieval preachers. As contemporary handbooks for the composition of sermons recommend, *Patience* ends with a conclusion which restates the opening theme (528–31).[2]

At a basic level, however, *Patience* resists classification as a homily. In the first five chapters of his *Form of Preaching*, the fourteenth-century Roger Basevorn defined the genre as 'the persuasion of many to meritorious conduct', with the understanding that 'we speak of the merit which pertains to eternal life', and that the speaker of the homily has

---

1. See Moorman (1963), Anderson (1969, 7–19), and Vantuono (1972).
2. On the practice of choosing a scriptural theme, and on recapitulating it at the end of the sermon, see Charland (1936, 113–14, 147–8).

distinguished himself in 'conscience', 'knowledge', and 'power'.[3]
Basevorn's definition puts in a nutshell what a medieval audience would
have expected from a homily, and what many readers have expected
from *Patience*. But on two accounts *Patience* fails to meet these expectations. The first concerns the relation between the narrator and his
audience. So far from 'persuading many', the narrator seems to direct his
advice about virtuous conduct not primarily at others but at himself
(Williams 1970). Only once does he address his audience from a position
of superior knowledge, as a preacher might, just before he embarks on
his retelling of the Book of Jonah:

> Wyl 3e tary a lyttel tyne and tent me a whyle,
> I schal wysse yow þer-wyth as holy wryt telles.
>
> (59–69)

(If you would wait a little while and listen to me for a moment I will tell you
what Holy Writ says.)

But when at the end of the *exemplum* the time has come for the narrator
to expound its relevance, he draws a moral appropriate to his personal
money-problems, representing himself not as someone who imparts
advice but as one who receives it:

> For-þy when pouerte *me* enprece3 and payne3 in-no3e,
> Ful softly with suffraunce sa3ttel *me* bihoue3
> For-þy penaunce and payne to-preue hit in sy3t
> Þat pacience is a nobel poynt, þa3 hit displese ofte.
>
> (528–31)

(And so when poverty and many pains oppress me, I should acquiesce
patiently, for penance and pain manifestly prove that patience is a noble
point, though it often displeases.)

The moral about patience may of course also apply to members of the
audience, but this view equally compels one to notice that the narrator
has placed himself on a par with his audience, showing no sign of the
special authority which Basevorn attributed to the homilist. By appear-
ing to listen to his own *exemplum*, the poet effectively abolishes the
distance that separates the speaker of the sermon from its hearers.

This identification with his audience characterizes the narrator
throughout *Patience*. Thus we encounter him in the prologue not as
preaching a sermon but as listening to one:

3. Ed. and trans. J.J. Murphy, *Three Medieval Rhetorical Arts* (Berkeley: University of
California Press, 1971).

I herde on a halyday, at a hyʒe masse,
How Mathew melede þat his mayster his meyny con teche ...
(9–10)

(I heard on a holy day, at high mass, how Matthew spoke about his master's teachings to his following ...)

In picturing himself at the receiving end of moral doctrine, the poet deploys a strategy familiar not from sermons but from contemporary Ricardian poets such as Gower or Chaucer. Their works may be edifying, but the voice of the poetic persona is likewise embodied by the learner, not the teacher. The Eagle in Chaucer's *House of Fame*, or the priestly Genius in Gower's *Confessio Amantis*, instruct, but like their audience, the narrators Amans and Chaucer must listen. These 'public poets', as Anne Middleton called them, claim no privileged position: 'The "I" of public poetry represents himself as, like his audience, a layman of good will ... "I" is like "you"' (Middleton 1978, 99).

There is another respect in which *Patience* resembles contemporary 'public' poetry, which brings us to the second point of contrast between *Patience* and the sermon. Whereas the sermon might be expected to guide us towards salvation, *Patience* concerns itself almost exclusively with worldly felicity, evincing the secular orientation typical of contemporary Ricardian poets. The narrator's choice of patience in the final stanza is not motivated by any considerations about the afterlife, but by the experience that impatience brings more 'penaunce and payne' than putting up with adversity. Undoubtedly, the *Gawain*-poet would have admired those for whom the rewards of heaven were sufficient reason for embracing suffering, but he himself did not aspire to such perfection. It is, at least on the surface, as a choice of the lesser evil that he enjoins patience on himself and his readers. The lessons he looks for are pragmatic rather than salvational, and it is precisely because he is not expressly concerned with the 'redeeming features' of patience that he can insist that patience is noble, without forgetting that 'it displese[s] ofte'.

Seeing *Patience* as a homily, the reader risks losing sight of the poet's representation of himself as the receiver of advice, and of the pragmatism of the wisdom the poem has to offer. *Patience* asks for a different approach, which is alive to the care the poet took to secularize his outlook and his poetic voice. With this different horizon of expectations, I want to turn in detail to the prologue of *Patience*.

'SUFFRAUNCE' IN THE PROLOGUE

Pacience is a poynt, þaʒ hit displese ofte.
When heuy herttes ben hurt wyth heþyng oþer elles,
Suffraunce may aswagen hem and þe swelme leþe,
For ho quelles vche a qued and quenches malyce.

For quo-so suffer cowþe syt, sele wolde folʒe,
And quo for þro may noʒt þole, þe þikker he sufferes.
Þen is better to abyde þe bur vmbe-stoundes,
Þen ay þrow forth my þro, þaʒ me þynk ylle.

$$(1-8)$$

(Patience is a point, although it often displeases. When heavy hearts hurt
with scorn or something else, sufferance may comfort them and calm the
fury, for she subdues all evil and quenches malice.

Prosperity follows the man who can put up with suffering, and he who
cannot endure it because of his impatience suffers the more. And so it is better for me to accept the blow when it comes than forever to give vent to my
impatience, although I might not like it.)

What does the virtue of patience involve for the narrator, and what did a
medieval audience think it involved?[4] To the first of these questions, the
opening stanzas suggest an answer. In the *Gawain*-poet's words patience
is synonymous with the word 'suffraunce'. The gloss is unlikely to
enlighten the modern reader, for the word 'sufferance' has become
obsolete. In medieval English, however, the word had a rich set of
meanings (Stokes 1983–4; *MED* under 'sufferaunce'). It could refer to
being in sorrow and pain, but also to one's capacity to endure these tribulations without protest, to bear them willingly. And the implied
presence of inner consent in the second meaning allows us to see the
link with its third meaning of 'permission', the sense that the verb 'suffer' also has in, for example, the Bible. 'Suffer it to be so now' (Matthew
3: 15) means 'allow it to be so now'.

The three meanings are related. They vary only in the relative prominence they give to the element of volition or consent. That today many
of the meanings of 'sufferance' or 'suffer' are obsolescent has everything
to do with a modern tendency to dissociate volition from enduring pain.
Suffering has by and large come to mean bearing pain involuntarily. The
idea that anyone should suffer willingly has become so alien that it

4. On the theme of patience in medieval literature and in *Patience* see the important collection of essays edited by Schiffhorst (1978), and Baldwin (1990).

survives only in some fossilized expressions, such as the adjective 'long-suffering'—being patient with those who inflict suffering—or the phrase 'on sufferance'—with permission, but reluctantly. The same dissociation of pain and volition is responsible for the inverse semantic narrowing of the word 'patience', which, like 'suffraunce', signified to medieval writers a state of affliction as well as calm endurance. The impoverishment of the word 'patience' differs from that of 'suffraunce' only in being restricted to the second rather than the first of this origin-ally double meaning. What the desynonymization of both words registers is that we have today come to regard suffering and good-will as mutually exclusive. We no longer combine the two in word, perhaps because we can hardly conceive of doing so in deed.

Patience, however, keeps the various meanings of 'suffer' and 'patience' continually in play. It is, at the simplest level, the experience of 'hurt' (2), which, as the narrator suggests, may be assuaged by 'suf-fraunce', by forbearing it. Then, our anger will subside, the 'qued' will become sufferable, and the 'malyce' we endure, or harbour against others, may be quenched. The 'qued' and the 'malyce' in the first stanza need not exclusively refer to the evil directed against ourselves, but also to the resentment felt towards others. Patience embraces both the way we live with ourselves and the way we live with others, and we shall see how the poet develops his point in the story of Jonah.

The opening of *Patience* suggests, then, that the proper approach to suffering is to take it on sufferance. The answer may appear tautological, yet while the poet's advice of 'suffraunce' still contains within it the word 'suffer', it nevertheless marks a change of attitude which makes all the difference, the difference namely between 'suffering' in the sense of 'forbearing' and the sense of 'smarting' (Stokes 1983–4). Patience, we might say, seizes on the semantic range of 'suffering', turning its negative meaning of experiencing pain into the more positive one of tolerating it. It follows that those who are impatient cannot accomplish this semantic conversion:

Who-so suffer cowþe syt, sele wolde folȝe,
And who for þro may noȝt þole, þe þikker he sufferes.

Unable to suffer in the one sense, they suffer for it in the other. True, the poet sees no easy way out of suffering, yet there is at least an option between the senses in which it can be taken. Within these confines, the poet concludes, the best one can do is to muster the good-will that can bring out its more positive meaning.

Some critics have been inclined to spiritualize this worldly-wise view
of suffering by, for example, reading 'sele' as heavenly bliss, and by
imagining that when the poet observes that the impatient will suffer 'þe
þikker', he was thinking of the pains of hell (Zavadil 1962, 39–40, 65).
Such a redemptive turn of thought might seem plausible for a medieval
Christian, but it is in fact not the narrator's, whose feet are planted too
firmly on the ground. The point appears clearly in his idiosyncratic
interpretation of one of the most exalted passages in the New Testament,
the Sermon on the Mount. As we have seen, the poet begins his paraphrase of the beatitudes by representing himself at the receiving end of
this sermon:

> I herde on a halyday, at a hyȝe masse,
> How Mathew melede þat his mayster his meyny con teche;
> Aȝt happes he hem hyȝt and vche-on a mede
> Sunderlupes for hit dissert vpon a ser wyse.
>
> Thay arn happen þat han in hert pouerte,
> For hores is þe heuen-ryche to holde for euer.
> Þay arn happen also þat haunte mekenesse,
> For þay schal welde þis world and alle her wylle haue.
>
> Þay are happen also þat for her harme wepes,
> For þay schal comfort encroche in kythes ful mony.
> Þay ar happen also þat hungeres after ryȝt,
> For þay schal frely be refete ful of alle gode.
>
> Þay ar happen also þat han in hert rauþe,
> For mercy in alle maneres her mede schal worþe.
> Þay ar happen also þat arn of hert clene,
> For þay her sauyour in sete schal se with her yȝen.
>
> Thay ar happen also þat halden her pese,
> For þay þe gracious Godes sunes schal godly be called.
> Þay ar happen also þat con her hert stere,
> For hores is þe heuen-ryche, as I er sayde.
>
> (9–28)

(I heard on a holy day, at high mass, how Matthew said that his master instructed his following. Eight blessings he showed them, and each its reward according to their various merits.

Blessed are those who have poverty in their hearts, for theirs is the heavenly kingdom, to keep forever. Also blessed are those who follow meekness, for they shall possess this world and will have all they want.

Blessed also are those who weep for sorrow, for they shall obtain comfort in many lands. Blessed also those that hunger after right, for they will be fed with all that is good.

Blessed also those who have pity in their hearts, for mercy will be their reward in all things. Blessed also those who are clean of heart, for they will see their Saviour on the throne.

Blessed also those who keep their peace, for they shall fittingly be called the sons of gracious God. Blessed also those who steer their hearts, for theirs is the heavenly kingdom, as I said before.)

With some exceptions, about which I shall have more to say later, this is a faithful translation of Matthew 5: 3–10. The poet's interpretation that follows, however, is very unusual, in particular in comparison with the other-worldly perspective from which Christ views suffering, a perspective which medieval commentators on the Sermon on the Mount had further underlined (Leclerq 1974).[5] Christ's Sermon exposes life on earth to the light of the life to come. It blesses those who suffer, as it looks beyond their current predicament into the celestial future that will bring a reversal of their fortunes. Arguably, the Sermon on the Mount sets the moment of reversal in this world. Unlike the other beatitudes, the first and the last announce the rewards of suffering in the present, not the future tense: 'quoniam ipsorum *est* regum caelorum', accurately translated by the *Gawain*-poet as 'hores *is* þe heuen-ryche' (14, 28). Might Christ's kingdom be a matter for the present? Certainly many of the oppressed in the Middle Ages took the Sermon in this way, for it was throughout the period a focus for millennial movements and rebellions, whose supporters were not going to wait until the end of time, or the end of their time, to reap the rewards of their misery. In contrast, the church tirelessly proclaimed that the needy and suffering were indeed blessed, as long as they did not anticipate their future bliss (Pellistrandi 1974). Their afflictions would be rewarded in heaven, provided they regarded that prospect as a sufficient rationale for their present suffering, and an adequate reason for accepting it gratefully.[6]

The way towards this spiritualization of the beatitudes, which made them conditional on patience, had been pointed by Augustine. There are three interpretative moves in Augustine's influential writings on the beatitudes which I want to single out for their relevance to *Patience*. The

---

5. See Hill (1968) for a convenient inventory of commentaries and sermons on the Sermon on the Mount. Unlike Hill, I would characterize the relationship between *Patience* and the commentary tradition as contrasting rather than overlapping.

6. See Mollat (1986, 88, 260–4) for the competing interpretations of the Sermon on the Mount by the church and the poor in the Middle Ages.

first is his insistence that in the first beatitude, 'Beati pauperes spiritu ...',
the word *spiritu* is the operative word. Poverty in spirit meant humility.
It applied to material poverty only if it was inwardly accepted.[7] Hence,
poverty borne not voluntarily but out of necessity was not redemptive
but damning. The moral was often repeated in the later Middle Ages, for
example, by Peter of Blois:

> Beati, inquit, pauperes spiritu, non omnes, sed tamen illi qui ducunt volun-
> tariam, non coactam, non necessariam, sed spontaneam paupertatem. Nam
> illud solum Deo acceptum est quod ex voluntate procedit.[8]

> (Blessed, he says, are the poor in spirit, not all the poor, but those who lead a
> life of voluntary poverty, not forced, not out of necessity, but a willed pov-
> erty. Because only what proceeds from the will is acceptable to God.)

The same spiritual slant was given by Augustine to the last beatitude:
'Beati qui persecutionem patiuntur propter iustitiam': blessed be those
who suffer for the sake of righteousness. In opposition to the Stoics, for
whom patience, constancy in prosperity and adversity, was simply man's
most reasonable and dignified response to the lamentable fickleness of
Fortune, Augustine elaborated a doctrine of patience that posited God
both as the source of suffering and as its end. He insisted that the suffering that counted as blessed was suffering 'for the sake of righteousness',
which Augustine glossed as suffering borne with God and the afterlife in
mind.[9] Tolerating suffering for other reasons—and again the idea was to
become a commonplace—was no true patience:

> Non igitur omnes qui persecutionem patiuntur beati sunt; siquidem iniqui se
> inuicem persequuntur; sed illi soli propter persecutionem sunt beati, qui eam
> propter justitiam patiuntur.[10]

> (Therefore not all those who suffer are blessed, since the unjust too persecute
> one another, but only those who do so for the sake of righteousness.)

Augustine's third argument was that Christ's insistence on an other-
worldly motivation in the eighth blessing was equally present in all the
previous blessings. Christ had stipulated 'for the sake of righteousness'

---

7. Augustine, *De sermone Domini*, ed. A. Mützenberger, *CC* 35 (Turnhout: Brepols,
   1967), 4; cf. his equally influential *Sermo 53*, *PL* 38, 364–73.
8. *Sermo 42*, *PL* 207, 689. Cf. Boniface, *De octo beatitudinibus*, *PL* 89, 850.
9. Augustine, *De patientia*, ed. and trans. Gustav Combès (Paris: Desclée de Brouwer,
   1948), 535–6, 542. Augustine's view of patience was alive and well in the later Middle
   Ages, and widely disseminated through Aquinas's *Summa Theologiae* (Gilson 1946).
10. Bruno Astensis, *Commentaria in Matthaeum*, *PL* 165, 100.

not as a new item to his list of beatitudes but to highlight a condition implicit in all the earlier beatitudes. That is why, as Augustine noted, the last maxim mirrors the first by repeating its phrase 'horum est regnum caelorum':

Octaua tamquam ad caput redit, quia consummatum perfectumque ostendit et probat ... nam octaua clarificat et quod perfectum est demonstrat.

(*De sermone Domini*, 9)

(The eighth maxim, returns, as it were, to the beginning: it presents and approves something consummate and perfect ... it clarifies and approves what is already complete.)

Thus, all afflictions mentioned in the earlier beatitudes were to be suffered for God's sake as well, with the humility and gratefulness that should accompany the promise of salvation (*De sermone Domini*, 13). We may call the view of suffering put forward by Augustine and espoused by the medieval church transcendental, since it places its meaning and *raison d'être* beyond time, but it was no more idealistic than the chiliastic and revolutionary attempts to anticipate Christ's promises by re-creating the world in heaven's image.

To return, after this brief sketch of medieval interpretations of the Sermon on the Mount, to the narrator's response is to land, with a shock, on the ground:

These arn þe happes alle aȝt þat vus bihiȝt weren,
If we þyse ladyes wolde lof in lyknyng of þewes:
Dame Pouert, dame Pitee, dame Penaunce þe þrydde,
Dame Mekenesse, dame Mercy and miry Clannesse,

And þenne dame Pes and Pacyence put in þer-after.
He were happen þat hade one, alle were þe better.
Bot syn I am put to a poynt þat Pouerte hatte,
I schal me poruay Pacyence and play me with boþe;

For in þe tyxte þere þyse two arn in teme layde,
Hir arn fettled in on forme, þe forme and þe laste,
And by quest of her quoyntyse enquylen on mede,
And als, in my vpynyoun, hit arn of on kynde.

For þer as Pouert hir proferes ho nyl be put vtter,
Bot lenge where-so-euer hir lyst, lyke oþer greme;
And þer as Pouert enpresses, þaȝ mon pyne þynk,
Much, maugre his mun, he mot nede suffer.

Thus Pouerte and Pacyence arn nedes play-feres;
Syþen I am sette with hem samen, suffer me by-houes;
Þenne is me lyȝtloker hit lyke and her lotes prayse,
Þenne wyþer wyth and be wroth and þe wers haue.

(29–48)[11]

(These are the eight blessings that we were promised if we would love these
ladies by imitating their manners: dame Poverty, dame Pity, dame Tribulation
the third, dame Meekness, dame Mercy, and pleasing Cleanness, and added
to them dame Peace and Patience. If the possession of one were a blessing,
having them all would be better still. But since I am reduced to a state called
Poverty, I will get myself Patience and play with them both. For in the text
where they are spoken of, they are formally linked, the first and the last, and
because of their graces they receive the same reward. And they are similar in
my opinion as well. For where Poverty presents herself she will not be put
outside, but she will stay where she likes, whether you like it or not. And
where Poverty puts herself forward, a man must suffer much, despite his
complaint, though he thinks it hard. Thus Poverty and Patience must needs
be playfellows. Since I am beset by both, I must suffer. And so it is better for
me to like them and praise their ways than to resist and be the worse for it.)

The poet's perception that the first and the last of the beatitudes are
'fettled in on forme' shows his keen eye for structural patterning, of
which his own poems are exquisite examples (Spearing 1970, 76). They
also suggest his familiarity with the Augustinian interpretation of the
beatitudes, perhaps as transmitted through the later-thirteenth-century
Speculum morale, once attributed to Vincent of Beauvais, which also
made the point that the eighth beatitude mirrors the first and had con-
cluded from this that 'paupertas comitem debet habere patientiam':
'poverty should have patience as a companion'.[12] The *Gawain*-poet put
it similarly: 'Pouerte and Pacyence arn nedes play-feres'.

But more striking than the similarities with medieval commentaries
on the Sermon are the differences, apparent even from the slightly different inflexion he gives to the dictum that the poor should be patient.
The narrator of *Patience* in contrast states that the poor cannot but be
patient; patience and poverty are not qualities spontaneously cultivated
but the unavoidable demands imposed by circumstance. The poet, in

11. I depart from Anderson's edition in capitalizing 'Poverty' and 'Pacyence' throughout
   this passage in order to bring out the gentle social comedy which the poet creates by
   personifying these two virtues as two obstreperous ladies who have forced their company on him.
12. *Speculum morale*, in Vincent of Beauvais, *Speculum majus* (Douay, 1624), III, 578, 684.

other words, does not regard his poverty and adversity as a blessing at all. Thus, his poverty, so far from being a voluntary 'poverty in spirit', or an objective correlative of his inner humility, is quite clearly material. Lady Poverty has not come on the poet's cordial invitation; she has forced her bad company on him. And since she will not be evicted without making things worse, the poet realizes that there is nothing for it but to put up with her, 'lyke oþer greme'.

Herein lies the kinship which the poet discerns between Poverty and Patience. Patience understood in the wider sense of 'suffraunce' is equally inescapable. One may not enjoy the company of either of these ladies, but whoever protests against them will be the worse for it. Cornered by Patience and Poverty, the poet can only make a virtue of necessity. He will therefore purport to like them, praise their irritating habits, and hope that they will soon go away. He has no choice in the matter of poverty or suffering, other than the attitude he takes to them: a narrow range of options, but the narrator makes it his playground.

To this pragmatic approach to adversity, the Sermon on the Mount and its metaphysical perspective have not made one iota of difference. Admittedly he draws some lessons from it, such as the link between Poverty and Patience, yet these only confirm the pre-existing 'vpynyoun'(40) of the poet. Doctrine does not shape his outlook and his experience; it is shaped by them. Thus, the poverty of spirit of the Sermon or Augustine becomes for the poor poet penury, while suffering 'for the sake of righteousness' becomes patience for lack of a better alternative. Hence it is the qualification 'for the sake of righteousness', elevated by Augustine as the touchstone for Christian patience, which disappears from the poet's paraphrase of the final beatitude: 'þay ar happen also þat con her hert stere ...'(27). The otherworldly motivation on which Augustine had insisted is lost from view in this secularization of patience, better suited to the narrator's level-headed 'vpynyoun'.

The narrator's worldly view of patience appears less obvious and uncontroversial when we realize that it is not unlike the Stoic ideal of patience as the most reasonable response to life's inevitable changes of fortune. The ideal had by the later Middle Ages become more acceptable than it had been for Augustine. Moral compendia like the popular twelfth-century *Moralium dogma philosophorum* turned freely to the pagan philosophers of Antiquity in an attempt to formulate a secular ethics for the layman. It is precisely in these texts, and not in the Church Fathers or in penitential manuals, that we find discussions of patience similar to the *Gawain*-poet's. This, for example, is what Brunetto Latini has to say on the subject in *Li livres dou tresor*, a didactic treatise heavily indebted to the *Moralium dogma* and to classical wisdom:

> Orasces dit, tout li mal ki sont a venir devienent plus legier par patience. Boesces dit, par non souffir te sera l'aventure plus aspre ke tu ne pués muer. Terrences dit, soufrons o bons corages ce que fortune nos aporte, car folie est de regiber contre aguilon.
>
> (*Livres dou tresor*, 270–1)[13]

> (Horace says that the misfortune that is to come becomes lighter through patience. Boethius says that by not suffering patiently, the situation you cannot change only becomes harder. Terence says we should suffer with good will what fortune brings us, for it is foolish to kick against a spike.)

This mundane approach to suffering also characterizes *Patience*. Compare Latini's gnomic wisdom with the homely proverb that concludes God's speech to Jonah (526–7): 'For he þat is to rakel to renden his cloþeȝ / Mot efte sitte with more vnsounde sewe hem to-geder' ('he who is too rash in tearing his clothes often must put up with more annoyance when he has to sew them together again'). With this thoroughly common-sensical advice, God sends Jonah on his way.

Among contemporaries, Chaucer's treatment of patience, in particular in his works set in pagan Antiquity, owes most to Stoic ethics (Burnley 1979, 74–98). We may think of Theseus's grand speech at the end of the *Knight's Tale*:

> 'Thanne is it wysdom, as it thynketh me,
> To maken vertu of necessitee,
> And take it weel that we may nat eschue
> And namely that to us alle is due.'
>
> (I, 3041–4)

On a less lofty note, Theseus's philosophy is put into practice by Criseyde. When she is trapped by a storm and invited to spend the night at Pandarus's house, she considers that, without a sensible alternative, she might as well bring herself to accept with good cheer what she cannot refuse:

> Criseyde, which that koude as muche good
> As half a world, took hede of his preiere;
> And syn it ron, and al was on a flod,
> She thoghte, 'As good chep may I dwellen here,
> And graunte it gladly with a frendes chere,

13. Ed. F.J. Carmody (Berkeley: University of California Press, 1948).

And have a thonk, as grucche and thanne abide;
For hom to gon, it may nought wel bitide.'

(III, 638–44)

ron: rained; *as good chep*: I might as well; *grucche*: complain

This is the principle of making 'vertu of necessitee' applied to the prac-
ticalities of everyday life. Significantly, the same irrefutable logic
convinces the narrator of *Patience* that, should his lord ask him to make
the arduous journey to Rome, he must do his bidding gladly:

ȝif me be dyȝt a destyne due to haue,
What dowes me þe dedayn oþer dispit make?
Oþer ȝif my lege lorde lyst on lyue me to bidde
Oþer to ryde oþer to renne to Rome in his ernde,

What grayþed me þe grychchyng bot grame more seche?
Much ȝif he ne me made, maugref my chekes,
And þenne þrat most I þole and vnþonk to mede,
Þe had bowed to his bode, bongre my hyure.

(49–56)

(If an appointed task were ordained for me, what good would it do me to be
indignant or defiant? Or if it pleased my liege lord to command me to go to
Rome on his errand, what would grumbling do but invite more trouble? I
would be lucky if he did not force me to go, despite my objections, receiving
threats and displeasure as my reward, when having done his bidding I might
have earned his thanks.)[14]

Since the powerless poet can be coerced into obedience, he sees no
point in protesting. The orders of lords have the finality of facts. Better,
then, to grin and bear it.

If this were the only lesson to be learnt from *Patience*, it might have
been a very bleak poem, and it may be worth asking ourselves what prevents this worldly-wise view of suffering from degenerating into an
apathetic indifference to the world. It is not the ability to see through a
world of suffering into heaven and its rewards, for, as we have seen, this
visionary outlook is not the poet's. Suffering for him is irreducibly real,
and other than suggesting that we accommodate ourselves to it, the narrator does not construct a dimension in which the realities of suffering
dissolve. What separates the narrator from the cynic is rather his trust

14. In my translation I follow Burrow (1989), who reads 'bongre' as a noun meaning
'gratitude' rather than a preposition 'in accordance with'. The parallel with *Troilus* is
also noted by Burrow.

that such a dimension none the less exists. As I shall show in the discussion of the epilogue, the reason for the narrator's reticence about it is that he no more pretended to have access to this dimension than his audience. It is only the *exemplum* of Jonah that gives us an assurance that it exists, an assurance which in the narrator's prologue can be felt only as a vague and undeclared source of optimism.

THE *GAWAIN*-POET AS A READER OF THE BIBLE

The story of Jonah is quickly summarized. Summoned to announce God's imminent vengeance to the Ninevites, a fearful Jonah instead takes to the sea in flight. His plans are thwarted by a violent storm, which, as the sailors sense, is directed against someone in the ship. A casting of lots points to Jonah as the culprit, and Jonah volunteers to be cast out into the sea. A giant whale swallows Jonah even before he lands into the water, and brings Jonah on his way to Nineveh. Here Jonah prophesies the city's destruction, but, touched by the repentance of the Ninevites, God changes his mind. Jonah, furious that his prophecies have been turned to lies, takes shelter under a luxurious gourd that God has made to grow for the prophet. Waking up the next morning, Jonah finds his protection gone after a God-sent worm has uprooted the woodbine. To the question of why God has turned against his prophet, God replies that if Jonah feels sorry for a plant that is not even of his own making, he should understand how much more God cares for the people of Nineveh, his own creation. He has been patient with the Ninevites; cannot Jonah be patient too?

The story in the Vulgate, which this plot follows, is a masterpiece in itself, and while critics usually stake claims for the quality of *Patience* on the poet's departures from his source, it seems to me that the poet's achievement lies largely in his insightful and sensitive reading of the biblical story. The *Gawain*-poet clearly relished this story for its own sake, for, although he added details, he left its larger implications untouched. He seems to have felt no need to represent Jonah's mission differently from the way his source suggested. His energy instead was spent on imagining how Jonah, or the whale, or the sailors might have experienced the events set down in the Book of Jonah (Spearing 1970, 82–4).

This consequent emphasis on the literal level contrasts markedly with a medieval tendency to read the Old Testament not for story but doctrine. The medieval tradition of Old Testament interpretation had developed as a defence of the Old Testament against the views of Marcion, who believed that its many lies and crudities meant it could not truly be God's revelation.[15] The weapon which the Church Fathers developed to refute Marcion was that of allegorical interpretation. Wherever history under the Old Covenant seemed in conflict with the teachings of the New Testament, it should be assumed that it actually meant something different. The 'carnal' level of the Old Testament should in these cases be interpreted 'spiritually', and those who did so would see that the Old Testament was actually in agreement with the New, both in the moral truths it presented, and in taking the coming of Christ as its subject. Many Old Testament events were prophecies of Christ's coming and his life on earth, and should be understood as shadows or figures of things to come. If the disagreement with Marcion over the value of the Old Testament led the Church Fathers to develop ways of transcending the literal level of Old Testament history by allegorizing it, they unfortunately ended up agreeing with their opponent in a very important sense: 'taken in its literal, historical meaning, the Old Testament had little to offer as a book for Christians' (Preus 1969, 10).

The medieval exegetical tradition that developed from the Church Fathers cannot of course be captured in a single paragraph, and I shall be suggesting that some hermeneutical refinements of the later Middle Ages may account for the poet's subtle use of the figural relation that was held to exist between Jonah and Christ. One may, however, safely generalize about a tendency to devalue the historical or literal level of Old Testament stories, certainly when, as was the case for the Book of Jonah, many fantastical elements could encourage, and had encouraged, incredulity (Bowers 1971, 1–60; Duval 1973, 13–15).

The *Gawain*-poet's familiarity with the exegetical tradition need not be doubted. Since Carolingian times, commentaries had found a secure place on the pages of the biblical text in the form of extensive glosses (Smalley 1984, 46–52). But the poet's retelling of the Book of Jonah takes as its subject the historical level, and it is not the least of his achievements to have preserved its integrity. A comparison of a few passages from the Bible with the poet's adaptation will bear this out. These are the words God speaks to Jonah in the Vulgate, with Jonah's response:

---

15. For two introductory studies of medieval Old Testament interpretation see Preus (1969), and Grant and Tracy (1984).

Arise and go to Nineveh to the great city and preach in it: for the wickedness therof is come up before me.

And Jonah rose up to flee into Tharsis from the face of the Lord: and he went down to Joppe and found a ship going to Tharsis. And he paid the fare thereof and went down into it, to go with them to Tharsis from the face of the Lord.

(1: 2–3)

Though one would not have guessed it from medieval biblical commentaries these lines are very funny. God speaks to his prophet, but his prophet will not hear. God's commands are resolute, and as the imperative mood suggests, absolute. The Bible does not spell out what Jonah makes of them. Any brief hesitation that they may have given him is already over when we reach the word 'And' in the third verse. Jonah's actions, from then on, are equally resolute, and he does not just disobey, but seems intent on doing precisely the opposite of what God has asked him to do (Holbert 1981). Going to Nineveh becomes fleeing to Tharsis; when ordered to 'rise up', Jonah goes 'down' to Joppe. But Jonah's determined contrariness gets him nowhere. As the rest of the story will show, the idea that one can escape from God is wishful thinking, for to imagine one can do so is to think God has a 'face' like ours, located in a particular place, and only capable of looking in one particular direction at a time.

The *Gawain*-poet adds a great deal to this passage, and I must quote his adaptation selectively:

'Rys radly', he says, 'and rayke forth euen;
Nym þe way to Nynyue wyth-outen oþer speche,
And in þat cete my saȝes soghe alle aboute,
Þat in þat place at þe poynt, I put in þi hert ...'

'... At alle peryles', quoþ þe prophete, 'I aproche hit no nerre;
I wyl me sum oþer waye þat he ne wayte after;
I schal tee in-to Tarce and tary þere a whyle,
And lyȝtly when I am lest he letes me alone.'

Þenne he ryses radly and raykes bilyue
Jonas toward port Japh, ay janglande for tene
Þat he nolde þole for no þyng non of þose pynes,
Þaȝ þe fader þat hym formed were fale of his hele.

'Oure syre syttes', he says, 'on sege so hyȝe,
In his glowande glory, and gloumbes ful lyttel

Þaȝ I be nummen in Nunniue and naked dispoyled,
On rode rwly to-rent with rybaudes mony.'

Þus he passes to þat port his passage to seche,
Fyndes he a fayr schyp to þe fare redy,
Maches hym with þe maryners, makes her paye
For-to towe hym in-to Tarce as tyd as þay myȝt.

Then he tron on þo tres, and þay her tramme ruchen,
Cachen vp þe crossayl, cables þay fasten;
Wiȝt at þe wyndas weȝen her ankres,
Spynde sprak to þe sprete þe spare bawe-lyn,

Gederen to þe gyde-ropes, þe grete cloþ falles,
Þay layden in on ladde-borde and þe lofe wynnes.
Þe blyþe breþe at her bak þe bosum he fyndes,
He swenges me þys swete schip swefte fro þe hauen.

(65–108)

('Rise quickly', he says, 'and go at once; take the way to Nineveh and in that city spread the words I will put in your heart there when the time comes.' 'Whatever the consequences', says the prophet, 'I will steer clear of it. I will go some other way, where he will not be watching. I shall go to Tharsis and stay there a while, and perhaps he will leave me alone when he has lost me.' Then Jonah rises quickly, and goes at once towards the port of Joppe, continually grumbling in his anger that there was no way he would put up with any of these hardships, though the father that created him were unconcerned about his welfare. 'Our lord', he says, 'sits on his high throne in resplendent glory, and wouldn't care if I were captured in Nineveh and stripped naked, grievously pierced on a cross by many wicked men.' Thus he goes to the port to find transport, and he finds a fair ship ready to sail. He teams up with the mariners, and pays them to carry him to Tharsis as soon as possible. Then he stepped on deck, and they get their gear ready. They hoist the square-sail, fasten the cables, quickly lift the anchors at the windlass, carefully fasten the spare bowline to the bowsprit, and tug at the guy-ropes. The big sail drops. They use their oars against the quay, and gain the luff; the merry wind catches the sail, and swings this lovely ship swiftly from the harbour.)

The stanzas I have left out give us more on Jonah's thoughts, which the Old Testament is content to pass over in silence. Jonah in *Patience* betrays himself explicitly as a suspicious prophet, but to attribute Jonah's disobedience to fear is to read the silences of the Old Testament in a way that makes, even to modern standards, for a highly plausible interpretation. Undoubtedly, it compares favourably with the standard presentation of Jonah in biblical commentaries on the Book of Jonah as a prophet who is reluctant to do pagans favours,[16] or with Philip of Harvengt's reading, which prefers to see Jonah as someone who prefers the contemplative over the active life.[17]

Moreover, the *Gawain*-poet was aware of the comic effect achieved in the Old Testament by the swift succession of God's orders and Jonah's evasion. What his poem loses by making the prophet pause before responding, is adequately compensated for by a series of adverbials that describe the prophet's hurry: 'radly', 'bilyue', and 'as tyd as þay my3t'. Nor was the humour of Jonah's deliberate contrariness lost on the poet. His Jonah, too, is determined not just to disobey orders but to invert them. If anything, the *Gawain*-poet's antithesis between God's words and Jonah's response goes one better than the Vulgate:

'Rys radly', he says, 'and rayke forth euen;
Nym þe way to Nynyue wyth-outen oþer speche ...'

Þenne he ryses radly and raykes bilyue
Jonas toward port Japh, ay janglande for tene ...

However, this Jonah, too, will be disappointed. The adverb 'ly3tly' in his own words (88) raises doubts about Jonah's ambitions even at this early stage. Like the prophet in the Vulgate, who believes God has a 'face' like ours, Jonah has the wrong idea about God's divine nature. Picturing him on a throne somewhere in the sky, Jonah wagers that God will not be able to see his prophet disappear. The mistake in Jonah's rationalizations lies in imagining that God has a body fixed in time and place.

The *Gawain*-poet's fancy next takes him to a lively description of the departure of Jonah's ship to Tharsis, full of the details that should convince the reader that when the poet talked of ships he knew the ins and outs. The inspiration for this description in the passage quoted above may have been Wace's *Brut*, which renders the moment of Arthur's fleet sailing out from Southampton with even more nautical jargon. I quote an extract from Wace's long description:

Quant es nés furent tuit antré
Et tide orente bon oré,
Donc veïssiez ancres lever,
Estrans traire, hobans fermer.

16. This line of interpretation was transmitted to the Middle Ages through Jerome, *In Jonam*, ed. and trans. Yves-Marie Duval (Paris: Editions du Cerf, 1985), 174–5. On Jerome's influence on later commentaries see Duval (1973).
17. *De Institutione Clericorum*, *PL* 203, 1108.

Mariniers vont parmi ces nés
Por hernechier voiles et trés.
Li un s'esforcent al vindas,
Li autre al lof et al betas …
… Estuins ferment et escotes
Et font tandre les cordes totes,
Uitagues laschent, trés avalent,
Boëlines saichent et halent,
Au vant gardent et as estoiles …
(*Brut*, 11218–31)[18]

(When they had all entered the ship, and had a favourable tide, you could have seen anchors being lifted, the stays made secure and the guy ropes fastened. The sailors rush about in the ships to unfurl the sails. Some are busy at the windlass, others at the luff and the yard-ropes. The stays and the cables are tightened, ropes are stretched or loosened, and the canvas comes down. The bowlines are pulled, the sailors check the wind and the stars …)

As usual, the Vulgate is far more economical, though certainly not without suggestive detail. Witness, for example, the 'naulum', the fare, which Jonah pays to the mariners. It adds nothing to the larger meaning of the Book of Jonah, and was not intended to do so. Its function lies precisely in its randomness, in the effect of reality it provides by confronting us, like life itself, with a moment of uninterpretability. The detail of the passage-money greatly taxed the ingenuity of biblical commentators, but by taking it to refer to Jonah's and, by implication, Christ's self-sacrifice, even the passage-money could be wrested from its context in the story and made to signify eternal verities.[19] In *Patience*, however, the verisimilar detail calls forth a close-up of the ship setting out to sea; it lured the *Gawain*-poet in the direction to which the little reality-effect in the Vulgate was beckoning. His visualization is of course, like so many medieval descriptions, blatantly anachronistic. The ship that leaves the harbour of Joppe is medieval, not the kind of vessel that might have existed in the remote past, 'þe termes of Judé' (61), in which the story is set. Those who look for careful reconstructions of past eras will be disappointed with the *Gawain*-poet, and medieval literature in general. One may find fault with these anachronisms, but they are the responses of people for whom history had not yet disappeared into an irrecoverable past, but continued to bear on the present: it was alive, and its relevance was immediate.

18. Ed. Ivor Arnold, 2 vols, SATF (Paris: Firmin Didot, 1938–40).
19. See Jerome, *In Jonam*, 182–3.

Another example of the poet's amplification of his source is his accomplished description of the storm. The Bible is brief:

> But the Lord sent a great wind into the sea: and a great tempest was raised in the sea, and the ship was in great danger to be broken. And the mariners were afraid and the men cried to their god: and they cast forth their wares that were in the ship into the sea, to lighten it of them ...
>
> (1: 4–5)

A small detail, that of the cargo thrown overboard, gives the story another effect of verisimilitude. The *Gawain*-poet took his cue from his source, and focused even more closely on the 'wares', so that they take on concrete shapes:

> Þer watȝ busy ouer-borde bale to kest,
> Her bagges and her feþer-beddes and her bryȝt wedes,
> Her kysstes and her coferes, her caraldes alle,
> And al to lyȝten þat lome, ȝif leþe wolde schape.
>
> (157–60)

> (They were in a rush to cast the packages overboard, and their bags, their feather-beds, their shining clothes, their chests, their cases, and all their casks. And all this to lighten the ship, in the hope of alleviating their distress.)

Again, the poet's additions do not lead us away from the story into abstract moralization but bring us closer to it, by closing in on what the Bible only gives in bare outline.

An element of rhetorical display is not alien to the poet, and he is clearly demonstrating his knowledge of conventional descriptions of storms when he evokes the sudden onslaught of the winds, where the Book of Jonah mentions only a 'mighty wind':

> For þe welder of wyt þat wot alle þynges,
> Þat ay wakes and waytes, at wylle hatȝ he slyȝtes.
> He calde on þat ilke craft he carf with his hondes;
> Þay wakened wel þe wroþeloker, for wroþely he cleped:

> 'Ewrus and Aquiloun þat on este sittes,
> Blowes boþe at my bode vpon blo watteres.'
> Þenne watȝ þere no tom þer bytwene his tale and her dede,
> So bayn wer þay boþe two his bone for-to wyrk.

> An-on out of þe norþ-est þe noys bigynes,
> When boþe breþes con blowe vpon blo watteres;
> Roȝ rakkes þer ros with rudnyng an-vnder,
> Þe see souȝed ful sore, gret selly to here.

Þe wyndes on þe wonne water so wrastel to-geder
Þat þe wawes ful wode waltered so hiȝe
And efte busched to þe abyme, þat breed fysches
Durst nowhere for roȝ arest at þe bothem.

When þe breth and þe brok and þe bote metten,
Hit watȝ a ioyles gyn þat Jonas watȝ inne,
For hit reled on roun vpon þe roȝe yþes;
Þe bur ber to hit baft, þat braste alle her gere ...
(129–48)

(For the wielder of wit, who knows all things, who always wakes and watches, has tricks up his sleeve. He called on the devices he made with his own hands. And since he called them angrily, they became all the fiercer: 'Eurus and Aquilon, who are in the east, blow on the dark waters at my commandment, both of you.' Then there was no delay between his speech and their execution, so eager were they to do his request. Promptly a loud noise starts from the north east, as both winds blew on the dark waters. Ragged clouds arose, suffused with a red glare, and the sea sighed so sorely that it was wondrous to hear. The winds wrestled together, and the waves in their anger mounted high and plunged back into the abyss so that big fish did not dare to stay at the bottom for fear. The boat Jonah was in was in a sorry state, when it met with the wind and the sea. It was tossed around on the rough waves. The gale took it abaft and shattered all their gear.)

Again, the *Gawain*-poet is more interested in the events themselves rather than in any allegorical significance. There is much in this lively passage which may remind readers of other medieval descriptions of storms, a topic that since classical times was something of a rhetorical commonplace (Jacobs 1972). The alliterative *Destruction of Troy*, also from the later fourteenth century, contains four set-piece descriptions of storms, with many of the motifs which the *Gawain*-poet also used. Here, for example, is a description of the tempest that overtakes the fleeing Antenor:

There a tempest hom toke on þe torres hegh:
A rak and a royde wynde rose in hor saile,
A myst and a merkenes was meruell to se;
With a routond rayn ruthe to be holde,
Thonret full throly with a thicke haile;
With a leuenyng light as a low fyre,
Blaset al the brode see as it bren wold.
The flode with a felle cours flowet on hepis.
Rose upon rockes as any ranke hylles.

So wode were the waghes & þe wilde ythes,
All was like to be loste, þat no lond hade.
The ship ay shot furth o þe shire waghes,
As qwo clymbe at a clyffe, or a clent hille,
Eft dump in the depe as all drown wolde.

(1983–96)[20]

(There a tempest took them onto mountainous waves. A fog and an angry wind rose in their sail, a mist and a darkness wondrous to see. With a roaring rain piteous to behold, it thundered terribly, with thick hail. The sea was ablaze with a gleaming light like that of a fire, as if it would catch fire. The flood mounted with cruel force; it rose over rocks like a steep hill, so angry were the tide and the wild waves. It seemed as if anything that was not on land would perish. The ship shot past on the clear waves, sometimes climbing steeply as if on a cliff or a precipitous hill, and then dropping back in the deep, as if all would be submerged.)

The violent winds, the eerie colour beneath the dark clouds, the angry waves, the heaving sea: these are some of the motifs that a poet well trained in the art of description had at his disposal. They had found their way into poems and commentaries on the Book of Jonah well before the *Gawain*-poet took them up (Rayé 1944; Duval 1973, 61). The anonymous *Carmen de Jona et Ninive*,[21] a poem long believed to have been a source for the *Gawain*-poet (Hill 1967), is one of the first treatments of the Book of Jonah to amplify the storm by using a rhetorical repertoire of motifs. The claim for a direct relation between the *Carmen de Jona et Nineve* and *Patience* founders, however, on similar amplifications of the storm in Jonah by later writers, such as Paulinus of Nola, the Pseudo-Fulgentius, or Marbod of Rennes (Duval 1973, 61), which make it possible to speak only of a common tradition to which the *Gawain*-poet was indebted. Moreover, the *Gawain*-poet's mention of 'Ewrus' and 'Aquilon' has no parallel in any adaptations of the Book of Jonah, or in contemporary alliterative poetry, but goes back directly to the classical writers which the *Gawain*-poet would have read at school. In Virgil's *Aeneid*, the winds are released by Aeolus, with the same devastating effect as in *Patience*:

... ac venti, velut agmine facto,
qua data porta, ruunt et terras turbine perflant.
Incubuere mari totumque a sedibus imis

20. Eds G.A. Panton and and Donald Davidson, 2 vols, EETS OS 29, 56 (London: Trübner, 1869–74).
21. Ed. Rudolf Peiper, *CSEL* 23 (Vienna: Akademie der Wissenschaften, 1891), 221–6.

una Eurus Notusque creberque procellis
Africus et vastos volvunt ad litora fluctus;
insequitur clamorque virum stridorque rudentum ...
... stridens Aquilone procella
velum adversa ferit, fluctusque ad sidera tollit ...

(I, 82–107)[22]

(... and the winds, as if in armed array, rush forth where passage is given, and blow in storm-blasts upon the sea, and from its lowest depth upheave it all—East and South winds together, and the South-wester, thick with tempests—and shore-ward roll vast billows. Then come the cries of men, and the creaking of cables ... a gust, shrieking from the North, strikes full on his sail, and lifts the waves to heaven.)

The *Gawain*-poet may have had the *Aeneid* in mind when he named his winds 'Eurus' and 'Aquilon'. Indeed, the close correspondence between Virgil's 'insequitur clamorque virum', and the *Gawain*-poet's dramatic 'and þenne þe cry ryses' suggests that the poet either had a good memory or a copy of the *Aeneid* in front of him while he was composing his own description of a storm.[23]

The *Gawain*-poet's familiarity with the specialized art of rhetorical *descriptio* is worth noting. After all, the poet himself, here as in the description of the passing seasons in *Gawain*, made a real effort to ensure that his competence in this field would attract notice (Pearsall 1955). His conspicuous rhetorical commonplaces advertised the author's learning and sophistication; they were the medieval poet's status symbols. This is not to say that they could not also be put to intelligent internal use. The names the *Gawain*-poet gives to the winds, for example, do more than imply his knowledge of Virgil; they help the poet to portray them as people, who, unlike Jonah, obey God's orders without further ado:

Þenne watȝ þere no tom þer bytwene his tale and her dede,
So bayn wer þay boþe two his bone for-to wyrk.

(135–6)

The winds demonstrate the 'suffraunce', the compliance with another's will, of which Jonah, a creature endowed with reason, has been incapable.

The contrast between an obedient universe and a rebellious prophet,

---

22. Ed. E.H. Warmington and trans. H. Rushton Fairclough, 2 vols, LCL (London: Heinemann, 1967).
23. Some other Virgilian allusions in the *Gawain*-poet's oeuvre are discussed in Chapman (1945).

highlighted by the *Gawain*-poet, is implicit in the Book of Jonah, most notably in its treatment of the great fish that swallows Jonah and transports him to a shore close to Nineveh:

> And the Lord prepared a great fish to swallow up Jonas: and Jonas was in the belly of the fish three days and three nights. (2: 1)

> And the Lord spoke to the fish: and it vomited up Jonas upon the dry land. (2: 11)

The fish is ready at God's command. God speaks to it, as he does to Jonah, and it obeys. The services it performs are unlikely, but for that reason all the more suggestive of God's power.

The *Gawain*-poet's whale enters into the picture somewhat earlier. The first hint of its movements comes in lines 143–4, which describe the effect of the tempest on the fish that normally rest at the bottom of the ocean: 'breed fysches / Durst nowhere for roȝ arest at þe bothem'. A hundred lines later the whale is back, on the surface of the water, just in time to gobble up Jonah as the sailors prepare to throw him overboard:

> A wylde walterande whal, as wyrde þen schaped,
> Þat watȝ beten fro þe abyme, bi þat bot flotte,
>
> And watȝ war of þat wyȝe þat þe water soȝte,
> And swyftely swenged hym to swepe and his swolȝ opened;
> Þe folk ȝet haldande his fet, þe fysch hym tyd hentes;
> With-outen towche of any tothe he tult in his þrote.
>
> (247–52)

> (As fate had ordained, a wild, wallowing whale that had been chased from the abyss was floating near the boat, and spotted the man who was headed towards the water. It swiftly swung around for the catch and opened its gullet —the folk were still holding his feet when the fish quickly grabs him. Without touching its teeth he tumbled into its throat.)

The sailors have not even let go of Jonah before the whale rises from the water to swallow its victim.

The manuscript illlumination in Cotton Nero A.x. depicts the scene accurately: Jonah, still held by his ankles, is already heading for the open jaws of the whale. The illumination may owe this nice touch to the text of *Patience*, but earlier manuscript illuminations of this scene from the Book of Jonah, such as the one reproduced on the cover of this book, likewise telescope the moments of Jonah being cast overboard and being swallowed by the whale. The telescoping of two consecutive events into a single tableau is an ingenious way in which the essentially static medium of manuscript illumination can represent sequence, and it seems likely that the *Gawain*-poet was influenced by visual representations of this scene, rather than the other way around (Friedman 1981). The reason why he may have chosen to incorporate the compression of sequence into his narrative is that it forcefully illustrates the inexorability of Jonah's destiny. The universe and its creatures run like clockwork, while the precision with which apparently fortuitous events interlock bears witness to the supreme control of its designer.

In this design the whale plays its allotted role. When it spews up Jonah, the poet again personifies the whale to reveal its obedience and Jonah's contrasting impatience:

> Thenne our fader to þe fysch ferslych bidde3
> Þat he hym sput spakly vpon spare drye.
> Þe whal wende3 at his wylle and a warþe fynde3,
> And þer he brake3 vp þe buyrne as bede hym oure lorde.
>
> (337–40)

> (Then our father fiercely bids the fish to spew him up quickly on the dry land. The whale performs his will and finds a shore, and there he vomits up the man as our lord had commanded.)

The whale, which in lines 143–4 is first making its way up so as to be in time to receive its passenger, is ready at God's will. Nor is the whale the only obedient creature. The sailors are obedient, the reformed Ninevites are, the winds are, even the worm is.

The Book of Jonah presents a universe in which only Jonah wages a fruitless battle against the divine will with which creation works in harmony. This will is a force so strong that it is foolish to stand in its way. Of what avail are the aspirations of a human being if the entire universe is willingly carried along in God's sway? The *Gawain*-poet rightly took this to be a central question of his source, and the reason why his adaptations of individual passages from the Vulgate seldom go against the grain is undoubtedly because he grasped their overall direction. In the Book of Jonah, human ambitions pale into insignificance in comparison with the divine will. The proper response, the *Gawain*-poet believed, was to 'suffer' it, to allow oneself to become an instrument of this will, rather than inflicting on oneself pain and frustration by swimming vainly against the tide.

For this moral, the Book of Jonah is singularly well chosen. Where else does it appear more difficult for a man to sail to Tharsis than for

God to predetermine the outcome of a casting of lots, to have a whale ready to swallow Jonah when the sailors cast him overboard, to have this whale carry Jonah in its belly for three days, and spew him up at a shore near Nineveh? And where else does it appear more sensible for Jonah to have avoided this troublesome detour by going to Nineveh immediately of his own accord and at his own convenience? The Book of Jonah needed no exegesis by the *Gawain*-poet to speak for the wisdom of 'suffraunce'. It made the point for him. The poet only underlined this moral, filled out the story with graphic detail, responded to its effects and implications, in ways only a perceptive reader could have done.

DRAMATIC IRONY IN THE STORY OF JONAH

Jonah's problem in *Patience* is not simply that he has desires of his own, but that these desires clash with God's grand scheme of salvation. As Schleusener (1971, 959) notes, the story of Jonah spells out the implications of a providential view of history:

> Men frame their goals to their own purposes, but because they are caught up in a greater plan conceived not by them but by God, the success or failure of their efforts depends on their conformity to his hidden will. For those who choose wrongly, unexpected consequences baffle action.

A view of history in which human beings are the instruments of God's overarching design would not seem to rate human experience very highly. If the phenomenal world participates in a divine purpose that is larger and of a different order than the way it appears to an individual human being, then surely one should approach man's experience of the phenomenal world with suspicion. It is precisely this suspicion that underlay the notion that suffering should be reinterpreted as a step towards salvation and hence as a blessing, and behind the practice of forms of exegesis that regarded the literal level only as a shadow of a true and higher level of meaning. The *Gawain*-poet, however, seems to have accepted the limitations of human experience, but without believing that things will thereby come to mean something else to us than they do. This outlook may be clarified by looking at the poet's use of the figural or typological dimension of Jonah.[24]

---

24. For discussions of the *Gawain*-poet's use of typology, see Andrew (1973), and Friedman (1981).

Few laymen in the poet's days would have known the wording of the Book of Jonah. With the exception of the Wycliffite Bible (c. 1382), no English translation of the work existed before *Patience*. It had been omitted in the popular medieval abridgements of the Bible, such as Peter Riga's *Aurora* and Peter Comestor's *Historia Scholastica*, and since verse adaptations of the Bible in French and English were largely based on these Latin abridgements (Morey 1993), the Book of Jonah would primarily have reached a Latinate audience.[25] On the other hand, even an illiterate church-goer of the fourteenth century would have known Jonah was a type of Christ. The origins of this typological link lie in the New Testament (Matthew 12: 38–41, and Luke 11: 29–32), where Christ's resurrection after three days and nights in the tomb is compared with Jonah's miraculous re-emergence from the whale, and where the repentance of the Ninevites is contrasted with the obduracy of those who heard Christ but would not listen:

> The men of Nineveh shall rise in the judgment with this generation and shall condemn it, because they did penance at the preaching of Jonas. And behold, more than Jonah is here.
>
> (Luke 11: 32)

In biblical exegesis these references had encouraged the commentators to search out the Book of Jonah for the most unlikely parallels between Jonah's history and Christ's.[26] Even the medieval layman would have been familiar with some of these parallels since they were depicted on the stained-glass windows of cathedrals and abbeys, in picture-book Bibles for the unlettered, in doctrinal best-sellers also intended for laymen, or alluded to in the mystery plays of the Chester and York cycles (James 1951; Woolf 1957; Bowers 1971, 1–60).

Not surprisingly, then, the *Gawain*-poet hints at the typological subtext of his story on several occasions. When, for example, Jonah disappears into the belly of the whale, the poet compares it to hell:

> And þer he festnes þe fete and fathmeȝ aboute,
> And stod vp in his stomak þat stank as þe deuel;
> Þer in saym and in sorȝe þat sauoured as helle,
> Þer watȝ bylded his bour þat wyl no bale suffer.
>
> (273–6)

---

25. In some medieval adaptations of the Bible, a condensed Jonah episode is interpolated after the mention of Jonah in II Kings 14: 25 (Bonnard 1884, 102).

26. The most extreme example of this typological exegesis is Rupert of Deutz, *Commentariorum duodecim prophetas minores*, PL 168, 401–42.

(And there he regains his footing, and gropes around, and he stood up in its stomach which stank like the devil, its grease and filth stinking like hell. There was made the bower of the man who would endure no hardship.)

The whale in Jonah had traditionally been associated with hell, and visual representations of hell's entry in manuscripts and wall paintings as the gaping jaws of the sea monster Leviathan must have made this association familiar to a medieval audience. It would have been equally well known that Christ had descended into hell to redeem mankind, to force open the gates of hell in order to release the righteous from captivity. The mention of the 'deuel' and 'helle' would instantly have called Christ's harrowing of hell to mind.

A second allusion to the harrowing of hell may be found in the whale's symptoms of indigestion after swallowing Jonah:

Ande euer walteres þis whal bi wyldren depe,
Þurȝ mony a regioun ful roȝe, þurȝ ronk of his wylle;
For þat mote in his mawe mad hym, I trowe,
Þaȝ hit lyttel were hym wyth, to wamel at his hert.

(297–300)

(And still the whale wallows in the hostile depths, in many rough regions, in the pride of his will. I think the morsel in his maw made him feel sick at heart, though it were tiny in comparison.)

Three days later the whale can finally relieve himself of his stomach-aches by vomiting Jonah up on the shore: 'he brakes vp þe buyrne as bede hym oure lorde' (340). The Vulgate has no equivalent to the sick whale. It is another example of the poet's efforts to recover the experiences of the characters in the story, by empathizing even with animals. But it also has a symbolic resonance, present in other writings on the Book of Jonah as well. An anonymous sermon, once attributed to Fulgentius, likewise focuses on the unfortunate whale:

Saginato ceto indigestus esurit. Rabies ventris satiatam feram per triduum consumpsit. Cruditate consumeris, fera. Negatur tibi quod tenes. Aestuans igitur bellua, per vastum aequoris navigans gravida atque nec assumens dapem digessit. Tunc cetus immanis dape onustus, jejunio aridus, imperio praeceptoris intimi sui ad aequoris metas celeravit, aequarum agmina navigio findens, ex opaco nigroque viscerum carcere fusum profugum praeda produxit, atque intactum ad limitem profudit.[27]

27. *Sermo 16*, PL 65, 880.

(Having stuffed itself, the sick whale remained hungry. A raging belly plagued the creature for three days. You are consumed by your food, sea-monster! What you hold is denied to you. In commotion, the whale traversed the vast waters, with a heavy stomach, but without being able to digest the meal it had eaten. Thus the great whale, burdened by its meal and famished because of his fast, hastened to the ends of the ocean on the order of its commander, and ploughing through the seas in its course, the animal brought forth as booty the run-away from the dark and black dungeon of its bowels, and spewed him up safe and sound on the shore.)

The links between this sermon and *Patience* are not necessarily direct. Both are informed by a trope that was commonly used to describe Christ's harrowing of hell. Christ had entered the 'bowels' of hell, but hell had been forced to 'vomit up' the 'indigestible bread' of Christ, just as the whale released the indigestible Jonah in the Old Testament (Bynum 1987, 32, 40).

The *Gawain*-poet, then, was clearly aware of the typological relation between Jonah and Christ. It would have been only a short step from here to argue that the story of Jonah should be understood differently and should be reinterpreted in terms of the Christ narrative. Medieval commentators typically took this step. As Duval puts it (1973, 234), the life of Christ influences, retroactively, their conception of Jonah. Their Jonah becomes *like* Christ, never impatient, always dignified. He is no longer the petulant prophet of the Old Testament story, no longer himself. I have already mentioned some of the noble motives which, in the process of reinterpretation, are attributed to Jonah's disobedience. He is said to prefer the contemplative life, or to be worried about doing favours to pagan Ninevites. The short poem *Naufragium Jonae prophetae* by the sophisticated poet Marbod of Rennes, known in medieval England and used by the *Gawain*-poet (see p. 8), comes closest to representing Jonah in all his weaknesses when it raises the possibility that Jonah may have shirked for fear:

> *Forte* timens fatum, non ivit vaticinatum.
> Nam quia portaret quod plebis corda gravaret,
> Nuntius interitus, satis foret undique tritus,
> Vel gladio stratus, vel forsitan igne crematus.
> At non est fortis, quis sic timet ultima mortis,
> Ut bene posse mori vitae postponat amori.
> Nec Dominum credit, qui non sibi tutus obedit.
> *Ergo causa fugae non convenit ista prophetae.*
> Sed Dominum norat, quia nos revocare laborat,

Et cito condonat, si quis mala pristina ponat ...
... Hoc timuit missus, quem conservavit abyssus,
Ne mentiretur, nisi dictum res sequeretur.[28]

(*Perhaps*, he did not go to prophesy because he feared his fate. Because as the
messenger of news that would aggrieve the people, he might be killed, or
beaten, or put to the sword, or perhaps burned at the stake. But he is not
strong who fears the throes of death so much that he prefers the love of life
to the art of dying nobly. Nor does the person who does not obey God in
trust really believe in him. *This reason does not therefore become our prophet.* But
he knew God; that he tries to call us back to him, and quickly has mercy if
someone renounces his former evil ... This is what the missionary, who survived the abyss, feared: that he would have lied if what he had announced
would not happen.)

In describing Jonah's worries, Marbod of Rennes veers towards the conclusion that Jonah may not be a Christ-like figure after all, yet the
thought that Jonah flees to save his own skin finally proves too much
even for Marbod, and he rejects it in favour of an interpretation that
exculpates Jonah by claiming that our prophet knew God would not
make Jonah's prophecy come true and that Jonah wished to avoid lying.

Significantly, it is the possibility from which Marbod finally shies
away which the *Gawain*-poet embraced. The boldness of this move
becomes all the more apparent when we realize that the *Gawain*-poet
was fully aware that Marbod had dismissed it. The *Gawain*-poet, after all,
knew Marbod's *Naufragium* (Fày 1975). Among other things, it had
given him the idea of depicting Jonah running through the various mis-
haps that might await him in Nineveh:

'If I bowe to his bode and bryng hem þis tale,
And I be nummen in Nuniue, my nyes begynes.

He telles me þose traytoures arn typped schrewes;
I com wyth þose tyþynges, þay ta me bylyue,
Pyneȝ me in a prisoun, put me in stokkes,
Wryþe me in a warlok, wrast out myn yȝen.'
(75–80)

('If I obey his bidding and bring them this message, and am captured in
Nineveh, my troubles will really begin. He tells me that these traitors are wicked
shrews. If I come with those tidings, they are sure to capture me, and put me
in prison, confine me in the stocks, torture me in foot-shackles, and stick out
my eyes.')

28. *PL* 171, 1676.

The possibility of a frightened Jonah has in *Patience* become a fact. As for Marbod's rejection of this possibility for one that makes Jonah come out better, the *Gawain*-poet decided to exercise his better judgement and disregard it, so that his Jonah could remain the imperfect character of the Old Testament story.

Whereas the figural relationship between Jonah and Christ led many medieval authors to rewrite Jonah as a Christ-like figure, the *Gawain*-poet managed to preserve Jonah's antic nature, without, however, ignoring the typological overtones which the Book of Jonah was supposed to contain. How did he achieve this delicate balance between the figural and the historical level? Simply by making Jonah in the story blissfully unaware of any of the figural significances that attach to his actions or words. As medieval people knew, Christ's self-sacrifice and resurrection mirrored Jonah's adventures, showing us how, to paraphrase Luke 11: 32, 'a man greater than Jonah' would respond to similar challenges involving patience and obedience. In *Patience*, however, this fulfilment lies outside of Jonah's control or volition. The reader may spot the typological references to Christ's harrowing of hell as Jonah descends into the belly of the whale, but they elude the prophet (Schleusener 1971). It is his destiny to be a type of Christ *despite himself*.

It is now possible to see why in *Patience*, in contrast with other medieval adaptations of the Book of Jonah, history does not come to be experienced differently by those who, like Jonah, participate in it. The adventures mean one thing to him, and another for the audience who can transcend the limitations of Jonah's historical moment, can look into the future of Jonah's history and see Christ's fulfilment of it. History has, to use the conceptual tools which Hugh of St Victor and Thomas Aquinas helped to develop, a *double significance*: the meaning perceived by the actors caught up in its drama is different from the meaning it has in God's cosmic design (Preus 1969, 51–3; Smalley 1984, 300; Charity 1966, 179–207). God wields, so to speak, a metalanguage, not available to human beings, unless it be through God's revelation or the gradual unfolding of his purposes through time.

Typology, at least as the *Gawain*-poet uses it, is precisely this added significance, apparent from the superior perspective of the audience, but neither grasped nor intended by Jonah. The presence of a double significance is felt whenever the *Gawain*-poet alludes to Christ, but nowhere more poignantly so than when Jonah complains about God's cruelty in sending him to Nineveh:

'Oure syre syttes', he says, 'on sege so hy3e,
In his glowande glorye, and gloumbes ful lyttel
Þa3 I be nummen in Nunniue and naked dispoyled,
On rode rwly to-rent with rybaudes many.'

(93–6)

('Our lord', he says, 'sits on his high throne in resplendent glory, and wouldn't care if I were captured in Nineveh and stripped naked, cruelly torn to pieces on a cross by many wicked men.')

God, it seems to Jonah, has withdrawn himself from human affairs, has become distant and heartless. Little does Jonah know that his words look forward to Christ's crucifixion, which, to the medieval mind, represented God's direct involvement in the world in its most dramatic form. In Christ, God had become man, and with Christ, God had suffered for man's sake. Rather than the 'glowande glorye' in which Jonah imagines God has taken up permanent residence, the crucifixion showed the full extent of human misery and agony which Christ, and hence God, had been willing to take on his shoulders (Kirk 1978, 92–4). If Jonah knew what he was saying, his own mission might seem lighter to him than it does. Instead, the picture of a caring God emerges from his words in spite of themselves. He prophesies Christ's death 'on rode', yet the prophetic words escape Jonah, as they must escape those who, unlike God or the reader, are not in possession of the meaning that future events will disclose in them. Rather than clashing with the meaning of the story of Jonah the poet's use of typology underwrites its central theme: man's powerlessness, his lack of control, even over his words.

I speak of man in general because Jonah is far from being the only protagonist in the *Gawain*-poet's oeuvre to be brought up against the limits of self-determination. The hero of *Sir Gawain and the Green Knight* experiences disillusionments similar to Jonah's. Gawain's role in the Beheading Game also hinges on patience, the surrender of his own will and the compliance with the demand of another. For the most part Gawain manages his task in exemplary fashion, but the offer of the green girdle gives Gawain an opportunity to regain control over his life which proves too tempting. When the poet depicts him in high spirits after his retention of the girdle the correspondences between Jonah and Gawain come to light:

Vche mon hade daynté þare
Of hym, and sayde, 'Iwysse,
Þus myry he wat3 neuer are,

Syn he com hider, er þis.'
    (*Gawain*, 1889–92)

(Everyone enjoyed his company, and said, 'Truly, this is the merriest he has
been, since he came here.')

Gawain's relief compares with Jonah's brief illusion of mastery, when his
boat finally sails out from the harbour into the open sea, apparently
beyond the reach of the Law:

Watȝ neuer so joyful a jue as Jonas watȝ þenne,
Þat þe daunger of dryȝtyn so derfly ascaped ...
                (109–10)

(Never was there so joyful a Jew as Jonah, when he had so neatly escaped
God's danger.)

But the bitter truth is that, while Gawain and Jonah believe themselves
to have outsmarted the Green Knight and God, they are unwittingly
caught out by a masterplot in which their own futile moves have already
been anticipated and overseen. Indeed, they are never more helpless
than when they try to assert control, never more exposed than when
they have recourse to stealth. Jonah, asleep in the bottom of the ship, is
soon to be dragged on to deck where a casting of lots will expose his bad
conscience. Gawain will soon be making his confession to Bertilac who,
as his revelation at the Green Chapel makes clear, had been a silent witness to Gawain's trickery all along.

As Jonah has failed to hide from God, so Gawain has proved totally
transparent to Bertilac. The stories of *Gawain* and *Patience* are shot
through with the terrible dramatic irony of two protagonists who think
they have taken charge of their destinies, but discover that the plots they
have woven had been pre-scripted by God or Bertilac. This dramatic
irony is essentially the double significance I have discussed in relation to
typology. Gawain thinks his adventure is a Beheading Game, while
Bertilac knows its true significance lies in a test of fidelity played out in
the Exchange of Winnings. Jonah believes he is going to Tharsis when
God knows he has in fact set out on his circuitous course to Nineveh;
finally Jonah thinks his words to the Ninevites will bring about their
destruction, only to find that they actually issue in their repentance and
salvation. Jonah and Gawain are like puppets in the hands of God and
Bertilac. Not surprisingly, both are infuriated by the retrospective
discovery of their powerlessness, and the *Gawain*-poet was clearly conscious of the similarities between his two poems when in God's final

communication to Jonah he gave God the same chastening line that Bertilac speaks to Gawain: 'Be no3t so gryndel' (*Patience*, 524; *Gawain*, 2338). From a poet who accepted the limitations of human control as a fact of life, we need expect no further apologies or condolences.

GOD AND MAN

Of the two poems, it is *Patience* which pushes man's powerlessness furthest, to the point where he appears the helpless victim of God's tyranny. We are easily inclined to dismiss the idea that God behaves unpleasantly as Jonah's interpretative error, yet the poet has no hesitation in conceding the experiential reality of this fact. God's manners in *Patience* are indeed thoroughly off-putting, and many of the poet's changes to the Vulgate make them even more so. Thus God's voice, not described in the Bible, is transformed in *Patience* to a harsh and booming voice that stuns its hearers:

> Goddes glam to hym glod þat hym vnglad made,
> With a roghlych rurd rowned in his ere ...
>
> (63–4)

(God's word came to him, which made him unhappy. With a harsh clamour it resounded in his ear ...)

From the outset the differences between God and man are sharply drawn. God dictates, as if from a megaphone; Jonah must obey. As Jonah soon finds out, he has no say in the matter, for he is not a creator but a creature. The moment Jonah forgets this, he suffers for it. Pain serves to recall him to humility, condemning any attempt to exercise his will independently of God to futility. Forced to recognize God's omnipotence when he is stuck inside a whale, Jonah notes how pain reminded him who is really in charge:

> For when þ'acces of anguych wat3 hid in my sawle,
> Þenne I remembred me ry3t of my rych lorde ...
>
> (325–6)

(For when the fit of anguish was hidden in my soul, I remembered my rich lord well.)

God's power, which Jonah had forgotten, becomes perceptible as 'anguych'.

It is not just a will of his own that is denied to Jonah, but all that we associate with selfhood: the right to secrets, to a private sphere that others will respect. As the sociologist Georg Simmel wrote in his analysis of discretion, 'an ideal sphere lies around every human being. Although differing in size in various directions and differing according to the person with whom one entertains relations, this sphere cannot be penetrated, unless the personality value of the individual is thereby destroyed' (Simmel 1950, 321). It is hard to think of a greater difference in the size of this 'ideal sphere' than that which holds between God and man. For while God's purposes are inscrutable, his secrets unfathomable, Jonah has to live with the fact that his private domain can continually be encroached upon by an intrusive God.

The *Gawain*-poet emphasizes God's indiscretion even more strongly than the Book of Jonah. His Jonah is forever throwing up protective barriers around his ideal sphere, trying to project himself beyond the fragile confines of his own body. As critics have noted, what Jonah creates for himself in the ship, in the whale, or under the woodbine, is comfort and shelter, an enclosure that protects him from the hostility of the outside world (Eldredge 1981; Stanbury 1987). Thus, we see Jonah hiding beneath the deck, making himself as comfortable as possible in his unfriendly surroundings:

> He watȝ flowen for ferde of þe flode lotes
> In-to þe boþem of þe bot, and on a brede lyggede,
>
> On-helde by þe hurrok, for þe heuen wrache,
> Slypped vpon a sloumbe-selepe, and sloberande he routes.
> Þe freke hym frunt with his fot and bede hym ferk vp;
> Þer Ragnel in his rakentes hym rere of his dremes!
> (183–8)

(He had fled for fear of the flood into the bottom of the boat, and he was lying on a plank, huddled up around the rudder-bank to escape heaven's vengeance, sunk in a deep sleep, and slobbering as he snored. The man prodded him with his foot and told him to get up; the devil in his chains rouse him from his dreams!)

We may laugh at Jonah, not because he is particularly ridiculous, but because the narrative and the sailor catch him at a moment when we all risk looking ridiculous. Asleep, neither we nor the 'slobbering' Jonah can interpose a screen between self and other by playing the social roles we are expected to play. That is why we sleep in private, somewhere, like Jonah, we believe we are not being watched by strangers. The

unpleasant sensation of waking up in a train compartment to the amused
eyes of fellow travellers may suggest how real the concern for one's ideal
sphere is. It is exposure that is at stake, and this is what Jonah experiences when the prodding foot of a sailor wakes him up.

The episode of the woodbine again sees Jonah looking for protection
and finding a home away from home in the shade of a plant:

> And euer he laȝed as he loked þe loge alle aboute,
> And wysched hit were in his kyth þer he wony schulde,
> On heȝe vpon Effraym oþer Ermonnes hilleȝ.
> 'Iwysse, a worþloker won to welde I neuer keped.'
>
> (461–4)

(And whenever he looked around his lodging he smiled, and wished it might
have been in the country where he ought to dwell, on high Ephraim or the
hills of Hermon. 'Truly, I have never cared to have a better dwelling-place.')

It is *Patience*, not the Bible, which reminds the reader that Jonah has
been forced out of his real home, and which makes the woodbine matter more to him than to Jonah in the Vulgate. It gives the homeless
Jonah a sense of privacy from the world outside, a refuge where Jonah
believes he can be off his guard:

> And quen hit neȝed to naȝt nappe hym bihoued;
> He slydes on a sloumbe-slep sloghe vnder leues,
> Whil God wayned a worme þat wrote vpe þe rote,
> And wyddered watȝ þe wod-bynde bi þat þe wyȝe wakned.
>
> (465–8)

(And when night approached he had to sleep. Slowly, he slipped into a heavy
sleep beneath the leaves, while God sent a worm that dug up the root. And
by the time the man woke up the woodbine had withered.)

But while Jonah sleeps, trusting he will be left alone, God, in character,
avails himself of the opportunity to destroy Jonah's shelter and expose
him to the natural elements. Naturally, Jonah is aggrieved, and the
Gawain-poet was ready to turn Jonah's despair in the Vulgate into a
powerful protest against God's 'maystery':

> And þen hef vp þe hete and heterly brenned;
> Þe warm wynde of þe weste, wertes he swyþeȝ.
> Þe man marred on þe molde þat moȝt hym not hyde.
> His wod-bynde watȝ away, he weped for sorȝe.
>
> With hatel anger and hot heterly he calleȝ:
> 'A, þou maker of man, what maystery þe þynkeȝ

Þus þy freke to forfare forbi alle oþer?
With alle meschef þat þou may, neuer þou me spareʒ ... '

(477–84)

(Then the heat increased and burned hotly, the warm western wind scorches the plants. The man who could not hide grieved; his woodbine was gone and he wept for sorrow. With bitter anger and hot fury he calls out: 'O you maker of man, what kind of achievement do you think it is to ruin your servant, of all people? You do not spare me any possible mischief.')

It is easy for the reader to say that Jonah is overreacting, but the poet has actually yoked the anger Jonah ventilates to the scorching heat that God inflicts on him. As the heat 'heterly brenned', Jonah calls 'heterly' with 'hot' anger. One cannot deny an appropriateness in the manner of Jonah's response.

What wisdom or consolation could come to Jonah's assistance at this moment? The narrator might say that Jonah should take God's will on sufferance, and that impatience will only exacerbate his situation. The story of Jonah has by this stage, however, broached a question which acquiescence fails to address. Resignation may well be desirable, but what exactly do we resign ourselves to? To the 'meschef' of a dictatorial God? Can anyone be patient when suffering is what God inflicts on his creatures to manifest his 'maystery', to reveal and reinstate the asymmetrical power relations between them?

The *Gawain*-poet has stretched these inequalities about as far as they will go. Jonah 'moʒt hym not hide', but God remains hidden. While Jonah cannot help sleeping, God 'ay wakes' (130), and mercilessly takes advantage of his moments of weakness to spring nasty surprises on his prophet. Jonah feels pain while God is impassible. It would seem that the Book of Jonah, and the *Gawain*-poet's retelling of it, illustrate Elaine Scarry's observation that the Old Testament figures man as body and God as voice, a distribution of power that when challenged, or disbelieved in, makes itself felt as pain, which reduces man to body while reminding him of the irrefutable reality of God's omnipotence (Scarry 1985, 200). It is a grim vision of God's relation to man in the Old Testament, but one which the *Gawain*-poet's Jonah shares when he denounces God's intolerable mastery.

God's final words to Jonah, however, reveal a very different relation between God and his creatures. Significantly, they shift the focus from God's alterity to his sameness, to his susceptibility to the same feelings of pain and anger that have driven Jonah to despair (Kirk 1978). As God bares his heart to the prophet, it becomes clear that he has not destroyed

the woodbine to demonstrate his supremacy, but rather to make Jonah
understand that he, too, feels attachment to creation:

> Þenne by-þenk þe, mon, if þe for-þynk sore,
> If I wolde help my honde-werk, haf þou no wonder.

> Þou art waxen so wroth for þy wod-bynde,
> And trauayled neuer to tent hit þe tyme of an howre,
> Bot at a wap hit here wax and away at an oþer,
> And ȝet lykeȝ þe so luþer, þi lyf woldeȝ þou tyne.

> Þenne wyte not me for þe werk, þat I hit wolde help,
> And rwe on þo redles þat remen for synne;
> Fyrst I made hem my self of materes myn one,
> And syþen I loked hem ful longe and hem on lode hade.
>
> (495–504)

(Then consider man, if you are aggrieved, whether it is strange that I would
wish to help my creation. You have become so angry about your woodbine,
and you never laboured to look after it for a moment, but at one stroke it
grew here and disappeared as suddenly, and yet it seems so awful to you that
you would give up your life. Then do not blame me for wanting to help my
creatures, and for pitying these helpless men who cry for their sins. First I
made them myself from matter and then I looked after them for a long time,
and took them in my care.)

God addresses himself directly to Jonah's assumption that God has saved
Nineveh only to annoy his prophet, that his grief must be a manifestation of God's heartlessness. But so far from confirming that pain and
sorrow constitute a point of radical difference between man and God,
God confesses to feeling strongly about his creation as well. If Jonah feels
sorry for a woodbine that came and went 'at a wap', as God puts it col-
loquially, then how much more must God love the creatures to whom
he gave existence and whom he raised with care? What God's argument
dismantles is the conclusion, which had seemed increasingly inescapable
to Jonah, that man is body while God is voice.

God in *Patience* is embodied and impassioned, and far more strikingly
so than in the Vulgate, as the poet's addition to his source shows:

> And if I my trauayl schulde tyne of termes so longe,
> And typ doun ȝonder toun when hit turned were,
> Þe sor of such a swete place burde synk to my hert,
> So mony malicious mon as mourneȝ þer-inne.
>
> (505–8)

(And if my work of such long duration should come to nought, and if I destroyed this town after its repentance, the grief about such a sweet place would sink to my heart, so many are the malicious men that now lament their sins there.)

As Jonah had been overjoyed with his woodbine, God looks with delight on the 'swete place' of Nineveh which he has created. Paradoxically, it is this love for Nineveh which is communicated through Jonah's grief. However inadequately, Jonah's vexation compares to God's infinite care for his creation, and the infinite 'sor' that he would have felt if he had destroyed it. Of course, this insight does not alter or belittle the fact that Jonah suffers. On the contrary, it raises suffering to a condition which God, too, experiences. And what it thereby does alter is the perception that suffering dramatizes the inherent inequalities between man and God, that the suffering of the one must be a sign of the power of the other. God, in short, reveals to Jonah his humanity, which the *Gawain*-poet had allowed his audience to glimpse briefly by alluding to the crucifixion of Christ, the Word made Flesh, Voice made Body.

The *Gawain*-poet fully realized the implications of God's recognizably human side for the virtue of patience. For if God suffers, then the need for patience does not fall unilaterally upon mankind, but devolves on God as well. And as God's patience with the Ninevites shows, it is an obligation he takes seriously, far more seriously, as God points out, than Jonah:

> Wer I as hastif as þou, heere, were harme lumpen;
> Couþe I not þole bot as þou, þer þryued ful fewe.
>
> (520–1)

(If I were as rash as you, it would be disastrous. If I could suffer no better than you, few people would thrive.)

The history of Jonah, ostensibly about the inescapability of human 'suffraunce', has actually traced the fortunate consequences of God's long-suffering, to which the Ninevites owe their existence. It is a story about God's emotions, as much as Jonah's.

The revelation that suffering may be shared by others must come as a surprise to Jonah, who, thoroughly preoccupied with his own troubles, has forgotten that God, or the Ninevites, might have feelings too. In this respect, Jonah's loneliness, the sense that he is at large in a cold and hostile universe, is of his own making. Suffering isolates him, because he does not suspect it in others, certainly not in God. The full impact of

God's revelation of his participation in 'suffraunce' can only be felt if we appreciate that the audience has been led to respond to Jonah's experiences in almost the same way that Jonah has. The narrator might have prepared us to see in them an example of how human beings should and should not respond to suffering, but who, without the benefit of hindsight, could have thought the story was actually about the way God suffers? It seems that we are not that different from Jonah in having imagined ourselves, and not God, at the centre of the story's attention.

No less than Jonah, we are forced by God's manifestation of his own 'suffraunce' to revise our interpretation of the narrative that has gone before. This revision leads us back even into the prologue, where the narrator's assertion that patience can assuage anger takes on a startlingly different complexion:

> When heuy herttes ben hurt wyth heþyng oþer elles,
> Suffraunce may aswagen hem and þe swelme leþe,
> For ho quelles vche a qued and quenches malyce.
>
> (2–4)

(When heavy hearts hurt with scorn or anything else, sufferance may comfort them and calm the fury, for she subdues all evil and quenches malice.)

I suspect I am not alone in having first read these lines as advocating patience as a medicine for the anger and 'malyce' which people might feel towards others or towards God. We take the 'hem' in these lines to mean 'us', quite simply because when we think of 'hurt' we, like Jonah, first think of ourselves. God's revelation to Jonah that he has curbed his malice against the Ninevites exposes the self-centredness of this interpretation. As it turns out, the 'hem' includes God, who, infuriated by the Ninevites' wickedness, contemplated vengeance against them. Here are his first words to Jonah, including the *Gawain*-poet's remarkable addition to his source implying that God has lost his patience:

> For iwysse hit arn so wykke þat in þat won dowelleʒ,
> And her malys is so much, *I may not abide*,
> Bot venge me on her vilanye and venym bilyue.
>
> (69–71)

(Truly, so many wicked men live in this town, and their malice is so great, that I cannot suffer it, but will avenge me on their villainy and venom at once.)

Patience does not come effortlessly, even to God. The humanization of God may clash with the doctrine that God is always patient without being impassioned, but patience for the poet involved a necessary struggle in oneself against feelings of impatience, from which no one is exempt.[29] How far the poet was willing to go in his insistence on the realities of these feelings may be gauged from the fact that even his God shows signs of strain.

But the struggle against impatience is one that God wages successfully. As his change of heart towards Nineveh shows, patience indeed 'quelles vche a qued and quenches malyce'. The surprise of *Patience* is that it is God who demonstrates the truth of this line. As the poem unfolds, we learn that patience is not only a bitter pill prescribed to human beings, but to God as well. There is no better measure of how the poet has enlarged our understanding of suffering and God's role in it than the radical revision of the prologue's meaning that the dénouement of Jonah's history forces us to undertake.

FROM REVELATION TO TRUST

With the disclosure of a humane and compassionate God working behind the scenes, the prologue and the story of Jonah release a far more optimistic moral than the narrator's wisdom that suffering allows us no other option but to 'suffer' it patiently. God's revelation is the last and only time that the *Gawain*-poet takes us beyond the realities of the physical world and allows his audience a glimpse into God's merciful nature:

'I may not be so malicious and mylde be halden,
For malyse is noȝ to mayntyne boute mercy with-inne.'
(522–3)

('I may not be so malicious and be considered mild, for malice is not to be practised without mercy within.')

Yet even in this sublime moment, where human suffering testifies to God's mildness, the *Gawain*-poet's God has no illusions about the fact that this mildness may be experienced on earth as 'malyce'. Suffering is the paradox of 'malyse' that has 'mercy with-inne', of a God both 'malicious' and 'mylde'. The paradox neatly expresses the concomitance of God's kind purposes and the unpleasant ways in which they may appear to human beings (Shoaf 1981).

29. On the doctrine of God's impassibility see, for example, Augustine, *De patientia*, 530, or the polemics of Bradwardine, the *Gawain*-poet's contemporary, discussed in Oberman (1957, 55).

I emphasize the validity of both meanings in *Patience*, for the *Gawain*-poet did not think he could resolve the paradox of 'malyce' and 'mercy' by making the experiential reality of suffering vanish behind the knowledge of God's benevolence. Like history, suffering has for the *Gawain*-poet what I have called a double significance, one in the phenomenal world to which Jonah, like most people, is bound, another from the perspective of those who can see beyond it into the secrets of God's divine plan. This separates our poet from many of his contemporaries, such as the mystic Walter Hilton, for whom the perception of God's love could take away the pain of suffering, and make patience effortless, even enjoyable:

> For one whose behaviour is governed solely by his own reason, it is very hard to be patient, peaceable, gentle, and charitable towards his neighbours when they vex him unreasonably or do him wrong, for he is inclined to retaliate with anger or resentment, either in word, or act, or both. Nevertheless, if although he is upset and troubled, he does not overstep the bounds of reason and restrains his hands and tongue, and is ready to forgive an offence when pardon is asked, he possesses the virtue of patience. It is as yet weak and unstable, but in so far as he desires to have it, and makes a real effort to control his irrational passions in order to acquire it, and is sorry that he does not possess it as fully as he should, his patience is genuine. But to one who truly loves God it requires no great effort to endure all this, because Divine Love fights for him and imperceptibly destroys these feelings of anger and resentment. His spiritual union with God and the experience of His blessed love renders his soul so quiet and peaceful, so patient and devoted, that he is unaffected by the contempt and criticism, disgrace or villainy inflicted upon him by men.
>
> (*Ladder of Perfection*, 216–17)[30]

The *Gawain*-poet's patience is, in Hilton's words, of the 'weak and imperfect kind'. A spiritual union with God, which according to Hilton makes perfect patience possible by allowing the sufferer to look through his afflictions into the ultimate reality of divine love, is too ambitious an aim for the poet. It is not that he would have doubted the existence of divine love, but he realized that for those who have not reached the heights of mystical transcendence the assurance of divine love is of a different order than the 'malyce' we experience. God's love may be manifest to visionaries and mystics, but for the poet it was not a matter of fact, like the feeling of pain, but a matter of faith.

---

30. Trans. Leo-Shirley Price (Harmondsworth: Penguin, 1988).

For this reason, the *Gawain*-poet's God concludes by recommending patience not with reference to a transcendental dimension in which suffering is transformed into mildness, but on the level of common experience where patience is quite simply the choice of the lesser evil:

> '... Be noȝt so gryndel, god-man, bot go forth þy wayes,
> Be preue and be pacient in payne and in joye;
> For he þat is to rakel to renden his cloþeȝ
> Mot efte sitte with more vnsounde to sewe hem to-geder.'
>
> (524–7)

('Don't be so angry, good man, but go your way. Be calm and patient in pain and in joy, for he who is too rash in tearing his clothes must put up with more annoyance when he has to sew them together again.')

It has seemed to many readers inconceivable that these down-to-earth lines should be spoken by God, and many editions punctuate this penultimate stanza as if it were part of the narrator's epilogue (Anderson 1969; Cawley and Anderson 1976; Andrew and Waldron 1978). Yet not only has God been extremely colloquial in his previous words to Jonah, but the lines clearly address someone who should not be 'so gryndel', which must refer to Jonah. The narrator of *Patience* is not one to address his audience directly; to expect him to do so in the singular of 'god-man', and as one who needs calming down, simply because we do not think God should utter a homely proverb, is to revert to the allegorical exegesis of many medieval commentators.

If it seems inappropriate that God should make his appeal to patience on the grounds of common experience, we should ask ourselves why. The answer, and the interest of the editorial misreading, is that these grounds seem to us, after God's revelation of his love for creation, incomplete. God had taught Jonah not simply that impatience makes things worse, but that he suffered at the hands of someone who wished him well. Yet when God sends Jonah on his way towards joys and pains to come, his advice makes no further mention of his good intentions. As God signs off and the poem looks towards the future, the certainty of God's benign purposes, apparent in God's revelations to his prophet, remains unspoken. This is so, however, not because of an oversight, but because the poet was aware that, after God has taken leave of his audience, the fact that suffering is for the best *will no longer be a certainty*, will disappear with God from the realm of experience into the realm of belief.

In God's final words, the assurance of his benevolence has already become the silence it must henceforth be for Jonah, and for the narrator, who in turn takes his leave in a similar tone of muted optimism:

> For-þy when pouerte me enpreceȝ and pyneȝ in-noȝe,
> Ful softly with suffraunce saȝttel me bihoueȝ;
> For-þy penaunce and payne to-preue hit in syȝt
> Þat pacience is a nobel poynt, þaȝ hit displese ofte.
>
> (528–31)

(And so when poverty and many pains oppress me, I should acquiesce patiently, for penance and pain manifestly prove that patience is a noble point, though it often displeases.)

It is, as I noted earlier, a conclusion that gives full weight to experience, both in its recognition that patience 'displese[s] ofte', and in choosing to argue the case for patience from the worldly wisdom that impatience entails even more 'penaunce and payne'. Yet in doing so, without reference to God's humanity, it likewise leaves the reader with the feeling that something has been left unspoken, that the narrator's resolution to suffer 'ful softly' intimates a belief in its larger purpose which the poem stops short of articulating.

Here, as in the previous stanza, it is the *Gawain*-poet's achievement to have made this silence palpable. The success with which he did so appears from the dissatisfaction of numerous editors who felt that there was something missing from God's homely words to Jonah. What is missing is, as I have suggested, the transcendental dimension to the question of suffering, to which the poet did not pretend to have any other access than through trust. The assurance of God's kindness existed for him not as a verifiable fact, but as a matter of faith. He communicated this to his audience in his tone of muted optimism, allowing his audience to hear his silence and sense the presence of an absence: to believe.

Chapter 4

Pearl

INTRODUCTION: *PEARL* AND ITS PROBLEMS

Pearl is the most ambitious of the *Gawain*-poet's works. His themes in the poem are human loss and the mysterious workings of heaven, in themselves hardly original themes, but all the more taxing in that many writers had gone before him. Moreover, neither human loss nor heaven lend themselves easily to verbalization: heaven, since it was believed to be fundamentally different from anything imaginable, beyond comprehension and articulation; bereavement, because it may be felt so strongly and personally that people cannot, or do not wish to, state it in a language that turns it into hard fact. Faced with loss, language seems often reduced to euphemisms or evasions, just as the ineffable otherness of heaven has mostly found expression in awesome silences, in analogies (heaven is *like* this), or negatives (heaven is *not* like this) (Schotter 1984; Watts 1984).

It is not surprising, then, that linguistic tensions are very much in evidence in *Pearl*. Indeed, the bulk of the poem, the debate between the Dreamer and the Pearl-maiden, consists of communicative short-circuits and misunderstandings. The prologue of *Pearl* is similarly opaque. While critics today tend to agree that the loss which the Dreamer laments in the opening section concerns his daughter,[1] the fact remains that he is obscure about what has actually happened. His lament is hedged about with figures of speech, as if he were unwilling to confront what has taken place, or taking refuge in formality.

The complex literary form which the *Gawain*-poet chose for his dream vision continually generates more verbal equivocations. The 101

---

1. See Eldredge (1975) for an overview of *Pearl*-criticism.

stanzas of the poem divide into twenty sections. The final line of each stanza in a section contains a similar refrain, while all stanzas are interlinked through the repetition of a key word from the last line of the previous stanza in the first line of the next stanza.

By repeating key words in different contexts, the poet sets their full semantic potential to work. His play on the double meaning of the word 'spot' is emblematic. In Middle English, as in Modern English, the word could mean 'blemish' or 'sin', as well as 'place' (Macrae-Gibson 1970). When it is first used, in the refrain of the first stanza, it seems to have the first meaning. The Pearl is unblemished ('wythouten spot') (12). However, in the first line of the next stanza, which repeats the key word 'spot', it is used in the second meaning of 'place':

> Syþen in þat spot hit fro me sprange,
> Ofte haf I wayted ...
>
> (13–14)

(Since the time it slipped away from me on this spot, I have often looked for it.)

With both meanings in play, subsequent references to the Pearl 'wythouten spot' become less clear. If 'spot' has been used in the two different senses of 'place' and 'sin', which should we choose when the narrator describes the garden in which he lost his Pearl?

> Þer wonys þat worþyly, I wot and wene,
> My precious perle wythouten spot.
>
> (47–8)

(There this noble lady lies, I am certain, my precious pearl without a spot.)

Like the narrator, we may take 'wythouten spot' in the sense of 'unblemished', and surrender to his belief that his lost Pearl is still locatable, that she still dwells ('wonys') on the spot where he lost her. But what if the Pearl no longer 'wonys' anywhere? What if his formulation that she 'dwells' among flowers and spices fends off the painful truth that his loss of the Pearl is irrevocable? This possibility opens the phrase 'wythouten spot' to an alternative interpretation: the Pearl may not only be without blemish, but also without a dwelling place.

And as the vision in which the Dreamer sees his Pearl in the glory of heaven demonstrates, she is indeed 'wythouten spot' in these two senses: unsoiled, and also in a state beyond time and place. She is in heaven, and, as medieval theologians argued, heaven was not a geographical place but a different realm of existence. The twelfth-century monk

Honorius Augustodunensis, who synthesized the essential articles of faith for the benefit of laymen in his *Elucidarium*, put it as follows:

> Discipulus: Est hic paradisus locus corporeus, vel ubi?—
> Magister: Non est locus corporalis, quia spiritus non habitant in locis corporalibus, sed est spiritualis mansio beatorum ... [2]

> (Pupil: Is this paradise a corporeal place, and if so, where is it?
> Teacher: It is not a corporeal place, because spiritual beings do not inhabit corporeal places, but the dwelling place of the blessed is spiritual.)

Pearl itself makes this point when, at the end of the dream vision, it shows the Dreamer trying to cross the river in an attempt to reach heaven. Of course, the attempt is doomed from the start, for what separates the Dreamer from heaven is not so much space as a different mode of being (Borroff 1982; Ginsberg 1988). The river is a gap which no amount of movement can reduce. It represents an ontological rather than a spatial divide.

The *Gawain*-poet's play on the word 'spot' establishes similar connections between physical space and spiritual conditions. The modern belief in the arbitrariness of the signifier, the belief that 'there is nothing in a name', has robbed punning of the intellectual prestige it enjoyed in the Middle Ages. But the serious interest in puns and word-play shown by medieval writers such as the *Gawain*-poet (or Dante and Langland) may be appreciated more if we acknowledge that 'word-play can be more than phonetic tinkering and become a fertile ground for intellectual activity when the criss-cross of sound represents a genuine complexity of real relations' (Ong 1947, 317). The pun on the double meaning of 'wythouten spot' is of this kind. It suggests a meaningful relation between being without sin and being without place that penetrates to a profound truth in the poet's theology: heaven, the transcendence of space, cannot be reached by travelling from one 'spot' to another, but only by being 'spotless'.

A word whose double meaning is similarly used by the *Gawain*-poet is 'mote'. Like 'spot', the word could refer both to a location, a 'city', and to a spiritual state, a 'sin'. Evidently, the *Gawain*-poet was conscious of the similarities between the two words 'mote' and 'spot'. In his translation of the Song of Songs 4: 7—'there is not a spot in thee' (*macula non est in te*)—he departs from the Vulgate by using both 'spot' and 'mote':

---

2. *PL* 172, 1157.

'Cum hyder to me, my lemman swete,
For *mote* ne *spot* is non in þe.'
(763–4)

('Come to me, my sweet lover, for there is no spot or blemish in you.')

The significance of the coupling of these two words emerges in section sixteen, where the poet performs the same pun on the word 'mote' as he had earlier done on 'spot'. Compare the meaning of 'mote' in lines 923–4 with that in lines 935–6:

'As ȝe ar maskeleȝ vnder mone,
Your woneȝ schulde be wythouten mote.'
(923–4)

('As you are unblemished under the moon, your dwellings should be without a spot.')

'If þou hatȝ oþer bygyngeȝ stoute,
Now tech me to þat myry mote.'
(935–6)

('If you have other stately houses, lead me to that joyful castle.')

The context still allows us to distinguish between the two different meanings of 'mote' in these passages: 'mote' as a state of being, and 'mote' as a location. The distinction is blurred, however, when the poet goes on to use the word twice in its different senses, in a single line:

'And as hys flok is wythouten flake,
So is hys mote wythouten moote.'
(947–8)

('And as his flock is without a stain, so his castle is without a spot.')

Like 'flok wythouten flake', the phrase 'mote wythouten moote' is deliberately bewildering. It is not that we have failed as readers if we find the two senses of 'mote' ('city' and 'sin') difficult to disentangle, for the confusion enables us to envisage the possibility that, in heaven, these senses *are inseparable*. Does not the Pearl-maiden, too, link the two when she warns the Dreamer that the heavenly city ('mote') is only for immaculate people 'wythouten mote' (972)? It would seem that in heaven, conventional distinctions between positions and dispositions collapse.

The *Gawain*-poet's originality lies not in the idea but in the way it is expressed. Any comprehensive medieval discussion of heaven could have informed us that the various 'mansions' which the heavenly company inhabit are not actual localities, but represent different degrees of happiness. But the poet does not take us from spaces to modes of being in a reasoned argument, but by fusing the two meanings of 'spot' or 'mote', by mirroring in his puns the heavenly transmutation of physical position into spiritual disposition.

As the examples suggest, the poet of *Pearl* did not indulge in verbal obscurities for their own sake. *Pearl* is a text that plunges us into the otherness of heaven and death, where language must convulse and stretch to reach what lies beyond it. This chapter is about how this truly extra-ordinary poem stages this confrontation with the 'beyond'. It will not always be following the poem sequentially. The *Gawain*-poet is not primarily developing a plot in *Pearl*. The story-line is very thin in comparison with, for example, *Sir Gawain and the Green Knight*. What is developed and deepened in the poem is rather the Dreamer's impression of a world entirely different from his own, a world from which he is excluded by seeing things he does not recognize; by being given things to understand that he cannot comprehend; and last but not least by being emotionally isolated: by having feelings which no one in heaven seems to share. The three main sections below focus on these three kinds of human alienation, the alienation of sense-perception, of reason, and of emotion.

MAKING HEAVEN STRANGE: THE DESCRIPTION OF HEAVEN

I

The first part of the plot of *Pearl* can be summarized quickly. After the Dreamer has fallen asleep in the garden where he lost his Pearl, his 'goste' enters a strange landscape of forests, cliffs, and meadows, which surround the heavenly city. As the Dreamer starts walking through this landscape, its beauties seem forever to increase. Feverishly, the Dreamer marches on, until a river blocks his way. In the early sections of *Pearl*, the plot is, however, subordinated to description. At least initially, it is through what the Dreamer sees that the drama of his encounter with heaven is communicated.

The originality of the poet's descriptive techniques can best be understood in the context of other medieval visualizations of heaven. Medieval answers to the question of what heaven looked like were no less assured for being unverifiable. Writers of the period seem on the whole to have had remarkably developed and remarkably similar ideas about heaven, which had been shaped in accordance with an inherited written tradition of heavenly visions. The truth of these visions could of course only be taken on trust, but as Chaucer's Prologue to the *Legend of Good Women* explains, the 'olde bokes' proved authoritative, not in spite, but by virtue of, being unfalsifiable. For, as Chaucer put it, what can not be 'assayed', must be believed:

> A thousand tymes have I herd men telle
> That ther ys joy in hevene and peyne in helle,
> And I acorde wel that it ys so;
> But, natheles, yet wot I wel also
> That there is noon dwellyng in this contree
> That eyther hath in hevene or helle ybe,
> Ne may of hit noon other weyes witen
> But as he hath herd seyd or founde it writen;
> For by assay ther may no man hit preve.
>
> (F 1–9)

acorde: agree; *noon*: no one; *assay*: experience

The reliance on a bookish tradition also explains the remarkable homogeneity of medieval descriptions or paintings of heaven.[3] In almost all of them, heaven is imagined as a city set in a pleasant garden, where flowers grow, where trees are always laden with fruit, where light, smell, and the song of birds please the senses:

> Illic flos purpureus rosarum numquam marcessit; illic florida nemora perpetua viriditate vernant; illic prata recentia semper melleis fluunt rivis: illic croceis gramina floribus redolent, et halantes campi jucundis admodum odoribus pollent.
>
> (Pseudo-Ambrose, *Acta S. Sebastiani martyris*)[4]

> (Here the purple-coloured blossom of roses never withers; here the trees and their flowers bloom in perpetual verdure: here mellifluous streams run through fresh meadows, here the lawns are redolent with golden flowers, and sweet-smelling fields are full of pleasurable odours.)

---

3. Medieval descriptions and visions of heaven are numerous. For general discussions of portrayals of heaven in literature and art see Hughes (1968), McDannell and Lang (1988), and Davidson (1994). A useful bibliography of medieval visions of heaven is Gardiner (1993).

4. *PL* 17, 1027. The description of heaven in the *Acta* became a literary model for the medieval period.

By the time the *Gawain*-poet wrote *Pearl*, these had become the commonplaces of literary descriptions of heaven, and the *Gawain*-poet
would have known them through, for example, Guillaume de Lorris and
Jean de Meun's *Roman de la Rose*, the immensely influential dream vision
of the thirteenth century. The *Roman* is one of the few non-biblical
works which the *Gawain*-poet explicitly mentions in his oeuvre. In
Cleanness he refers to it as the 'clene Rose' by 'Clopyngnel', the name
under which Jean de Meun introduces himself in the *Roman de la Rose*
(10569–70). The *Roman de la Rose*, which relates the quest of the
narrator for his rose, is by no means a heavenly vision, but the description of the Garden of Pleasure is modelled on the conventional
descriptions of paradise. Here, too, are the flowers that never wither, the
delightful song of birds, and trees bearing fruit throughout the year. Not
surprisingly, the narrator is convinced that he has set foot in heaven:

> Et sachez que je cuidai estre
> Pour voir en paradis terestre;
> Tant estoit li leu delitables
> Qui sembloit estre esperitables ...
> (*Roman de la Rose*, 635–8)[5]

> (Believe me, I thought that I was truly walking in the earthly paradise; so
> delightful was the place that it seemed to me to be spiritual.)

The features of the garden are so typical of descriptions of paradise that
the narrator confidently concludes he must be in heaven. After a long
tradition of texts that represented heaven as the garden of our dreams, it
had become instantly recognizable, and entirely predictable.

The *Gawain*-poet might have represented the landscape in which the
Dreamer finds himself in a similar vein. The *Roman de la Rose* was a text
he knew, and drew on in *Pearl* (Pilch 1970). Twice *Pearl* echoes the
Roman. Like the narrator of the *Roman*, the Dreamer in *Pearl* senses he
has entered heaven:

> ... vrþely herte myȝt not suffyse
> To þe tenþe dole of þo gladneȝ glade;
> Forþy I þoȝt þat Paradyse
> Watȝ þer ouer gayn þo bonkeȝ brade.
> (135–8)

---

5. Guillaume de Lorris and Jean de Meun, *Roman de la Rose*, ed. and trans. Armand
   Strubel (Paris: Librairie Générale Française, 1992).

(An earthly heart could not sustain a tenth part of those joyous joys.
Therefore I thought Paradise lay beyond the wide shores.)

Then follows the Dreamer's description of the stream that prevents him
from going further, which probably draws on the artificial conduit in the
Garden of Pleasure in the *Roman de la Rose*:

> Par petiz roissiaus et conduiz
> Qu'ot fet faire danz deduiz,
> S'en aloit l'eve aval, fesant
> Une douce noise et plesant.
> (*Roman de la Rose*, 1387–90)

(The water ran along little brooks and conduits which Pleasure had planned
there, and it made a sweet and pleasant sound.)

> I hoped þe water were a devyse
> Bytwene myrþeȝ by mereȝ made …
> (*Pearl*, 139–40)

(I thought the water was a conduit joining pleasure-gardens made by the side
of pools.)

But even while *Pearl* draws directly on the *Roman de la Rose*, the
Gawain-poet creates a landscape that is fundamentally different from
the paradisiacal garden of the *Roman*. There may be 'gladneȝ glade' in
the celestial setting of *Pearl*, but the joy has a depth which his 'vrþely
herte' cannot plumb. Moreover, unlike the Dreamer in the *Roman*, who
participates in the merry-making when he is invited to join in a courtly
dance, the Dreamer of *Pearl* remains an outsider.

The stream which separates him from the beauties beyond the water
bring his exclusion home to us. The menacing river is a far cry from the
decorative conduit of the *Roman de la Rose*, and potent with symbolic
meaning:

> Bot þe water watȝ depe, I dorst not wade,
> And euer me longed ay more and more.
>
> More and more, and ȝet wel mare,
> Me lyste to se þe broke byȝonde;
> For if hit watȝ fayr þer I con fare,
> Wel loueloker watȝ þe fyrre londe.
> Abowte me con I stote and stare;
> To fynde a forþe faste con I fonde.
> Bot woþeȝ mo iwysse þer ware,
> Þe fyrre I stalked by þe stronde.   (143–52)

(But the water was deep, and I dared not cross. And ever I longed more and more. More and more, and still more I wished to see what lay beyond the stream. For if the land where I was wandering was fair, the land in the distance was fairer still. I stopped and stared around me, and tried hard to find a ford. But the further I walked along the bank, the more dangers there were.)

Manifesting itself as a separation in space, the Dreamer's exclusion from the bliss beyond the river awakens in him an insatiable desire to advance, from the 'fayr' meadows where he is now, to the 'loueloker' lands that still lie before him. To the Dreamer, the grass is always greener on the other side of the fence, and no matter how fast he walks, still greater beauties forever loom up before his eyes:

> I welke ay forth in wely wyse;
> No bonk so byg þat did me dere3.
> Þe fyrre in þe fryth, þe feier con ryse
> Þe playn, þe plontte3, þe spyse, þe pere3 ...
> (101–4)

(I kept on walking on, blissfully. No banks, however high, could stop me. The further I went into the woods, the more beautiful were the meadows, the shrubs, the spice-plants, and pear trees ...)

There is something tantalizing about this journey, in which the Dreamer is always allowed to glimpse his destination—the still more beautiful land on the horizon—without ever getting closer to it. His desire to reach the point where his own surroundings are no longer inferior to the scenery ahead urges him on, but with each step he takes the object of desire recedes further into the background. The river that eventually prevents him from reaching his goal has, in some sense, always been present. It is a 'device', not simply in the sense it has in the *Roman de la Rose* of a 'conduit', but in its possible other sense in Middle English of a 'boundary', a 'dividing line' which cannot be crossed, and which marks the difference between himself and the blessed in heaven.[6] Beyond the stream, desire has reached fulfilment, while for the Dreamer, and for all human beings, the quest for satisfaction never ends:

> As fortune fares þer as ho frayne3
> Wheþer solace ho sende oþer elle3 sore,
> Þe wy3 to wham her wylle ho wayne3
> Hytte3 to haue ay more and more.
> (129–32)

---

6. On the different meanings of the Middle English *deuyse* see Gordon's editorial note on lines 139–40.

(While fortune acts as she wills, whether she allots comfort or care, the man to whom she turns her favour always seeks to have more and more.)

The landscape in *Pearl* allegorizes this predicament of human desire, of always wanting 'more and more'. The symbolic meaning of the river deepens further when we consider it is a 'deuyse / Bywtene myrþeӡ'. Following a suggestion by Gordon (1974, 52), Cawley and Anderson (1976) translate the phrase as 'a device (i.e. an artificial conduit) joining pleasure gardens'. But the phrase might equally well mean 'a division between two kinds of mirth': on the one hand the perfect mirth in heaven where, as Peter Abelard wrote, 'desire never aspires beyond its object, and is never under-rewarded',[7] and on the other hand the imperfect happiness in a world ruled by fortune. Editors face an impossible task here in deciding which of the two meanings, the literal meaning or the figurative one, is intended. For the point of the pun is to activate both meanings at the same time, in defiance of the logic that tells us that a 'deuyse' cannot at once be a river and an ontological divide. The pun contains the same impossibility that characterizes heaven, the realm where the corporeal places are figures for spiritual conditions. If we cannot logically understand this, the play on the double meaning of the 'deuyse bytwene myrþez' nevertheless allows us to imagine how the physical and the metaphysical might merge.

The changes which the *Gawain*-poet made to the garden from the *Roman de la Rose* tell us something about his treatment of the topoi of the heavenly description as a whole. If we had first recognized in the 'deuyse' the familiar conduit from the *Rose*, closer inspection reveals dimensions which might well make us 'stote and stare' like the Dreamer. Other standard paradisiacal motifs also take on unfamiliar faces in *Pearl*. The trees are indigo-blue (76), their leaves are like polished silver (77), the gravel consists of precious pearls (82), the slopes are like 'fyldor fyn' (106). Unlike the cosy garden of the *Roman de la Rose*, the *Gawain*-poet gives us lawns and forests that are surprisingly *unnatural*.

II

Let us consider two examples of the poet's technique of defamiliarization in more detail. In both cases, the poet's artistic choices may be illuminated by comparing them with two close analogues in a thirteenth-century Italian poem: the *De Jerusalem Celesti* by Giacomino da Verona,

---

7. '... Ubi non praevenit rem desiderium / Nec desiderio minus est praemium'. Quoted from Abelard, 'O quanta, qualia sunt illa sabbata' (7–8), PL 178, 1786.

a description of the heavenly Jerusalem whose direct influence on Dante, and, through Dante, on later-medieval poetry generally, was considerable. Like the *Gawain*-poet, Giacomino describes a river full of jewels that runs through the meadows:

> Clare è le soe unde, plui de lo sol lucento,
> Menando margarite d'oro fin e d'arçento
> E pree preciose sempro mai tuto 'l tempo
> Somiente a stelle k'è poste êl fermamento.
> (93–7)

(Its waters are clear, shining brighter than the sun. Pearls of gold and silver and precious stones are carried along in it, forever dazzling and manifold, like stars set in the firmament.)

This may be compared with the river in *Pearl*:

> In þe founce þer stonden stoneȝ stepe,
> As glent þurȝ glas þat glowed and glyȝt,
> As stremande sterneȝ, quen stroþe-men slepe,
> Staren in welkyn in wynter nyȝt ...
> (113–16)

(At the bottom stood bright stones, glowing and glistening like a beam of light through glass, like twinkling stars, which shine in the heavens on a winter night when human beings sleep.)

The river filled with precious stones is a commonplace in descriptions of heaven, but the same is not true for the comparison that both poets make between the jewels on the shore and the stars shining in the firmament. This is a powerful and surprising image, evoking that sense of awe that we have when we gaze at a part of the universe to which we have no access. But the simile does more: what we are asked to imagine looking *down* into the river of heaven is what, in this world, we see when we look *up* into the sky. The image creates an instant of vertigo, a feeling of being in a world where things are upside down. In this regard, it bears comparison with the striking image of the moon rising in broad daylight, which the *Gawain*-poet uses later in his poem to introduce the procession of the Lamb:

> Ryȝt as þe maynful mone con rys
> Er þenne þe day-glem dryue al doun,
> So sodanly on a wonder wyse
> I watȝ war of a prosessyoun.
> (1093–6)

(Just as the powerful moon rises before the light of the day sinks, so I suddenly and miraculously became aware of a procession.)

The effect of this simile is equally disorientating. Light belongs to the day and the moon belongs to the night; when such basic distinctions collapse, the laws of the universe can appear momentarily out of sync. The image of the rising moon is appropriate in the context of heaven for this very reason: it evokes wonder by eliciting an equivalent feeling of being in a universe whose laws have changed.[8] By so doing it briefly transports us to a world where day is night, just as the comparison of stones with stars transports us to a strange place where 'up' is 'down'.

If the *Gawain*-poet was in any way indebted for the star-simile to Giacomino's *De Jerusalem Celesti*, he added a touch of mystery of his own. Giacomino's heavenly stones shine like stars; the poet's stones shine like stars at night '*quen stroþe-men slepe*' ('when human beings sleep'). The function of the qualification is not primarily to help the reader visualize the glimmering stones. It serves rather to evoke a sense of a world that is perpetually hidden from our consciousness. For what do stars look like when we are asleep? The question is not in fact answerable. Without being awake, 'stroþe-men' cannot see the stars, just as they cannot see whether the light in the fridge is still on after they have shut the door. We have, then, an image for the heavenly jewels which, rather than facilitating the visualizing process, curiously obstructs it. The comparison is with something that *cannot* be seen—a fitting comparison since human beings cannot see heaven or its jewels either. Both go beyond experience: this is the strength of the simile, and the reason why we are none the wiser for it.

The choir of birds in the *Gawain*-poet's heaven similarly keeps us wondering. No medieval description of heaven was complete without birds. Thus we find them in Giacomino's *De Jerusalem Celesti*, singing their songs on boughs of gold and silver:

> Calandrie e risignoli et altri begi oxegi
> Corno e nioto canta sovra quigi arboseli
> Façando li soi versi plus preciosi e begi
> Ke no fa viole, rote nè celamelli.
>
> (113–16)

---

8. This appropriateness explains why the same simile of the rising moon can be found in two other famous otherworldly visions, Dante's meeting with Brunetto Latini (*Inferno*, xv, 13–9), and Aeneas's vision of Dido in the underworld (*Aeneid* VI, 451–4). The *Gawain*-poet may well have taken it from either of these poems (Chapman 1945).

(Larks, nightingales, and other beautiful birds sing day and night on these trees, making their verses more precious and beautiful than a viol, a fiddle, or a flute might.)

This is both similar and dissimilar to the birds in *Pearl*:

Fowleȝ þer flowen in fryth in fere,
Of flaumbande hweȝ, boþe smale and grete;
Bot sytole-stryng and gyternere
Her reken myrþe moȝt not retrete;
For quen þose bryddeȝ her wyngeȝ bete,
Þay songen wyth a swete asent.
(89–94)

(Birds flew together in the forest, with flaming colours, small and great; but neither citole-string or lute could imitate their joyful song. For as they flew, they sang in sweet harmony.)

Like the *Gawain*-poet, Giacomino assures us that the bird-song surpasses musical instruments. But we are nevertheless entirely at home in his quatrain: larks and nightingales we have seen before. In contrast, the *Gawain*-poet defamiliarizes the motif of the heavenly birds, by giving them 'flaumbande hweȝ'. What birds are these? When all recognition fails, we realize like the Dreamer that we are strangers to this place. The poet's technique in sections two and three is intended to produce this realization in us. Unlike the stylized heaven of most medieval descriptions, his landscape continues to surprise: rivers disclose unsuspected symbolic meanings; similes take us beyond our realm of experience; birds or trees have changed beyond recognition.

III

These effects of estrangement or defamiliarization culminate in the Dreamer's final description of the heavenly city of Jerusalem, which draws heavily on the Book of Revelation, or 'Apokalypce', as the poet calls it:

In the Apokalypce is þe fasoun preued,
As deuyses hit þe apostel John.

As John þe apostel hit syȝ wyth syȝt,
I syȝe þat cyty of gret renoun ...
(983–6)

(In the Apocalypse the matter is proved, as it is described by the apostle John. As John the apostle saw it with his eyes, so did I see that city of great renown.)

Just as John saw the heavenly city in 'Apokalypce', the poet saw it in his private revelation. The two visions, one by an apostle, the other by a vernacular English poet, are presented as mutually verifying.

But we should observe one large area of discrepancy between the two works. John's Apocalypse is, as the title implies, apocalyptic: it foretells the last resurrection and the Day of Judgment, when the city of Jerusalem will 'come down from heaven' (Revelation 21: 2) to replace the old world, and the faithful will walk in God's presence for eternity. Not surprisingly, the Book of Revelation proved influential with medieval (and later) writers who sought to convince their audience that the end of the world was nigh. The *Gawain*-poet's use of Apocalypse stands out among these doom-prophets for not being apocalyptic at all.[9] His description of the heavenly city is not intended—as it is in his biblical source—to herald man's permanent absorption into the kingdom of God, but to underline his continued exclusion from it. Hence, there is no mention in *Pearl* of a Second Coming; there is only the sequence of surreal images in which the heavenly city is mediated to 'John' in the Apocalypse.

The *Gawain*-poet, for example, borrowed from his source the enigmatic symmetry of the celestial city: it has twelve foundation stones —'foundementeʒ twelue' (993)—the twelve tiers are formed by twelve precious stones (994–1020); the walls are twelve furlongs long (1030);[10] the city has twelve gates (1035); the trees in it bear twelve kinds of fruit, twelve times a year (1978–9). Like the heavenly Jerusalem glimpsed by 'John', the *Gawain*-poet's city stands frozen in the timeless symmetry of the number twelve. The mysterious recurrence of this number in the geography of heaven simultaneously invites and defies explanation— why twelve?—while creating a stillness that likewise attracts and repulses at the same time. On the one hand its order suggests beauty and perfection, on the other its static quality calls forth 'our resistance to stasis— our sense that there is something unnatural, unhuman about it' (Mann 1994c, 194).

The heavenly city is clearly unlike anything in nature. In addition to its fearful symmetry, its streets are paved with gold and transparent like glass (1025); it is illuminated by the bright radiance of a Lamb (of all

---

9. It should be noted that, while unusal, the *Gawain*-poet is not alone in drawing on the Apocalypse without being apocalyptic. Emmerson (1992) gives a useful overview of the different kinds of uses to which the Book of Revelation was put in the medieval period.

10. The Book of Revelation (21: 16) reads twelve *thousand* furlongs.

things), who leads a stately procession of thousands of maidens dressed in white; who has seven horns of gold; who rejoices while bleeding from his side; and who sits on a throne from which flows a river 'bryȝter þen boþ þe sunne and mone' (1056).

These psychedelic images, taken from Revelation, support the *Gawain*-poet's presentation of heaven as a shockingly alien world. The capacity to accept its coherence without rubbing one's eyes would seem to require not just a suspension of disbelief but an hallucination, an alteration in the forms of our very consciousness. Heaven in *Pearl* thus departs from the common iconography of heaven as a pleasant garden. Rather than being cosy and inviting, it shuts people out; unless, of course, they cease to be human. By reminding us of that precondition for total imaginative participation in the world of heaven, the *Gawain*-poet shows himself to be not only an original poet, but a good theologian.

REASON AND REVELATION: THE DEBATE ABOUT HEAVEN

I

The inaccessibility of heaven is not restricted to the level of sense-perception. Heaven in *Pearl* also proves inaccessible to human reason, the limitations of which become painfully clear once the Dreamer starts talking to his dead daughter, whom he recognizes in the glorious maiden whom he sees from across the uncrossable river. I want to reserve the intensely personal drama of this encounter for a later section, and turn here to the more abstract debate about the mysteries of heaven. 'Debate' —the word has become commonplace in *Pearl*-criticism—is an unfortunate misnomer for the exchange of words between the Dreamer and the Pearl-maiden. Debates are possible only between people with a shared understanding of the logic by which certain positions may legitimately be arrived at, defended, or faulted. The parties in a debate may hold different views, but they must agree on what is arguable, and what is unreasonable. Between two people who are locked into different ways of reasoning, argument can only result in mutual incomprehension. And in *Pearl*, this is precisely what happens.

From a poet who insisted on the absolute difference between the realms of earth and heaven, the fact that the Dreamer and the Pearl-maiden can communicate at all is perhaps more surprising than the fact that they continually talk at cross-purposes. What, according to medieval Christians, made communication across this otherness possible was the principle of accommodation, the deliberate adjustment of divine revelation to the limits of human understanding, an adjustment which typically relied on the use of homely analogies. At first sight, accommodation appears to be the exact opposite of defamiliarization. But, as I shall show in this section, accommodation may better be understood as a strategy akin to defamiliarization. It seems to make concessions to our ordinary ways of thinking, but it is actually out to expose their helplessness before the divine otherness.

One simple example will make clear that accommodation in *Pearl* is never truly accommodating. Towards the end of the debate, if so it may be called, the maiden speaks of heaven as 'Jerusalem'. The Dreamer promptly brings his geographical knowledge to bear on her revelations:

> 'Þou tellez me of Jerusalem þe ryche ryalle,
> Þer Dauid dere watz dyʒt on trone,
> Bot by þyse holtez hit con not hone,
> Bot in Judee hit is, þat noble note.'
>
> (919–22)

('You are talking to me of Jerusalem, rich and royal, where David was enthroned. But it cannot be in these areas. The noble city lies in Judea.')

The reason why the Dreamer can no longer follow the Pearl-maiden is that he looks on heaven from his worldly perspective, confusing the heavenly city with Jerusalem on earth. Yet clearly, the Pearl-maiden's accommodation *invites* him to think along these lines: it is she who called heaven Jerusalem in the first place. He has been lured into human ways of understanding, only to discover that they are dead ends. Accommodation thus plays upon familiar modes of comprehension with the purpose of alienating us from them. It throws our logic into disarray.

To see the effects of accommodation on the Dreamer in more detail, we need to look at the debate more closely, beginning with the moment in *Pearl* when the Dreamer first broaches the question of the Pearl-maiden's new life in heaven:

> 'Bot now I am here in your presente,
> I wolde bysech, wythouten debate,
> ʒe wolde me say *in sobre asente*
> What lyf ʒe lede erly and late.
> For I am ful fayn þat your astate
> Is worþen to worschyp and wele, iwysse;

Of alle my joy the hyʒe gate,
Hit is in grounde of alle my blysse.'

'Now blysse, burne, mot þe bytyde',
Þen sayde þat lufsoum of lyth and lere,
'And welcum here to walk and byde,
For now þy speche is to me dere.
Maysterful mod and hyʒe pryde,
I hete þe, arn heterly hated here.
My Lorde ne loueʒ not for to chyde,
For meke arn alle þat woneʒ hym nere;
And when in hys place þou schal apere,
Be dep deuote in hol mekenesse.
My Lorde þe Lamb loueʒ ay such chere,
Þat is þe grounde of alle my blysse.'

(389–408)

('... But now that I am here in your presence, I would ask you, without
further argument, that you would tell me in simple agreement what life you
lead, early and late. For I am very pleased that you have risen to honour and
wealth. It is the mainspring of all my joy, and the ground of all my bliss.'
'Now, happiness, sir, be yours', then said she, lovely of face and limb. 'And
feel free to walk and dwell here, for now I like your words better. Arrogance
and pride—I warn you—are greatly disliked here. My Lord does not like to
chide, for all people who live near him are meek. And when the time comes
for you to appear in this place, be devout in sincere humility. My Lord the
Lamb, who is the ground of all my bliss, always likes such behaviour.')

Having first addressed the Dreamer with some stinging rebukes, the
Pearl-maiden appears to be in a more conciliatory mood when
the Dreamer asks her about her status in heaven. Having chastened the
Dreamer into submission, she finally approves of his tone: 'now þy
speche is to me dere'. But, even at her kindest, the maiden does not
move an inch. She may agree with the Dreamer that they ought to have
no 'debate', but the two seem to have very different ideas about who
must give in to whom to reach agreement. Whereas the Dreamer asks
her to speak 'in sobre asente', the Pearl-maiden responds approvingly, as
if she has understood him as saying *he* will speak 'in sobre asente'. The
Pearl-maiden is coming at the question of 'asente' from an entirely different angle. Submission must come from man, not from God or from
the blessed whom he has endowed with perfect understanding.

The point repeats the moral of the previous section of the poem, in
which the key word is 'deme' (meaning both 'to speak' or 'to decide'),

and the key question is who can 'deme' in the one sense and who can 'deme' in the other:

> '... þou most abyde þat he schal deme.
>
> Deme Dryȝtyn, euer hym adyte,
> Of þe way a fote ne wyl he wryþe.'
>   (348–50)

('You have to put up with what he ordains. Go on and censure God, and arraign him! He will not budge.')

People may of course argue with God, and attempt to prove him wrong, but this is of little or no consequence to what will eventually happen. God alone has the power to make words count. This fact is brought into focus through the repetition of 'deme' in different meanings and contexts. Whether or not the word has the decisive sense of 'ordaining' depends entirely on who is the subject of the verb: God or man.

The words that come under scrutiny in the long passage quoted above (390–408) are 'grounde of alle my blysse'. First used by the Dreamer, they refer to his joy at seeing his daughter's elevation in heaven (397), but when the Pearl-maiden repeats the phrase, she changes its reference:

> 'My Lorde þe Lamb loueȝ ay such chere,
> Þat is þe grounde of alle my blysse.'
>   (407–8)

The 'grounde' of *her* bliss is not her glory but Christ. In her apparent echo of the Dreamer, his words return to us in an altered perspective; they have been made strange. As so often in *Pearl*, repetitions are not affirmations but disconfirmations.

When the Pearl-maiden responds to his query concerning her status in heaven, the Dreamer is momentarily allowed to stand on firmer ground:

> 'A blysful lyf þou says I lede;
> Þou woldeȝ knaw þerof þe stage.
> Þow wost wel when þy perle con schede
> I watȝ ful ȝong and tender of age;
> Bot my lorde þe Lombe þurȝ hys godhede,
> He toke myself to hys maryage,
> Corounde me quene in blysse to brede
> In lenghe of dayeȝ þat euer schal wage;
> And sesed in alle hys herytage
> Hys lef is. I am holy hysse:

Hys prese, hys prys, and hys parage
Is rote and grounde of alle my blysse.'
(409–20)

('You say I lead a blissful life, and would like to know my status. You know
well that when your pearl departed, I was young and tender of age. But my
Lord, in his divinity, chose me for his marriage, and crowned me queen, to
live in bliss for a length of days that will last forever. And his beloved is pos-
sessor of all of his heritage. I am his entirely. His worth, his excellence, and
lineage are the root and ground of all my bliss.')

The Pearl-maiden tells the Dreamer that she has become the bride of
Christ, that she has been crowned queen in heaven, and now shares
in Christ's inheritance. As ways of talking about the fate of the blessed in
heaven, these are all conventional expressions, echoing Revelations 19:
7 and Romans 8: 17 in the Bible:

Let us praise and rejoice, and give honour to him, for the marriage of the
Lamb is come, and his wife hath prepared herself also.

And if sons [of God], heirs also; heirs indeed of God, and joint heirs with
Christ: yet so that, if we suffer with him, we may also be glorified with him.

With these analogies to worldly forms of affiliation, the Pearl-maiden
accommodates heavenly realities to the Dreamer. But of what help are
her homely analogies? Do they necessarily make things easier to understand for the Dreamer? The Dreamer's response suggests not:

'Blysful', quod I, 'may þys be trwe?
Dyspleseʒ not if I speke errour.
Art þou þe quene of heueneʒ blwe,
Þat al þys worlde schal do honour?
We leuen on Marye þat grace of grewe,
Þat ber a barne of vyrgyn flour;
Þe croune fro hyr quo most remwe
Bot ho hir passed in sum fauour?'
(421–8)

('You happy girl', I said, 'can that be right? Pardon me if I am wrong. Are
you then the queen of blue heaven, whom all this world should honour? We
believe in Mary from whom grace came, who bore a child in maidenhood.
Who might take the crown from her, unless she surpassed her in some way?')

The Dreamer has listened to the Pearl-maiden's words carefully, has
pondered their consequences, and is led, ineluctably, to a problem. If she
has been crowned queen, has she not in the process ousted the Virgin

Queen, Mary, from her throne? And, to anticipate an objection the Dreamer later raises, if Christ has married her, how has she managed to put herself forward before all other desirable and eager young ladies suing for his hand? Or are we to believe Christ is polygamous? Our first inclination may be to criticize the Dreamer for his obtuseness, but it should be noted that these questions follow *entirely logically* from the Maiden's words. The Dreamer's problem is not that he interprets her words unreasonably—for he takes her words to mean exactly what they say—but that he interprets them too rationally. Paradoxically, it is reason that leads the Dreamer astray, into a maze of questions and objections where the Maiden's apparently straightforward propositions no longer make sense to him. Her 'accommodating' language, which seemed at first to cater for his ordinary ways of understanding, ends up by showing its inadequacy as a vehicle for the mysteries of heaven.

What, then, is the relation between the Maiden and the Virgin Queen? As the Pearl-maiden puts it, it is not rivalry but harmony:

'The court of þe kyngdom of God alyue
Hatȝ a property in hytself beyng:
Alle þat may þerinne aryue
Of alle þe reme is quen oþer kyng,
And neuer oþer ȝet schal depryue,
Bot vchon fayn of oþereȝ hafyng,
And wolde her corouneȝ wern worþe þo fyue,
If possyble were her mendyng.
Bot my Lady of quom Jesu con spryng,
Ho haldeȝ þe empyre ouer vus ful hyȝe;
And þat dyspleseȝ non of oure gyng,
For ho is Quene of cortaysye.'

(445–56)

'The court of God's kingdom has this inherent quality: all those who enter in it are queens or kings of the whole realm, and yet no one will deprive another, but everyone is glad with what the other has, wishing that the other's crown were worth five times more, if that were possible. But my Lady from whom Jesus sprang, rules high above us all. And no one in our company is displeased by this, since she is the Queen of courtesy.')

This is the heaven that is typical in medieval descriptions, a place that is hierarchical, but where all are equally pleased with their own places and with those of others (Dinzelbacher 1979). If this coexistence of hierarchy and equality is difficult to conceive, the maiden's talk of courts, kings and queens is likely to make it even more so. For what is clear is that heaven is in fact not at all like a conventional court, where royal favour is the object of fierce rivalry between its members. If we draw on our knowledge of the way courts work—the maiden's idiom after all invites us to do so—we discover that we would be better off without it. Appeals to our ordinary world are a hindrance rather than a help.

Word-play again comes closest to communicating the mysteries of heaven. If our knowledge of the world stands in the way of understanding, puns can confuse our terms of reference, by blurring the linguistic distinctions in which our knowledge of the world is expressed. The phrases on which the poet puns in section seven are 'Quene of cortaysye' and 'quene by cortaysye', the first of which the poet consistently uses to refer to the Virgin Mary (432, 444, 456), while the second is used for the women in heaven (468, 480). The capital letters are an editorial intervention, an attempt to sort out the same problem that bothers the Dreamer: how can heaven reward all women with queenship, while still granting pride of place to Mary? This is where the similarities and differences between the phrases 'Quene of cortaysye' and 'quene by cortaysye' become important. They are like each other, the more so when we realize that in Middle English the preposition 'of' could also mean 'by'. Note, for example, the second usage of the preposition 'of' from section seven of *Pearl*:

> 'For ho is Quene of cortaysye.
>
> Of courtaysye, as sayt3 Saynt Poule,
> Al arn we membre3 of Jesu Kryst ...'
> (456–8)

> ('For she is the Queen of courtesy. By courtesy, as Saint Paul says, we are all members of Jesus Christ ...')

Unlike Queen Mary who is the 'Quene of cortaysye', the blessed are queens 'of courtaysye' only in the second sense of the preposition: 'by courtesy' of God's kindness. The play on 'Quene of cortaysye' and 'quene by cortaysye' offers an imaginative solution to the problem of how all women can be queens like the Virgin Mary, and she remain different from them. It moves beyond the logical impasse by showing how in these two phrases sameness and difference can coexist.

I have so far tried to avoid talking of puns as explanations of the Dreamer's problems, for the same reason that I have avoided talking of the Dreamer's failure to understand the Pearl-maiden's words. As we have seen, the Dreamer's problem is his logical thinking. His failure, it follows, consists in not being able to *mis*understand the Pearl-maiden's words, to realize that they do not mean what they say. As the Dreamer puts it when he sees the pearl on the maiden's breast, human beings cannot grasp the ineffable until their comprehension fails:

A manneʒ dom moʒt dryʒly demme,
Er mynde moʒt malte in hit mesure.

(224–4)

(Human reason would be be utterly confounded, before his mind could comprehend its limits.)

Comprehension, then, is conditional on confusion. And the efficacy of the pun lies precisely in generating the essential misunderstanding on which illumination depends.

II

It would take us too long to go through the poet's full repertoire of puns and *double-entendres*.[11] Instead, I want to pursue the theme of human reason and divine revelation in the Pearl-maiden's retelling of the Parable of the Vineyard. The apparent function of the parable is to resolve the Dreamer's continued scepticism about the appropriateness of the maiden's rise to queenship. She had, after all, spent less than two years on earth in God's service; hardly enough to merit an immediate elevation to the highest rung of the hierarchical ladder:

'That cortaysé is to fre of dede,
ʒyf hyʒ be soth þat þou coneʒ saye.
Þou lyfed not two ʒer in oure þede;
Þou cowþeʒ neuer God nauþer plese ne pray,
Ne neuer nawþer Pater ne Crede;
And quen mad on þe fyrst day!
I may not traw, so God me spede,
Þat God wolde wryþe so wrange away.
Of countes, damysel, par ma fay,
Wer fayr in heuen to halde asstate,
Oþer elleʒ a lady of lasse aray;
Bot a quene! Hit is to dere a date.'

(481–92)

('That courtesy is too generous, if you are indeed telling me the truth. You lived less than two years on earth. You could not please or pray to God, and

---

11. On word-play in *Pearl* see Wilson (1976, 30–45); Thomasch (1989); and Donner (1989).

did not even know your Lord's Prayer or your Creed. And made a queen on the first day! I don't believe it—so help me God—that God would turn so unjustly from the right path. On my word, young lady, to be a countess in heaven would be wonderful, or perhaps a lady of lesser rank, but a queen! That is too exalted a goal.')

The Dreamer raises objections that are at the heart of a fourteenth-century controversy regarding the relationship between good works and the divine gift of salvation, between what we do on earth and the reward that awaits us in the life to come (Simpson 1990, 75–85). According to the Dreamer, the relationship between the two must be commensurate, so that the longer we labour on earth, the higher we may expect God's reward to be, and the sooner we may expect to receive it. Common sense seems to be on the Dreamer's side, for the time we spend in someone's service may be presumed to be a measure for the wages we will earn. Not surprisingly, the Pearl-maiden's instant promotion to the status of queen after only two years in God's service seems a blatant injustice to the Dreamer, a breach of convention and propriety. If the Pearl-maiden is right about her elevation, a whole way of thinking about merit and salvation comes under threat. 'Hit is to dere a date' is the Dreamer's indignant stand on behalf of common sense and God's decency.

The Pearl-maiden responds, in the first instance, by denying the validity of the notion of measure altogether:

> 'Þer is no date of hys godnesse',
> Þen sayde to me þat worþy wyȝte,
> 'For al is trawþe þat he con dresse,
> And he may do noþynk bot ryȝt.
> As Mathew meleȝ in your messe
> In sothfol gospel of God almyȝt,
> In sample he can ful grayþely gesse,
> And lykneȝ hit to heuen lyȝte.
> "My regne", he saytȝ, "is lyk on hyȝt
> To a lorde þat hade a uyne, I wate.
> Of tyme of ȝere þe terme watȝ tyȝt,
> To labor vyne watȝ dere þe date."'
> (493–504)

('There is no limit to his goodness,' that noble lady answered, 'for all he does is just, and he can only do what is right. As Matthew says in your mass, in the true gospel of almighty God—speaking fittingly in a parable and finding an analogy for our bright heaven—"My kingdom", he says, "is like a lord who had a vineyard. The season had come: it was high time to work in the vineyard."')

There is no 'date', no limit, to his goodness, and no way, therefore, of calculating one's eventual reward on the basis of the units of time (date) spent in his employment. Measurements such as these do not apply to God. Clearly, this reply is no answer to the Dreamer's objection that work-time and reward ought to be commensurate. It merely dismisses the objection, by denying that the criterion of 'date' is relevant to what God ordains. If the Dreamer thinks God is unjust, then that is his problem, not God's:

> 'For al is trawþe þat he con dresse,
> And he may do noþynk bot ry3t.'

On the question of whether God rightly elevated her, she states simply that God is by definition right—'truth by assertion', as the strategy is known today. If anything should remind us that the Pearl-maiden does not answer the objection that the Dreamer raises, it is the ease with which she reasserts the dogma of God's justice, when this dogma is precisely what the Dreamer had called into question.

Judging by the rules of any ordinary debate, the Pearl-maiden's practices are grossly unfair, the more so in that the Pearl-maiden for her part does not hesitate to subject the Dreamer's premisses to close inspection. Continually, she repeats his words, before taking them apart, as if it were indeed an exercise in scholastic argumentation:

> 'Þou says þou trawe3 me in þis dene ... '
> (295)

> 'Anoþer þou says ... '
> (297)

> 'A blysful lyf þou says I lede ... '
> (409)

But despite appearances, the Dreamer is up against propositions that are essentially not debatable, at least not by mortal beings. They cannot reason their way up to them, which is why in this 'debate' the Dreamer does not stand a chance against the Pearl-maiden. Her views are, of course, *a priori* correct, but she cannot be held answerable for them.

Having first rejected the Dreamer's question on the grounds that its presuppositions concerning 'date' are invalid, the Pearl-maiden rekindles our hopes for some explanation when she promises an illustrative story, a 'sample' (409). From the outset, the Parable of the Vineyard from Matthew 20: 1–16 promises to be amenable to the Dreamer's modes of apprehension, for the story begins by resurrecting the concept of 'date' which the Pearl-maiden had earlier deemed inadmissible: 'To labor vyne watʒ dere þe *date*'. Before long, the parable has immersed us in the realities of everyday life. Above all, these are the pressures of 'date', of time. Already in Matthew, the passing of time is charted in painstaking detail. The lord of the vineyard sets out 'early in the morning' (20: 1), to contract labourers. Offering them the price of a penny for a day's work, he sends them off to work in his vineyard. 'About the third hour' (20: 3) he sees some men standing idle, whom he asks to join his workforce. The process repeats itself 'at the sixth hour' and 'the ninth hour' (20: 5), at the 'eleventh hour' (20: 6), until, an hour later, the time has come for the labourers to receive their wages.

The Pearl-maiden's retelling of the parable traces the progress of time with the same precision, from the 'date of ʒere' (505) to sunrise, from sunrise to afternoon, and from afternoon to evensong:

'At þe date of day of euensonge,
On oure byfore þe sonne go doun,
He seʒ þer ydel men ful stronge
And sade to hem wyth sobre soun,
"Wy stonde ʒe ydel þise dayeʒ longe?"
Þay sayden her hyre watʒ nawhere boun.
"Gotʒ to my vyne, ʒemen ʒonge,
And wyrkeʒ and dotʒ þat at ʒe moun."
Sone þe worlde bycom wel broun;
þe sunne watʒ doun and hit wex late.
To take her hyre he mad sumoun;
Þe day watʒ al apassed date.'

(529–40)

('At the time of evensong, one hour before sunset, he saw able men standing idle, and he said to them in a calm voice: "Why are you doing nothing the whole day long?" They said their hire had not been arranged anywhere. "Then go to my vineyard, young yeomen, and work as hard as you can." Soon the day became dark. The sun sank and it became late. He announced they could fetch their wages; the day had passed.')

In contrast to Matthew, who measures time in numbers, not in seasons and setting suns, the passage of time in *Pearl* appeals directly to the world of our senses, as well as to our preconceptions about the way the world works. At last, the Pearl-maiden places the Dreamer and the reader in a heaven in which they can feel at home, a heaven where the Lord keeps track of time, and promises rational wages:

'Why stande ʒe ydel?' he sayde to þos.
'Ne knaw ʒe of þis day no date?'

(515–16)

('Why are you standing idle?' he said to them. 'Do you think the day will never end?')

'What resonable hyre be naʒt be runne
I yow pay in dede and þoʒte.'

(523–4)

('Whatever reasonable wages you will have earned for yourselves at night, I will pay you, in deed and in thought.')

But we do not savour the joys of recognition or the lyrical evocations of nature for long: the Lord lines up his workforce and pays them all a penny each, beginning with those who started work last. Like the Dreamer's sense of injustice at his daughter's swift coronation, the response of the workmen who have been slaving away all day long is predictable as well as reasonable:

'More haf we serued, vus þynk so,
Þat suffred han þe dayeʒ hete,
Þenn þyse þat wroʒt not houreʒ two,
And þou dotʒ hem vus to counterfete.'

(553–6)

('We think that we, who have endured the heat of day-time, have worked harder than these men who haven't worked for more than two hours. And yet you are giving them the same treatment.')

There is a danger that our familiarity with the ending of the parable blinds us to the nasty surprise it springs on us. For it is not just the labourers who have been busy calculating the hours they have worked, in the expectation of commensurate pay. Their claims are substantiated by the story itself, which from the very beginning has been measuring the progress of time in disproportionate detail. And like the workers in the vineyard, the audience expects some return for the energy they have spent keeping track of it. But the parable that keeps on harping on the importance of 'date' ends up by shrugging off its relevance. All receive the same reward. More perversely still, the last to start work are the first to receive their penny. And does the Lord of the Vineyard justify his ways? Not in the least. He merely says he stands by his decision, and dismisses the complaints:

Þenne sayde þe lorde to on of þo:
'Frende, no waning I wyl þe ȝete;
Take þat is þyn owne, and go.'
(557–9)

(Then the lord said to one of them: 'Friend, I am not going to offer reductions. Take what is yours, and go.')

Surely, the Dreamer cannot be blamed for being disappointed by the explanatory power of this story.

None of these disillusionments will be felt by the Pearl-maiden. She had said all along that there is no 'date' to his goodness. The parable which had first adopted our measures of 'date', finally discards them as well, and returns us to the mystery of divine generosity it had purported to explain.

The maiden's exegesis of the parable which follows only deepens this mystery. Medieval exegetes had generally followed Augustine, who had interpreted the various hours of the day in which the Lord of the Vineyard hires his labourers as the stages of life in which human beings respond to God's calling. In his interpretation, the Parable of the Vineyard ought to remind us that it is never too late to convert to Christianity:

Tamquam prima hora vocantur, qui recentes ab utero matris incipiunt esse christiani; quasi tertia, pueri; quasi sexta, juvenes; quasi nona, vergentes in senium; quasi undecima, omnino decrepiti: unum tamen vitae aeternae denarium omnes accepturi.

(*Sermo* 87)[12]

(Those who become Christians soon after emerging from their mother's womb, are like those called at the first hour; children are like those called at the third hour; youths like those at the sixth; those who are getting old are like those called at the ninth; the very decrepit like those at the eleventh. And yet all will receive the penny of eternal life.)

In the Pearl-maiden's exegesis, however, those called at the eleventh hour are not people who convert late in life, but those who, like herself, have died in infancy, and are therefore least tested:

'Wheþer welnygh now I con bygynne—
In euentyde into þe vyne I come—
Fyrst of my hyre my Lorde con mynne:

12. *PL* 38, 533.

I watȝ payed anon of al and sum.
Ȝet oþer þer werne þat toke more tom,
Þat swange and swat for long ȝore,
Þat ȝet of hyre noþynk þay nom,
Paraunter noȝt schal to-ȝere more.'
(581–8)

('Even though I had only just begun—I came into the vineyard in the evening—the Lord nevertheless first looked after me. I was promptly paid in full. But there were others that took more trouble, who laboured and sweated for ages, and still they did not get their pay, and perhaps they won't for quite some time yet.')

Unlike most exegetes, then, the maiden interprets 'eventyde' as infancy, while those who have lived 'for longe ȝore' are likened to the labourers who started work at the dawn of day. Evening turns into the dawn of life, and morning into old age. It seems that the *Gawain*-poet has muddled up the exegesis of the Church Fathers. Attempts have been made to tidy up the muddle (Robertson 1980), but, as Theodore Bogdanos has suggested, there may be a purpose to the confusions about time:

Through transference, the dawn becomes the evening, and the evening the dawn. We have an illogical syllogism, which in its absurd dialectic incarnates another inscrutable principle governing God's mercy: his view of time. To him, the past, the present, and the future are an Eternal Time.

(Bogdanos 1983, 96)

Being an eminently reasonable man, neither the parable, nor the maiden's exegesis makes sense to the Dreamer. Again, it is not that he has made the wrong logical inferences. In fact he responds to them quite coherently when he interrupts the maiden as follows:

'Me þynk þy tale vnresounable ...
... Now he þat stod þe long day stable,
And þou to payment com hym byfore,
Þenne þe lasse in werke to take more able,
And euer þe lenger þe lasse, þe more.'
(590–600)

('I think your tale is not reasonable ... Suppose someone worked hard all day long, and you got paid first, then less work would mean more pay, and ever alike, the less, the more.')

The Pearl-maiden's tale is indeed 'vnresounable'. Anyone who thinks of deserts in terms of time and measurable quantities, as reason compels us to do, will rebel against its conclusion, just as the labourers in the Parable of the Vineyard do. The parable and the maiden's exegesis, in other words, raise the same problems that they were supposed to solve. They cannot therefore be expected to convince the Dreamer; only those who needed no convincing in the first place will be persuaded by them.

Readers, perhaps, feel that they are not excluded from the meaning of the Pearl-maiden's words in the way the Dreamer is. If parables divide listeners into insiders and outsiders (Kermode 1979, 23–47), we perhaps consider ourselves to be on the other side of its meaning from the Dreamer:

> To you it is given to know the mystery of the kingdom of God, but to them that are without, all things are done in parables: that seeing they may see and not perceive; and hearing they may hear and not understand ...
>
> (Mark 4: 11–12)

I quote these lines from Mark because they raise the same question as *Pearl* asks us to consider, namely what the grounds for our better perception might be. Does not *Pearl*, by insisting that these grounds cannot be the powers of reason, also suggest that no amount of seeing and hearing can put us inside the mysteries if we were not there already? The Pearl-maiden can only make sense to the converted. These are implications that critics and readers who sit in judgment on the Dreamer, and regard him as naïve and dim, must confront: that what allows them to do it is not their superior intelligence, but a stronger faith. They believe more lightly than the Dreamer.

To dismiss the Dreamer's problem as one of misinterpretation, or as 'literalism', is to miss the point that the figurative meaning of the maiden's talk of 'courts', 'queens', or heavenly 'marriages' is not a matter of fact ('for by assay ther may no man hit preve', as Chaucer put it) but a matter of faith. As the Dreamer's reasoned approach to the Pearl-maiden's revelations shows, they cannot be made to yield meaning by trying to convert them into logical propositions, with which they are incompatible. They are what Stanley Fish has called 'dialectical' rather than 'rhetorical', digestible not by 'taking the mind from point to point, according to the laws of logic', but 'by *changing* the mind into an instrument congruent with the reality it would perceive' (Fish 1972, 19). This explains why the Dreamer, who remains sensible throughout, is also permanently incapable of understanding the maiden.

III

I want to conclude this section by returning once again to the puns in *Pearl*, for the pun epitomizes the problems of the Pearl-maiden's 'dialectical' discourse, which becomes meaningful only through a conversion of the mind. Characteristically, the Pearl-maiden's response to the Dreamer's dissatisfaction with her account of God's justice hinges on a pun, this time on the word 'pay' and its double meaning, 'to pay' and 'to satisfy' (Mann 1983). These are her words to the Dreamer:

> 'Of more and lasse in Godeʒ ryche',
> Þat gentyl sayde, 'lys no joparde,
> For þer is vch mon payed inlyche,
> Wheþer lyttel oþer much be hys rewarde ... '
>
> (601–4)

On first reading the line 'For þer is vch mon payed inlyche' we probably decide to take 'pay' in its most common sense of 'to pay', glossing the line as 'Here each man is paid the same'. It is an apparently straightforward reading, until the next line—'Wheþer lyttel oþer much be hys rewarde'—flatly contradicts the proposition of equal payment which we thought was contained in the previous line. At this point, we are prompted to consider the alternative reading 'Here everyone is equally satisfied', taking 'paid' in the sense of 'contented' which it clearly has in, for instance, line 1177: 'Me payed ful ille to be outfleme / So sodenly of þat fayre regioun' ('It did not please me a bit to be banished from that fair region so suddenly'). As the poetry takes us from 'payed' (paid) to 'payed' (contented), it offers us in a pun another reflection of a divine mystery which the Pearl-maiden is trying to communicate: to be paid in heaven is necessarily to be satisfied. If in our world payment and satisfaction have become different things altogether, the pun momentarily obliterates the logical distinction and allows the audience to enter into the Pearl-maiden's world where they are one and the same thing.

Clearly, some insight makes it possible for this pun, or any other pun in *Pearl*, to become visible, and in the light of the discussion about 'dialectical' discourse, it is interesting to ask the question of where the change that produces this insight occurs: in the word 'payed', or in our minds? The question may be approached by considering a phenomenon similar to word-play, known as the 'ambiguous picture' or the 'visual pun'. The best-known example of this is the duck/rabbit picture. This picture of a duck may be stared at for minutes, before we see in it, in a moment of insight that stands in no proportion to the time we have spent analysing it, the likeness of a rabbit. This sudden realization, which Wittgenstein called 'noticing an aspect', radically transforms our perception. When we look at the picture again we longer 'see' a duck, but can see it *as* a duck. It has become possible to 'read' the picture at different levels. Yet, while it seems to us that the picture has taken on a new meaning, it is clearly no different from what it was before. If we see it differently, it is because *we* have changed (Wittgenstein 1953, 220).

The verbal pun demands a similar mental conversion from the reader. As in the duck/rabbit picture, reason will not necessarily get us anywhere. The idea that ducks are rabbits, and that payment is the same as satisfaction, actually runs counter to common experience. Its full meaning is revealed only to those who, first, believe, despite our logical assumptions, that there can indeed be more to the picture or the word than meets the eye, and who then make the imaginative leap that renders the different levels of meaning visible.

What I have said about puns applies to the Pearl-maiden's accommodating revelations as a whole. They baffle the Dreamer, not because he is literal-minded—for that would imply that other levels of meaning were visible to him—but because he does not 'notice their aspect'. Like a person staring at the duck/rabbit picture and only seeing a duck, he listens to the maiden's talk of heavenly brides, queens, or cities, without being able to take them for anything else. If we can, this is so because we trust, against the grain of our logic, that these words indeed contain a deeper meaning. As in the pun, it is only a 'conversion' that allows the interpreter of revelation to see *and* to perceive, to hear *and* to understand.

Granted, the mental conversion needed to see a pun is not of the same order as the conversion that would be needed to put us inside the otherness of heaven. It is clear that the poet thought that only death, the ultimate transformation, could produce in human beings the perfect 'cnawyng' that he attributed to the Pearl-maiden. The *Gawain*-poet's puns nevertheless illustrate the process of illumination through conversion. He may have thought of them as a foretaste of heaven.

THE UNKINDNESS OF HEAVEN

I

I have so far presented the encounter between the Dreamer and the Pearl-maiden as one between a man of reason, condemned *for that reason* to remain an outsider to the mysteries of heaven, and a maiden securely placed within them, but therefore equally incapable of crossing the divide between them and of meeting the Dreamer on his own ground. This account may appear to do little justice to the profoundly tragic nature of this encounter, which strikes us more and more strongly as it becomes progressively clearer that the Dreamer and the Pearl are a father and his lost daughter. But if I have until now postponed a discussion of the personal drama of the meeting between the Dreamer and the Pearl-maiden, it is not because I wish to deny its emotional impact. We are mistaken, however, if we think the tragedy can be heightened by down-playing their strangeness to one another. On the contrary, it is only when we recognize their otherness that the full extent of the tragedy becomes visible. The tragedy is, after all, not that a father and a daughter should meet in heaven, but that she should have become estranged from him. While the Dreamer is still as attached to his daughter as he was before her death, she appears to have formed a new attachment to the Lamb and his following.

The difference in the ways in which the Dreamer and the Pearl-maiden use the pronoun 'we' brings this new conflict of their loyalties to the fore. When used by the Dreamer the first-person plural pronoun ('we', 'oure', 'vs') refers to himself and her, to the two of them together (251, 387–9, etc.). In the Pearl-maiden's usage, however, the 'vs' is the exclusive 'us' in heaven, as opposed to 'you' on earth (455, 458, etc.). Unlike the Dreamer, the Pearl-maiden insists that there is no community which she and the Dreamer have in common, no 'vs' that includes the two of them.

Another seemingly trivial point of contention that discloses the barrier that has interposed itself between the two is their different understanding of who or what is 'makeleȝ'. In line 780, the Dreamer praises the Pearl-maiden, his 'pearl', as a 'makeleȝ may and maskelleȝ' ('a peerless and spotless maiden'), but she promptly ticks him off for choosing the wrong words:

> 'Maskelles', quod þat myry quene,
> 'Vnblemyst I am, wythouten blot,
> And þat may I wyth mensk menteene;
> Bot "makeleȝ quene" þenne sade I not.'
>   (781–4)

('Spotless I am', said that pleasant queen, 'unblemished I am, without blot, and that I can affirm with propriety; but "peerless queen" I did not say.')

With impressive composure, she accepts one part of the Dreamer's compliment as factually correct (spotless she *is*), but repudiates the other part as an elementary error (peerless she is *not*), presumably thinking about the 144,000 brides of Christ who are her equals in heaven.

The interest in the Pearl-maiden's lesson lies in its exposure of a double misunderstanding: first, a symptomatic error on the part of the Dreamer, and, secondly, a curious lack of insight on her part into the real reason for the Dreamer's confusion. The seeds of his confusion are sown some lines earlier, where the Pearl-maiden expounded the virtues of the priceless 'pearl' from the parable of the merchant (Matthew 13: 45–6), the merchant who sold all his goods for a 'pearl of great price', the kingdom of heaven:

'[Þe jueler] solde alle hys goud, boþe wolen and lynne,
To bye hym a perle watȝ *mascelleȝ*.

This *makelleȝ* perle, þat boȝt is dere,
Þe joueler gef fore alle hys god,
Is lyke þe reme of heuenesse clere ...'
(731–5)

('The jeweller sold all his goods, both wool and linen, to buy himself a pearl that was spotless.

This peerless pearl, which is dearly bought, and for which the jeweller gave all his goods, is like the bright realm of heaven ...')

This passage helps to account for the Dreamer's 'mistake' in two ways. First of all, a careful reading of these lines shows that the Dreamer's confusion between 'mascelleȝ' and 'makeleȝ' is inherent in the Pearl-maiden's own words. The refrain word in the last line of each of the stanzas in section thirteen is 'mascelleȝ', and in all other sections of the poem, this refrain word is duly picked up by the opening line of the next stanza. In the extract above, however, the opening line of the new stanza (line 733) does not repeat the refrain word 'mascelleȝ' but instead has 'makelleȝ'. This could, of course be a scribal error, but, as Gordon observes in his editorial note to these lines, the same irregularity in the pattern of concatenation occurs in the fourth stanza of section thirteen as well, where the opening line (line 757) again reads 'makeleȝ' instead of the expected 'mascelleȝ'. The Dreamer, then, is hardly alone in mixing up the words 'mascelleȝ' and 'makeleȝ': the text seems to treat the two as interchangeable as well.

The Pearl-maiden's mention of a 'makelleȝ *perle*' further explains the

Dreamer's erroneous reference to her as 'makeleȝ'. Because the Pearl-maiden is herself also called a 'perle' by the Dreamer, her phrase leaves plenty of room for ambiguity: of which pearl (the maiden or heaven) is 'makelleȝ' the attribute? Now, the Maiden would no doubt answer that, in her usage, 'pearl' always refers to heaven, but the problem seems to be that the Dreamer has taken 'makelleȝ perle' to mean *her*. While the Pearl-maiden's mental universe has been restructured around God, the Dreamer's is still centred on his lost daughter, so that whenever she says pearl, he naturally thinks of her first. His praise of her 'peerlessness' is more than a slip of the tongue: it is a symptom of an emotional life entirely unlike hers. And so radical is this unlikeness that the Pearl-maiden, too, cannot understand the source of his confusion, as is apparent from her belief that the Dreamer's 'mistake' can be corrected simply by reminding him of the meaning of the word 'maskeleȝ', which she kindly glosses twice for him:

> 'Maskelles', quod þat myry quene,
> 'Vnblemyst I am, wythouten blot ... '

An error that betrays the Dreamer's involvement with her is reduced by the Pearl-maiden to a straightforward matter of linguistic incompetence, as if his problem were not his emotional absorption but his ignorance of what exactly the adjective 'maskelles' means.

The painfulness of the Dreamer's encounter with the Pearl-maiden arises from the nasty truth that is illustrated by these mutual misunderstandings: that in the course of their long 'meeting' they never really meet. As the Dreamer puts it in a moment of despair, their encounter is *both* a meeting *and* a separation:

> 'Why schal I hit boþe mysse and mete?'
> (329)

The impact of the poem depends on this simultaneous perception of the close bond they once shared and of the gap that has now opened up between them. An appreciation of the emotional force of *Pearl* might therefore well begin by asking how the *Gawain*-poet makes us conscious of the altered relations between the Dreamer and the Pearl-maiden, while continuing to remind us of their former closeness. To answer this question we must go back to the prologue of *Pearl*, and look at the ways in which the Dreamer keeps the past alive, in his memory, and in in his hopes that the Pearl of his memories may still be recovered.

II

Perle, plesaunte to prynces paye
To clanly close in golde so clere,
Oute of oryent, I hardyly saye,
Ne proued I neuer her precios pere.
So rounde, so reken in vche araye,
So smal, so smoþe her sydeȝ were,
Quere-so-euer I jugged gemmeȝ gaye,
I sette hyr sengeley in synglere.
Allas! I leste hyr in on erbere;
Þurȝ gresse to grounde hit from me yot.
I dewyne, fordolked of luf-daungere
Of þat pryuy perle wythouten spot.

Syþen in þat spote hit fro me sprange,
Ofte haf I wayted, wyschande þat wele,
Þat wont watȝ whyle deuoyde my wrange
And heuen my happe and al my hele.
Þat dotȝ bot þrych my hert þrange,
My breste in bale bot bolne and bele;
Ȝet þoȝt me neuer so swete a sange
As stylle stounde let to me stele.

(1–19)

(Pearl, pleasing for a prince to set in pure gold! I dare to say that, among pearls from the orient, I never found her equal. So round, so radiant in every setting, so small, so smooth her sides were, that wherever I judged the value of beautiful pearls I set her apart as unique. Alas! I lost her in a garden; it went from me through the grass to the earth. I pine away, smitten by love-longing for my own spotless pearl.

Since the time it slipped away from me, I have often looked for it, longing for her grace which was wont to drive away my sorrow and heighten my happiness and well-being. It only makes my heart hurt grievously, and my breast rages and festers with pain. Yet I thought there was never so sweet a song as the one which the quiet hour allowed me to hear.)

In a rereading of the prologue to *Pearl*, we inevitably come to it with a clearer understanding about the nature of the Dreamer's loss: the loss of a young daughter. In many ways, the opening lines betray signs or symptoms of this human loss, yet they never explicitly admit to it. At least ostensibly, the Dreamer laments the loss of a precious pearl. Of course, there are good reasons that may persuade us that the pearl represents a woman (Spearing 1970, 137–40). For one thing, the 'perle', or as

the *Gawain*-poet calls it elsewhere, the 'margyrye' (99, 206, 1037), conjures up a long tradition of texts—mostly love-lyrics—which exploit the
many meanings of 'margarita': pearl, daisy, but of course also the
woman's name 'Margareth'. Equally suggestive are the narrator's
description of her 'smoþe sydeȝ' and his choice of the pronoun 'her'.
Finally there is the Dreamer's emotional despair, the pain, which, as he
puts it, he suffers because of 'luf-daungere'. The phrase evokes the
despair of the lover in the *Roman de la Rose*, whose efforts to approach
his beloved Rose are frustrated by the allegorical character 'Daunger',
who represents the Lady's stand-offishness (Barron 1965).

It is important to recognize, however, that the narrator's use of the
conventions of love-lyric and romance is as misleading as his talk of a
lost jewel. There is, after all, as fundamental a difference between a lost
pearl and a lost person as there is between the absent or stand-offish lady
of medieval love-poetry and a dead one. Taken singly, both tropes
throw a veil over the death that has taken place. The 'pearl' metaphors
admit to the loss, but deny that the lost object is human; the rhetoric of
courtly love admits that the despair is over a lady, but denies she has
been lost forever. It is only when we see the two tropes as partial admis-
sions, and put one and one together, that something like the truth begins
to emerge.

In these stanzas and in the prologue as a whole, the *Gawain*-poet
leaves it to his audience to piece together a picture of the traumatic
event that has taken place. Why? Obviously, because he wanted *us* to
discover it. Yet I would also suggest that the reason why we must rely
on our own resources in sorting out what has happened is that the
Dreamer refuses to confront it openly. His evasiveness hides from us that
his daughter has died, because he is hiding it from himself. In the
laments of this man, who haunts the grave of a loved one, lingers a hope
that she is in fact not dead at all. It is not that he denies her absence, for
this is a reality that cannot be denied. What he disavows is rather the
finality of her absence. Thus he imagines it as the spatial separation of
the lover and his lady in romance, or as the loss of a pearl, which may be
found again, if he looks for it:

> Syþen in þat spote hit fro me sprange,
> *Ofte haf I wayted*, wyschande þat wele,
> Þat wont watȝ whyle deuoyde my wrange
> And heuen my happe and al my hele.

The search, as we know, is in vain, but 'In Auguste in a hyȝ sesoun' (39) the Dreamer returns to the spot where his Pearl was lost, and where, it sometimes seems, he still believes the Pearl to dwell:

> Þer *wonys* þat worþyly, I wot and wene,
> My precious perle wythouten spot.
>
> (47–8)

But while the Dreamer takes comfort in metaphors and tropes which prolong her existence in his mind (Aers 1993), the reader is placed in the uncomfortable position of knowing she will not return. We become the bearers of the tidings which the Dreamer finds too painful to hear, implicated in the tension which the poet produces by pitting the past happiness to which the Dreamer clings against the realities of the present. The tension disturbs both the Dreamer and the reader. In the Dreamer it produces the wish to deny the present, in us the wish that the Dreamer may let the past go.

In the Dreamer's vision of heaven, the past is at least for a short moment left behind when the stunning vistas around him distract his mind:

> The dubbement dere of doun and daleȝ,
> Of wod and water and wlonk playneȝ,
> Bylde in my blys, abated my baleȝ,
> Fordidden my stresse, dystryed my payneȝ.
>
> (121–4)

(The priceless adornments of the downs and dales, of the wood, the waters, and the lovely meadows fostered happiness in me, quietened my grief, removed my anguish, and took away my pain.)

Yet, if forgotten by the Dreamer, these lines keep his 'stresse' and his 'payne' alive in the mind of the audience.

The precariousness of his joy becomes all too apparent when the sight of a maiden across the river reminds the Dreamer of the Pearl he has lost:

> I knew hyr wel, I hade sen hyr ere.
> As glysnande golde þat man con schere,
> So schon þat schene an-vnder schore.
> On lenghe I loked to hyr þere;
> Þe lenger, I knew hyr more and more.
>
> The more I frayste hyr fayre face,
> Her fygure fyn quen I had fonte,
> Such gladande glory con to me glace

As lyttel byfore þerto watȝ wonte.
To calle hyr lyste con me enchace,
Bot baysment gef myn hert a brunt.
I seȝ hyr in so strange a place.
Such a burre myȝt make myn herte blunt.

(164–74)

(I knew her well, I had seen her before. Like glistening gold cut by men, so beautifully shone she on the bank. For a long time I looked at her; the longer I did, the surer I felt I knew her.

I looked harder at her fair face, and having perceived her fine figure, bliss glided towards me, as in the past it had done only rarely. Joy prompted me to call out to her, but a shock dealt my heart a blow. I saw her in such a strange place. It was a blow that could stun my heart.)

The passage is extraordinarily reticent about what the Dreamer thinks after he has been struck by the maiden's likeness. Joy and pain take hold of him in rapid succession, but they seem so overwhelming that rational control is helpless against them. Feelings are personified, as if they had the power to think and to act in the Dreamer's place. What semi-conscious thoughts may be flitting through the Dreamer's mind can only be inferred from his fluctuating emotions. First there is 'gladande glory', the joy of having found his daughter alive and well, which makes him want to call out to her. But the surge of hope is dashed by doubt. If, as the Dreamer senses, he is in heaven, does not this mean that she is dead after all? As the implications of her presence in 'so strange a place' hit home, joy suddenly gives way to a sharp feeling of pain: 'Bot baysment gef myn hert a brunt'. The pangs of pain are in turn succeeded by a third emotion, dread:

More þen me lyste my dred aros.
I stod ful stylle and dorste not calle;
Wyth yȝen open and mouth ful clos
I stod as hende as hawk in halle.

(181–4)

(Against my will my fears arose. I stood still, and dared not call; with open eyes and mouth closed, I stood, frozen like a hawk in a court.)

Having first taken her to be alive, then dead, the Dreamer ends up para-lysed by fear. Unable to settle either for the certainty of her survival, or for the certainty of her death, he remains suspended in between. The feeling of 'dred' captures this feeling of uncertainty with great precision. Having swung from joy to pain, his emotions, as ever beyond his control, come to rest at a mid-point: in hope and fear. As in the garden, the knowledge that he may not be reunited with her lies buried under the hope that things may still be as they were before.

This hope is about to be crushed, for the apparently familiar face of the Pearl-maiden masks a disconcerting transformation that has taken place in her. We expect a great deal from scenes of recognition in literature (Cave 1988), but this reunion is deliberately disappointing. For it soon transpires that the Pearl-maiden has not only moved to a 'strange place', but has become strange herself. This, of course, is what Christian teaching tells us. People in heaven will no longer be as we knew them on earth. They live in perpetual bliss, unburdened by the miseries that afflict human beings on earth, and no longer conscious of past suffering. Towards the end of his universal history, the twelfth-century writer Otto of Freising gave a useful summary of the 'facts' about the afterlife, among which he included the following:

> Sicut ergo sancti habebunt omnium, quae delectare possunt, plenam memoriam, sic nichil, quod officere possit, eorum tanget conscientiam, ut plene habeant, unde redemptori suo gratias agant, et nichil recolant, unde leso corde de priorum recordatione doleant ...
>
> (Otto of Freising, *Chronica*, VIII, xxviii)[13]

> (Just as all the saints will have full memory of all that is pleasurable, so nothing harmful can touch their consciousness. Thus, they possess in fullness all the things for which they thank their redeemer, and have, when they think of the past, no memory of things that could cause them grief.)

Once in heaven, memory becomes selective, conscious only of pleasure and not of harm.

It is so customary for medieval writers to regard this 'brainwashing' of the dead as a great blessing that it may not have occurred to us, before reading *Pearl*, how awful their altered consciousness can be. The moment that this becomes clear to the Dreamer is when he first exchanges words with the maiden he has missed so much. Seeing her happiness, he is upset by the fact that the pain of separation is not mutual. But the Pearl-maiden has yet another surprise in store for him, for she replies to his cry for commiseration without a trace of sympathy, as if he were a perfect stranger:

'O perle,' quod I, 'in perleȝ pyȝt,
Art þou my perle þat I haf playned,

13. Ed. Walter Lammers (Darmstadt: Wissenschaftliche Buchgesellschaft, 1961).

Regretted by myn one on ny3te?
Much longeyng haf I for þe layned,
Syþen into gresse þou me agly3te.
Pensyf, payred, I am forpayned,
And þou in a lyf of lykyng ly3te,
In Paradys erþe, of stryf vnstrayned.
What wyrde hat3 hyder my iuel vayned,
And don me in þys del and gret daunger?
Fro we in twynne wern towed and twayned,
I haf ben a ioyle3 iuelere.'

That iuel þenne in gemme3 gente
Vered vp her vyse wyth y3en graye,
Set on hyr coroun of perle orient,
And soberly after þenne con ho say:
'Sir, 3e haf your tale mysetente,
To say your perle is al awaye,
Þat is in cofer so comly clente
As in þys gardyn gracios gaye,
Hereinne to lenge for euer and play,
Þer mys nee mornyng com neuer nere.
Her were a forser for þe, in faye,
If þou were a gentyl iueler.'

(241–64)

('O Pearl', I said, 'adorned with pearls, are you my pearl, which I have
mourned and grieved for, all alone at night? I have hidden away my longing
for you, since you slipped away from me in the grass. I am sorrowful,
dejected, and suffering, and you lead an easy life in paradise, untouched by
grief. What fate has taken my jewel here, and left me in misery and despair?
Ever since we were severed and divided in two, I have been a joyless jeweller.'

   That gentle jewel with gems adorned, lifted up her face and her grey eyes,
put on her crown of oriental pearls, and said gravely in response: 'Sir, you do
not know what you are saying when you claim your pearl is gone, when it is
beautifully enclosed in the casket of this splendid garden, to dwell there for
ever and to play, where misery and mourning never come near. Here would
be a casket for you, in faith, if you were a noble jeweller.')

What is striking about the Dreamer's first words to the Pearl-maiden is
that, so far from consoling him, the Pearl-maiden's joyful afterlife in
heaven only adds to the grief he feels. That 'ther ys joy in hevene' he
can see for himself. But what good will do that do him, if heaven does
not include him?

Even to a sympathetic reader, such as A.C. Spearing, the Dreamer's dissatisfaction with the joy in heaven appears thoroughly misguided:

> Along with the genuineness of his suffering, which arouses our compassion, this last question, coming from a Christian, is almost ridiculously inept. What else could he have expected to find?
>
> (Spearing 1970, 150)

The Pearl-maiden, too, responds to the Dreamer in this way when she rebukes him for having 'mysetente' his 'tale'. But she pursues her case more rigorously than Spearing when she refutes the Dreamer's despondent 'tale' by denying the reality of the loss he has incurred. She is not 'al awaye', but lives on in the gracious gardens of heaven. Her rigour shows up a problem in Spearing's argument. One cannot at the same time dismiss the Dreamer's disillusionment with heaven as inept, and also accept the 'genuineness' of his suffering. As the Pearl-maiden argues, the reason why heaven should work for him is that it demonstrates that his loss is *not genuine*. In her opinion, the Dreamer has absolutely nothing to mourn for.

As we have seen her do so often, the Pearl-maiden only 'answers' the question of loss and mourning by pointing out that they are the wrong questions to ask. As the early Church Father Ambrose had said long before her, for Christians who believe in an afterlife these are problems that need not arise:

> Intersit inter Christi servulos, idolorumque cultores; ut illi fleant suos, quos in perpetuum existimant interiisse: illi nullas habeant lacrymarum ferias, nullam tristitiae requiem consequantur, qui nullam putant requiem mortuorum. Nobis vero quibus mors non naturae, sed vitae istius finis est; quoniam in melius ipsa natura reparatur, fletus omnes casus mortis abstergat.
>
> (Ambrose, *De excessu fratris sui Satyri*, I)[14]

> (Let there be a difference between Christians and idol-worshippers. Let the latter mourn the dead, whom they believe to have disappeared forever. Let them have no rest from crying, no peace from sorrow, who believe there is no resting place for the dead. But for us death is not the end of our nature, but only of this present life. And because our nature is renewed in a better form, the coming death should not cause us tears.)

But the dreamer finds no consolation in the eternal happiness of the daughter he has lost. True, heaven may have all the right answers for her, but he mourns not for her, but for himself. And for his experience

---

14. *PL* 16, 1312.

of loss, heaven offers no solutions, other than assuring him that his loss does not actually exist. If from the maiden's point of view, the Dreamer's disconsolateness is ridiculously inept, from the Dreamer's perspective it is the maiden's consolation that is at a tangent. True, the blessed in heaven cannot be expected to share our concerns. As we have seen, they were believed to know no sorrow, and to have no sad memories. But only a few poets went as far as to suggest that this might leave them totally insensitive to human beings who do.

Dante, whose *Divina Commedia* the *Gawain*-poet had probably read, was one of these few.[15] In a scene in the *Purgatorio*, whose disturbing power the *Gawain*-poet seems to have felt, Dante suddenly finds himself abandoned by the man who has so far guided him through the otherworld: Virgil. Still in tears, Dante recognizes, on the other side of the river, the familiar face of Beatrice, the girl he loved. It is a reunion that Dante has been longing for throughout the *Divina Commedia*. But instead of a welcome or some words of consolation, Beatrice scolds him for crying about Virgil's disappearance, concluding her well-placed rebukes with the curiously unhelpful remark that there is no grief in heaven:

> 'Guardaci ben! Ben son, ben son Beatrice.
> Come degnasti d'accedere al monte?
> non sapei tu che qui è l'uom felice?'
> <div align="right">(<i>Purgatorio</i> XXX, 73–5)[16]</div>

> ('Look at me well; I am indeed Beatrice. How dare you approach the mountain? Did you not know that here man is happy?')

As Steven Prickett has argued in his fine discussion of this scene, there is a doctrinal necessity in the disillusionment which Dante is made to feel. Heaven simply does not pander to the emotional needs and expectations of human beings. Yet our knowledge that this is so does not make the harshness with which it is experienced at a personal level any more tolerable (Prickett 1986).

Pearl creates precisely this tension between doctrine and experience, and I suspect that the *Gawain*-poet had Dante's *Purgatorio* in mind when he had the Pearl-maiden say to the doleful Dreamer that there is no place in heaven for sorrow: 'þer mys nee mornyng com neuer nere'. As

---

15. On the influence of Dante on *Pearl*, see Kean (1967, 120–32); Payne (1989, 27–58), and Shoaf (1990).
16. *The Divina Commedia*, ed. and trans. Charles S. Singleton, Bollingen Series (Princeton: Princeton University Press, 1973).

in Beatrice's rebuke to Dante, the Pearl-maiden's comment is all the worse for ignoring the Dreamer's grief altogether. This disregard, to be fair on the Pearl-maiden, is not deliberate. The Pearl-maiden *cannot* address the grief he feels for his loss, both because her nature excludes her from experiencing grief herself, and, more importantly, because, from her perspective, this 'loss' does not exist.

The Dreamer is acutely aware that the Pearl-maiden takes no notice of his suffering. Yet, feeling his loss to be real enough, he cannot pretend it does not exist. If the Pearl-maiden is unmindful of it, it falls to him to remind her:

> 'Rebuke me neuer wyth worde3 felle,
> Þa3 I forloyne, my dere endorde,
> Bot kyþe3 me kyndely your coumfourde,
> Pytosly þenkande vpon þysse:
> Of care and me 3e made acorde,
> Þat ere wat3 grounde of alle my blysse.'
> (367–72)

('Don't rebuke me with cruel words, even if I err, my love, but show me your kind comfort, and think mercifully on this: you who used to be the ground of all my bliss acquainted me with sorrow.')

> 'In blysse I se þe blyþely blent,
> And I a man al mornyf mate;
> 3e take þeron ful lyttel tente,
> Þa3 I hente ofte harme3 hate.'
> (385–9)

('I see you joyously placed in bliss, and I a man mournful and sad. You do not take much notice of this, though I often suffer burning pain.')

The repeated exhibition he makes of his own sorrow has struck many critics as rather indulgent, but it is important to remind ourselves of the circumstances that prompt the Dreamer to talk repeatedly about his loss. As we have seen, the Pearl-maiden does not and cannot recognize his grief, and it follows that the only one who can take pity on it, and prove it exists, is the Dreamer himself. Nor is the Dreamer's pity only self-centred. When, in his vision of the City of Jerusalem, he sees Christ, the Lamb, bleeding from his wounds, his reaction is characteristically humane:

> Bot a wounde ful wyde and weete con wyse
> Anende hys hert, þur3 hyde torente.

Of hys quyte syde his blod outsprent.
Alas, þoȝt I, who did þat spyt?
Ani brest for bale aȝt haf forbrent
Er he þerto hade had delyt.

(1135–40)

(But a wide and wet wound was visible close to his heart, through his torn skin. From his white side the blood spurted out. Alas, I thought, who did that awful thing? Any heart should have been consumed with sorrow rather than take delight in it.)

Instinctively, this response to the bleeding Lamb seems appropriate. As a late-medieval English poem on Christ's passion puts it, it would be unkind not to feel sorry for the suffering Christ:

Quan mannes soule hat in mynde
Þe blod þat cryst let for mankynde
With teres & woundis smerte,
Man, *fynde þou non unkyndnesse*
Quan þe wey of swetnesse
Wyl entryn in-to þin herte:
Sey, 'a, ihesu, quat hast þou gylt.'
('An ABC on the Passion of Christ', 201–7)[17]

(When man's soul remembers the blood that Christ shed for mankind with tears and hurtful wounds, man do not be unkind when the way of sweetness wants to enter into your heart; say: 'Ah, Jesus, how did you deserve this?')

And yet, strangely enough, Christ and his company show precisely this 'unkyndnesse'. Despite his gaping wounds, Christ and his company show only delight:

The Lombe delyt non lyste to wene.
Þaȝ he were hurt and wounde hade,
In his sembelaunte watȝ neuer sene,
So wern his glenteȝ gloryous glade.

(1141–44)

(No one could doubt the Lamb's delight. Even though he was wounded and hurt, it did not show in his appearance, so gloriously happy did he look.)

As if there were no occasion for the compassion which the spectacle arouses in the Dreamer, the bleeding Lamb and the Pearl-maiden make

17. Ed. F.J. Furnivall, *Political, Religious and Love-Poems*, EETS OS 15 (London: Trübner, 1866).

'much of mirþe' (1149). The pity which the Dreamer takes on himself thus appears as misplaced as the pity he feels for the Lamb (Bogdanos 1983, 138–40).

These revelations confound the Dreamer *and* the reader, challenging our cherished assumptions that sympathy for suffering and sorrow over death cannot be anything other than laudable. Yet these are the very assumptions that the Pearl-maiden questions when she upbraids the Dreamer as follows:

> 'Þou blameʒ þe bote of þy meschef,
> Þou art no *kynde* jueler.'
>
> (275–6)

'You blame the remedy for your misfortune. You are no kind jeweller.')

The temptation for the reader is to side without further ado with the Pearl-maiden against the Dreamer. But as much as we might like to grant the maiden her point, we can only do so by changing our basic understanding of what 'kindness' in our language means. Is it not 'kind' —the word meant both 'kind' and 'natural' in Middle English—for a human being to be distressed by the loss of a loved one? Is what is natural for us and the Dreamer really unnatural? This is not a question which the *Gawain*-poet asks us to settle in favour of either the Dreamer or the Pearl-maiden. There is no position from which we could measure the truth of the two views objectively, for the simple reason that what the Dreamer and the Pearl-maiden find natural depends entirely on their nature. The question only throws into relief the maiden's otherness, a difference not of rank or place, as the Dreamer likes to believe, but a difference of *kind*. Hence also the futility of the Dreamer's poignant appeals to the maiden's humanity:

> 'Rebuke me neuer wyth wordeʒ felle,
> Þaʒ I forloyne, my dere endorde,
> Bot kyþeʒ me *kyndely* your coumfourde … '
>
> (367–9)

Given her difference in nature, her 'kindness' cannot but manifest itself to the Dreamer as 'unkindness': she can only be kind after her fashion.

III

As I have suggested, the dialogue between the Dreamer and the Pearl-maiden is most poignant when our consciousness of the rift between the

Dreamer and the Pearl-maiden collides with the Dreamer's refusal to accept the finality of his loss. This is what happens when, after the Pearl-maiden has called him an unkind jeweller, he confesses himself greatly cheered by her words and her survival:

> 'Iwysse', quod I, 'my blysfol beste,
> My gret dystresse þou al todrawe3.
> To be excused I make requeste;
> I trawed my perle don out of dawe3.
> Now haf I fonde hyt, I schal ma feste,
> And wony wyth hyt in schyr wod-schawe3,
> And loue my Lorde and al his lawe3
> Þat hat3 me bro3t þys blys ner.
> Now were I at yow by3onde þise wawe3,
> I were a ioyful jueler.'
>
> (279–88)

('Indeed', I said, 'my dearest, you take away my great sorrow. Please excuse me; I thought my pearl had died. Now that I have found it, I will be happy, and live with it in these bright groves, and love my Lord and all his laws, since he brought me so close to this bliss. If I were now with you beyond these waves, I would be a joyful jeweller.')

In the Dreamer's mind, heaven only confirms his lingering hopes that the Pearl was not lost definitively. As he says to the Pearl-maiden, he has found her again, and will now live with her in joy: '*Now haf I fonde hyt*, I schal ma feste, And *wony* wyth hyt in schyr wod-schawe3 ...'. What these lines highlight is not only that the Dreamer continues to cling to false hopes, but that these hopes feed on the same metaphors that he had earlier used to describe his daughter's death:

> Alas! I *leste* hyr in on erbere ...
>
> (9)

> Þer *wonys* þat worþyly, I wot and wene ...
>
> (47)

We still prefer to euphemize death, to speak of it as 'loss', or of 'rest', but the fiction of survival implicit in euphemisms for death is taken literally by the Dreamer. Another example of the way the Dreamer takes shelter in the ambiguity of language involves the euphemism of death as a 'separation':

> 'And, quen we departed, we wern at on;
> God forbede we be now wroþe,

We meten so selden by stok oþer ston.'
(378–80)

('And, when we separated we were as one. God forbid that we be angry now, we meet so rarely around the place.')

As in the prologue, where he troped death as the absence of the lover—'I dewyne, fordolked of luf-daungere' (11)—the euphemism of death as a 'departure' allows the Dreamer to maintain the illusion that they can continue to meet up once in a while in future, 'by stok oþer stone'. That stock phrase of Middle English poetry is here used to great effect: it captures the Dreamer's attempt to spread a web of everyday words on this strange encounter, to convince himself that this vison of his daughter in heaven is no different from meeting her 'around the place' on earth. Euphemisms do not console the Dreamer; they enable him to inhabit the fantasy that his daughter never died.

Clearly, he deludes himself when he thinks he can be reunited with the Pearl-maiden. Between the inhabitants of heaven and the people on earth lies, as we have seen, a world of difference. But while we know that the Dreamer is foolish to deny this, the enormity of his self-deception is itself a measure of the undiminished strength of his attachment to the daughter he lost. Accepting heaven's inaccessibility would be to let her and the past go. And so the Dreamer wages a fruitless battle against our knowledge that it cannot be otherwise by insisting we are wrong.

At moments such as these in *Pearl*, when compassion for the Dreamer might well lead us to wish we were wrong about the finality of death as well, we understand why it is a fact that the Dreamer denies. Unfortunately, however, we know that we are right, and that the Dreamer cannot escape the truth by forcing it into the mould of his wishes.

PATIENCE AND PROTEST IN THE EPILOGUE

The Dreamer, too, finally faces the conflict between the way things must be and the way he would like them to be. No words will persuade him of how foreign and inaccessible the territory of the Pearl-maiden is. The maiden then guides him to the Heavenly Jerusalem, which he is allowed to see from beyond the river that he may not cross. In Dante's *Divina Commedia*, the vision of the heavenly city is, at least for Dante himself, the climax of his journey. For a brief moment, his imagination leaps over the divide between the world of mortals and the celestial world, and achieves the ineffable union with the divine. Inevitably, Dante must here desert his audience, for this achievement lies beyond the limits of thought and representation, beyond memory and words. To become one with the otherness of heaven, Dante has to be 'unkind' to his readers, who must stay behind while Dante's mind soars up to God.[18]

In contrast, the *Gawain*-poet and his persona in the dream remain true to their nature. The *Gawain*-poet's determination never to leave his audience behind is nowhere more apparent than in the Dreamer's vision of the heavenly Jerusalem and the Lamb of God. At what for Dante and many medieval mystics was to be the culmination of their visionary experience, the Dreamer only sees, as the key words of section seventeen continually remind us, what John saw in his 'Apocallypse', his Book of Revelation (Nolan 1977, 157). It is no exaggeration to say that this section of *Pearl* is largely a string of quotations from this biblical text. By the end of it, we know no more about the City of God than what we could have read for ourselves in the Bible. Perhaps this is a disappointment, but it is indicative of the modesty of a poet who did not presume he could see any further than his audience.

Ever hopeful that he can join his daughter in heaven, the Dreamer again falls victim to his kindness. Seeing the Pearl-maiden amidst her fellows in heaven, he makes ready to plunge into the river that separates him from her:

> Delyt me drof in yʒe and ere,
> My maneʒ mynde to maddyng malte;
> Quen I seʒ my frely, I wolde be þere,
> Byʒonde þe water þaʒ ho were walte.
> I þoʒt þat noþyng myʒt me dere
> To fech me bur and take me halte,
> And to start in þe strem schulde non me stere,

---

18. Dante's abandonment of the reader is implicit in his famous address to the reader:

> Or ti riman, lettor, sovra 'l tuo banco,
> Dietro pensando a ciò che si preliba,
> S'esser vuoi lieto assai prima che stanco. (*Paradiso* X, 22–5)
> (Now remain, reader, upon your bench, reflecting on this of which you have a foretaste, if you would be glad far sooner than weary.)

This is the first time in the *Divina Commedia* that the reader is located in space (on the bench) and imagined bodily. As Leo Spitzer observed: 'Here Dante truly has "created his reader"—in the moment in which he must leave him behind' (Spitzer 1988, 190).

To swymme þe remnaunt, þaȝ I þer swalte.
Bot of þat munt I watȝ bitalt:
When I schulde start in þe strem astraye,
Out of þat caste I watȝ bycalt:
Hit watȝ not at my Prynces paye.

Hit payed hym not þat I so flonc
Ouer meruelous mereȝ, so mad arayde.
Of raas þaȝ I were rasch and ronk,
Ȝet raþely þerinne I watȝ restayed.

(1153–69)

(Delight assailed my eyes and ears, and my human mind gave way in frenzy; when I saw my fair one, I wished to be there, even though the water kept her from me. I thought nothing could harm me, by fetching me a blow or by making me stop, and that no one could prevent me from jumping in the stream, and from swimming the rest, even if I should die. But I was shaken from my plan: when I wanted to rush astray in the stream, I was summoned to abandon this purpose: it was not to my Prince's liking. It did not please him that I should leap across these strange waters, in a state of madness. Though in my haste I was rash and impetuous, I was promptly checked in the attempt.)

At this point the Dreamer wakes up, cast out from heaven at the moment he prepares himself to make a run for it. Yet again the Dreamer comes up against a barrier he cannot cross. His final attempt costs him his vision.

As the Dreamer's rude awakening approaches, the *Gawain*-poet already detaches us from the dream world. We no longer perceive events through the eyes of the Dreamer but through the perspective of someone who looks back on it, and who has learnt the lesson about the otherness of heaven and the irrevocability of his loss. His reflections on the foolishness of the Dreamer's attempt to cross the river reveal that the dream is, after all, an event that occurred in the past. It is a tribute to the poet's capacity to absorb us in the dream that, until the final section, we forget that the centre of consciousness in *Pearl* is not the Dreamer, but the narrator to whose recollection we have been listening all along (Russell 1988, 127). In the course of the Dream, the reader also falls asleep, taking the world of the vision to be the only reality, until, in these stanzas, we wake up to the voice of the narrator who tells us about a dream he once had. Recognizing that the maiden cannot be retrieved from heaven, he takes on his own shoulders the burden of truth which the Dreamer's self-delusion had for so long forced the reader to carry.

We are no longer embroiled in the conflict between the way things must be and the wish that they may be different. It is not that the conflict disappears, but the narrator has come to fight it within himself.

His words 'Hit watȝ not at my Prynces paye' show his awareness of the necessity that opposes his will. He also knows it is futile to fight it. Nothing expresses this futility better than the way the many subjunctives that convey the Dreamer's will are answered by a brief clause in the passive voice. The Dreamer would like to reach the other shore, thinks that nothing might prevent him from doing so, would like to jump in the stream, but, without ever materializing into action, the subjunctives founder on a curt passive:

> Bot of þat munt I watȝ bitalt ...

> Out of þat caste I watȝ bycalt ...

> Ȝet raþely þerinne I watȝ restayed ...

The use of grammar makes the narrator's point perfectly. *Homo proponit, Deus disponit.* It is for human beings to wish, but for God to act. The only way people can act at all is by conforming to his will. Their resistance can make no difference to what happens. It will only turn them into subjects in a passive clause: not in control of events, but at their mercy.

This, we remember, is what Jonah in *Patience* discovers as well. Having set his will against God's omnipotence, he is reduced to a puppet, and forced to become an instrument of the divine will despite himself. Like his counterpart in *Patience*, the narrator in *Pearl* sees no alternative but to suffer patiently, rather than making things worse by trying to resist the irresistible. *Pearl* closes, therefore, with a narrator determined to let the past go, and to substitute the vain hope of finding his Pearl again for the hope of obtaining the pearl which the maiden had said mattered most. This pearl, for which the merchant of Matthew 13: 45–6 sold all his possessions, is the kingdom of heaven.

The epilogue, it should be said, does not represent a narrator who has submitted to God's will, but one who is struggling to do so (Sklute 1973):

> Þen wakned I in þat erber wlonk;
> My hede vpon þat hylle watȝ layde
> Þer as my perle to grounde strayd.
> I raxled, and fel in gret affray,
> And sykyng, to myself I sayd,
> 'Now al be to þat prynces paye.'

Me payed ful ille to be outfleme
So sodenly of þat fayre regioun,
A longeyng heuy me strok in swone,
And rewfully þenne I con to reme:
'O perle', quod I, 'of rych renoun,
So watȝ hit me dere þat þou con deme
In þys veray avysyoun!
If hit be ueray and soth sermoun
Þat þou so stykeȝ in garlande gay,
So wel is me in þys doel-doungoun
Þat þou art to þat Prynseȝ paye.'

(1171–88)

(Then I woke up in that lovely garden, my head lying on the hill where my pearl had fallen to the ground. I stretched myself and fell into great fear, and sighing I said to myself: 'Now let all be as the prince desires.'

It did not please me at all to be so suddenly cast out from these fair lands. A heavy longing struck me down in a swoon, and sorrowfully I cried out: 'O pearl', I said, 'of great renown, what you said to me in this true vision was so dear to me! If it is true and a fact that you are set in this gay garland, then I am content in this doleful dungeon that you please that prince.')

For modern readers, habituated to thinking of patience and protest as mutually exclusive responses to power, the narrator's resolve to comply with God's 'paye' is easily mistaken for a surrender of his own will. However, accepting the impossibility of resisting God's will and making this will one's own are two very different matters. As the narrator in *Patience* continues to grumble while making a virtue of necessity, so the narrator of *Pearl* does not miss the opportunity to point out that his 'prynces paye' is not his own:

Me payed ful ille to be outfleme
So sodenly of þat fayre regioun …

Moreover, the miserable life to which his banishment from heaven has reduced him still appears distinctly unpalatable to him:

'… If hit be ueray and soth sermoun
Þat þou so stykeȝ in garlande gay,
So wel is me in þys doel-doungoun
Þat þou art to þat Prynseȝ paye.'

True, the narrator says he is happy on earth—as he should be if he were content with his 'Prynces paye'—but can anyone who goes on to liken himself to a prisoner in a 'doel-doungoun' really mean this? The truth is that, for all the narrator's deference to God's will and what this will expects of him, his heart is not in it. If it were, there would be no need to resign himself to it, no need to say to himself: 'Now al be to þat prynces paye'. As Ian Robinson observes: 'What is the point of saying "Thy will be done" unless our will is in conflict?' (Robinson 1982, 232).

Patience might itself be seen as a form of protest, for it presupposes, in the words of the medieval mystic Ramon Lull, a 'dominion' over one's will:

> The Beloved [Christ] asks the Lover if he possesses patience. He answers: 'All things please me, and therefore I do not need patience, for he who has no dominion over his own will cannot be impatient.'
>
> (Book of the Lover and the Beloved, 221)[19]

But unlike the self-effacing mystic, the Dreamer in *Pearl* does need patience, and in summoning it he draws attention to the 'dominion' he has over his will. But, as *Pearl* shows, his wilfulness is a mixed blessing. If it endears him to readers who also have wills of their own, it is at the same time what costs him his vision of heaven, and what makes the loss of his daughter, and the loss of his vision, so difficult to bear. It is a high price to pay, but 'kindness' in *Pearl* does not come cheap.

---

19. Trans. Kenneth Leeds (London: Sheldon Press, 1979).

Chapter 5

Cleanness

INTRODUCTION

Despite the significant differences between *Cleanness* and the works I discussed in the previous chapters, this poem is unmistakably by one and the same author. With *Pearl* it shares most noticeably the image of the immaculate pearl, symbol of purity:

> Perle praysed is prys þer perre is schewed,
> Þaȝ ho not derrest be demed to dele for penies;
> Quat may þe cause be called bot for hir clene hwes,
> Þat wynnes worschyp abof alle whyte stones?

> For ho schynes so schyr þat is of schap rounde,
> Wythouten faut oþer fylþe, ȝif ho fyne were ...   (1117–22)

(The pearl is valued highly where jewels are displayed, even if she is not deemed to have the highest value in pennies. How can this be explained if not by its clean colours, which win honour before all other white stones? For she shines so brightly in her round shape, without blemish or filth—well might she be called fine ...)

Like *Patience*, *Cleanness* draws on Old Testament stories, which the poet brings to life in his characteristic way. Imagining himself to have been an eyewitness of the histories he reports, he describes in close-up the events which the Old Testament leaves shadowy. But, as in his retelling of the Book of Jonah, the details which the *Gawain*-poet gives us in *Cleanness* again rarely distort the overall sense of his Old Testament stories. The difference between the *Gawain*-poet's version and his biblical source is largely one of focus, and the experience of reading his retelling after the original is rather like looking at the same picture through a more power-ful lens. Also familiar from *Patience* (see 123–4) is the paraphrase of Psalm

93.9 in *Cleanness*, included to remind us humans that we are always objects of God's panoptical gaze:

> Bot sauour, mon, in þyself, þaȝ þou a sotte lyuie,
> Þaȝ þou bere þyself babal, byþenk þe sumtyme
> Wheþer he þat stykked vche a stare in vche steppe yȝe,
> Ȝif hymself be bore blynde, hit is a brod wonder ...
>
> (581–4)

> (But ponder in yourself, man, though you live like an idiot, and behave like a fool; consider for once whether it would not be a great miracle if he who put the power of sight into every bright eye were himself born blind ...)

God sees whatever we see, and more; he sees all that our necessary involvement in what we observe disables us from seeing. His perception is not constrained by a position in the field of vision, and, as I shall argue later, this freedom from human limitations confers on God in *Cleanness* a nature entirely unlike ours.

Cleanness, however, differs from all the *Gawain*-poet's other works in structure. It does not tell a single and coherent story, but several stories, which are related at the level of theme rather than that of plot. All are told with the purpose of showing us the disastrous consequences of uncleanness, and the good fortune that attends those who are clean. The composite nature of *Cleanness* is clear from the *Gawain*-poet's own words at the end of his poem, where he sums up his method and moral:

> Þus vpon þrynne weyss I haf yow þro schewed
> Þat vnclannes tocleues in corage dere
> Of þat wynnelych lorde þat wonys in heuen,
> Entyses hym to be tene, telled vp his wrake.
>
> And clannes is his comfort, and coyntyse he louyes,
> And þose þat seme arn and swete schyn se his face.
>
> (1805–10)

> (And so I have shown you in three ways that uncleanness sticks in the noble heart of that gracious lord who lives in heaven, incites him to become angry, and arouses his vengeance.
>
> And cleanness is his comfort, and refinement he loves, and those who are comely and pleasant shall see his face.)

The 'þrynne weyss' presumably refer to the three Old Testament stories which he has recounted. Apart from the short retelling of the Parable of the Wedding Feast (49–164), these Old Testament stories are the poet's main *exempla*.

The three *exempla* may be summarized as follows. The first, based on Genesis 6–10, is the story of the Flood (249–540). As a punishment for the sexual perversions of the antediluvians God resolves to drown all living creatures on the face of the earth. Noah, the only righteous man alive, is ordered to build an ark. When Noah has constructed the ark the Flood strikes, sparing only the animals and human beings in Noah's ark.

The second *exemplum*, a paraphrase of Genesis 18–19, is a longer and more complex narrative (601–1056). It begins with Abraham's reception of three visitors in his house in Mamre. They announce to Abraham God's intention to wipe out the sinful cities of Sodom and Gomorrah, upon which Abraham bargains with God in an attempt to save the city-dwellers. The story then shifts focus to Lot and his wife who live on the outskirts of Sodom and give hospitality to two angels. In the evening their house is surrounded by foul-mouthed Sodomites who demand that the two angels be handed over so that they can have intercourse with them. Lot is rescued from his plight by the angels, who strike the Sodomites with blindness. In the early morning they order Lot and his relatives to flee from their homes, since the destruction of the city is at hand. In full flight, Lot's wife looks back, despite the angels' strict injunction not to. She had been disobedient before when she served the angels salted food, and is therefore changed into a pillar of salt.

The third *exemplum* focuses on Belshazzar's feast and God's punishment of his presumption (1157–1804). It suggests the poet's deep familiarity with the Old Testament, as it is pieced together from relevant material in at least three different Old Testament books: the Book of Daniel 4–5, from which the *Gawain*-poet took the central episodes of Belshazzar's ostentatious feast, his desecration of the sacred vessels, and the metamorphosis of his father Nebuchadnezzar into a beast; and II Chronicles 36 and Jeremiah 52, which the poet used to place these episodes in the broad historical context of the Babylonian captivity. The resulting story is on an ambitiously grand scale. It opens with the destruction of Jerusalem by Nebuchadnezzar and the commander of his forces, Nebuzarredan. The downfall of Jerusalem is God's punishment for the wickedness of the city's ruler, Zedekiah, and his subjects, who have lapsed in their faith and have taken to worshipping idols. The Jews who survive the massacre are enslaved or imprisoned in Babylon, and their sacred vessels are brought as spoils to Nebuchadnezzar who, out of respect for their holiness, stores them in his treasure-house. Nebuchadnezzar's son, Belshazzar, lays on a lavish feast and, carried away by the occasion, orders the holy vessels to be brought in, so that they may serve as cups for his guests and concubines. Suddenly, a hand appears that scratches three words on the wall. Only Daniel, Belshazzar's prisoner, is able to decode the message. As Daniel explains, Belshazzar has forgotten God. His father, Nebuchadnezzar, had at one point been equally foolish, and was promptly exiled from his empire and turned into a beast. Belshazzar ought to have learnt the lesson that God taught his father. Now he, too, will be punished for his pride, and his empire will pass to the Persians. That night, after the feast has ended, Daniel's prophecy comes true. Darius's army invades the city of Babylon and Belshazzar is slain by enemy soldiers.

As the summary suggests, the *exempla* are quite different in content, and if all three are about God's hatred of uncleanness, as the *Gawain*-poet writes in his conclusion to *Cleanness*, then it is clear that uncleanness for him encompasses many different things: 'unnatural' sexual behaviour in the case of Adam's descendants and the Sodomites, salting the food of angelic visitors in the case of Lot's wife and, to name only a few other 'unclean' acts from the final *exemplum*, pride, idolatry, and the profanation of sacred objects.

The list does not end here, for interspersed with the *exempla* is a variety of homiletic material which applies cleanness and uncleanness to a range of other activities. Priests who appear before God's altar and handle the eucharist must be pure; we should be clean when we enter heaven, lest we be thrown out like the guest who turns up in filthy rags in the Parable of the Wedding Feast; like Christ who hates dirt and breaks bread 'cleanly' into two pieces, we should avoid defilement, and should double our efforts to remain pure once we have 'cleansed' ourselves in confession.

Clearly, the poet's exemplary materials are heterogeneous, but knowing the *Gawain*-poet's ability to produce tightly structured works such as *Pearl* or *Sir Gawain*, we must assume that he wanted it this way. And it is perhaps not that difficult to understand why, when we realize that the disparateness of the *exempla* allowed the poet to build up a far wider range of meanings for cleanness and uncleanness than we find in works by his contemporaries. The handbooks for preachers, a reliable guide to the associations that vices and virtues would have triggered in the minds of laymen and clerics, typically define cleanness simply as virginity or chastity.[1] In *Cleanness*, too, this association is present—witness the poet's description of Mary's Virgin Birth:

---

1. See, for example, the preacher's handbook by the fourteenth-century Dominican John of Bromyard, the *Summa praedicantium* (Nuremberg, 1518), which defines cleanness (*munditia*) as '*virginitas vel castitas*' (cap. 232), and the anonymous *Tabula exemplorum*, which glosses cleanness as '*castitas interior et pudicitia exterior*': ed. J.T. Welther (Paris: Guitard, 1926), 70.

When venkkyst watȝ no vergynyte, ne vyolence maked,
Bot moch clener watȝ hir corse God kynned þerinne.
(1071–2)

(When no virginity was vanquished, and no violation was done, but her
body was all the cleaner for God being conceived in it.)

But virginity is only one of many meanings gathered up in the *Gawain*-
poet's use of the word *clannes*. On a more mundane level, cleanness
refers, for example, to the state of our clothes, as when the poet insists
that our 'wedeȝ ben clene' (165), or to standards of personal hygiene,
which brook no 'handeȝ vnwashen' (34).

Taking on different shades of meaning from each of the contexts in
which cleanness and uncleanness are put to use, the words become
entangled in an increasingly dense web of associations. They accumulate
meaning, and the growing complexity and length of the three main
exempla are a reflection of the ever-expanding semantic field which
cleanness and uncleanness come to occupy. From the 289 lines covering
the Flood, we move to the 455-line story of Sodom and Gomorrah,
which is followed in its turn by 649 lines about Belshazzar's desecration
of the vessels and the historical events leading up to it. Moreover, while
in all these stories the consequences of uncleanness affect human beings
in their thousands, the extinction of unnamed multitudes provides the
background or the possible future against which a steadily increasing cast
of individual characters must make their choices for clean or unclean
behaviour—each in his or her own unique circumstances. In the *exemplum* of the Flood, only Noah emerges from anonymity. The second
exemplum begins in Mamre in Abraham and Sarah's house, then branches
off to focus on Lot and his family, and returns finally to Abraham, who
from his home surveys the dust and ashes to which the cities of Sodom
and Gomorrah and its inhabitants have been reduced. The third *exemplum* jumps from Zedekiah in Jerusalem to Belshazzar in his palace in
Babylon; it then takes us back in time to his father Nebuchadnezzar, and
finally returns to Belshazzar's death and the capture of the city. As more
and more meanings crystallize around the concepts of purity and impurity, the narratives designed to exemplify these concepts similarly become
increasingly long. And the greater the ramifications of cleanness and
uncleanness and the number of situations on which they bear, the more
the narrative tends to branch out into different directions and plot-lines,
as if the poet were attempting to cast the net of his narrative more and
more widely.

This accretive structure of *Cleanness* is very different from that of *Gawain*. It lacks the tightness and symmetry of the *Gawain*-poet's Arthurian romance, which, like the pentangle on Gawain's shield, is a seamless whole, 'withouten ende at any noke' (*Gawain*, 660). A metaphor that comes closer to describing the structure of *Cleanness* is that of a tree. It may today seem an unlikely poetic emblem, but as a way of conceptualizing the organization of a work, and as a standard by which to measure its success, it was commonplace in the Middle Ages. The theme of a work, as later-medieval arts of preaching and arts of poetry put it, is like the seed or the root of a tree. As the author considers the various divisions of his theme, he may pursue its implications, the branches that spring from this root, and these implications may split off again, like offshoots on a branch (Charland 1936, 113; Kelly 1992, 280–1). The *Gawain*-poet develops the theme of cleanness in just this way. It gathers meaning, grows along the branches of his main *exempla*, which in their turn spread out into smaller narrative strands.

This kind of organization has the disadvantage of leaving many loose ends, but it is clear that what *Cleanness* loses in compression it gains in reach. The effect is not unlike the rhetorical *tour de force* by the Pardoner in the *Canterbury Tales*, whose sermon on avarice seems to digress aimlessly on the vices of gambling, drunkenness, and swearing, until the *exemplum* shows how all these three vices rear their heads after the discovery of a treasure which each of the three rioters intends to keep for himself. Avarice, as the Pardoner had stated at the outset, is the root of all evil. And as all other vices spring from avarice, so the apparently irrelevant excursions turn out to have been merely the ramifications of the Pardoner's theme.

By tying the theme of cleanness to a wide range of different exemplary narratives and different activities, from washing hands to obeying God, the *Gawain*-poet similarly suggests that there is hardly any situation, however trivial, that does not fall within the purview of his theme. Given its span, and the cataclysmic disasters that befall the characters in *Cleanness* who do not practise what the poem preaches, it is a theme which the *Gawain*-poet does not allow his audience to ignore.

UNCLEANNESS AND THE CONFUSION OF KINDS

As I have argued in the previous section, the range of the *Gawain*-poet's exemplary stories is a measure of the reach of his theme. But what explains the elasticity of this theme? What allows cleanness and uncleanness to stretch across so many different situations without coming unstuck at any of the contexts to which the *Gawain*-poet attaches them? To answer this question we must discover the logic that holds the disparate material in *Cleanness* together. I want to begin my exploration of the many meanings of cleanness and uncleanness by considering part of the poet's second *exemplum*—Lot's reception of two angels and his confrontation with the Sodomites—since it is an apparently straightforward illustration of the poet's concluding moral: those who are unclean bring upon themselves God's anger, while those who are clean flourish.

Cleanness and uncleanness would seem here to be first of all a matter of sexual preferences. The homosexual Sodomites perish, while the staunchly heterosexual Lot and his family, with the exception of his disobedient wife, live to tell the tale. The distinction between homosexuals and heterosexuals is definitely one of the many ways in which the opposition between the clean and the unclean may be restated. And there is no doubt that this crude sexual morality seemed entirely unproblematic to the *Gawain*-poet. This much is clear from Lot's curious attempt to reform the Sodomites by offering up his two daughters to their lust. The source for this is Genesis 19: 7–9, which presents Lot's offer as a desperate bid to protect his guests from harm:

> Do not so, I beseech you, my brethren, do not commit this evil. I have two daughters who as yet have not known men. I will bring them out to you and abuse you them as it shall please you, so that you do no evil to these men, because they are come under the shadow of my roof.
>
> But they said: Get thee back thither. And again: Thou comest in, said they, as a stranger, was it to be a judge? Therefore we will afflict thee more than them.

It does not appear from this passage that Lot is particularly concerned with the relative merits of homosexual or heterosexual sex. He thinks, rather, of the duty of a host to protect his guests. This obligation demands terrible sacrifices, from which Lot does not shrink. His sense of duty goes so far that he surrenders his two daughters and his own dignity in an act of public self-humiliation. Lot in Genesis twists and turns, but he is not out to lecture the Sodomites. If they counter by accusing him of being judgemental, it is only to let him know that they have not been taken in by Lot's humility, that his manoeuvres and peace overtures are not going to distract them from their purpose.

The *Gawain*-poet's Lot strikes a very different tone. His humility and the offer of his daughters are no longer a decoy. They are intended to teach the Sodomites a timely lesson about good manners and about the superiority of heterosexual sex:

> Þenne he meled to þo men mesurable wordeȝ,
> For harloteȝ with his hendelayk he hoped to chast:
>
> 'Oo, my frendeȝ so fre: your fare is to strange;
> Dotȝ away your derf dyn, and dereȝ neuer my gestes.
> Avoy! hit is your vylaynye, ȝe vylen yourseluen;
> And ȝe ar iolyf gentylmen, your iapeȝ ar ille.
>
> Bot I schal kenne yow by kynde a crafte þat is better;
> I haf a tresor in my telde of tow my fayre deȝter,
> Þat ar maydeneȝ vnmard for alle men ȝette;
> In Sodamas, þaȝ I hit say, non semloker burdes.
>
> Hit arn ronk, hit arn rype, and redy to manne;
> To samen wyth þo semly þe solace is better;
> I schal biteche yow þo two þat tayt arn and quoynt,
> And laykeȝ wyth hem as yow lyst, and leteȝ my gestes one.'
>
> (859–72)

(Then he addressed these men with courtly words, intending to chasten the rascals with his good manners.

'O, my dear friends, you behaviour is too strange. Let your great clamour be, and do not harm my guests. For shame! It is to your disgrace that you degrade yourselves; if you are worthy gentlemen, your jokes are in bad taste.

But I shall show you a skill that is better and in accordance with nature. I have a treasure in my home, consisting of my two pretty daughters, who are maidens as yet undefiled by any man. In Sodom no better-looking girls can be found, if I say so myself.

They are grown, they are ripe, and ready for men. It will be more fun to sleep with these attractive girls. I will bring you those two who are lively and charming. Play with them as you please, and leave my guests alone.')

While Lot in Genesis tries to appease the Sodomites, Lot in *Cleanness* tries to bring them to their senses by setting an example and by appealing to what better standards of taste they might possess. Sex between a man and a woman is, in Lot's mind, simply better, and the description of his daughters' beauty is intended to convince the Sodomites of this fact. This, for once, is entirely at odds with the biblical passage. It may have been inspired by an early Christian poem which was once attributed to the Church Father Tertullian, *Carmen de Sodoma*, in which Lot is similarly at pains to praise his daughters in an attempt to sell straight sex:

Nunc, si fas iuuenale habet uastare pudorem,
sunt intus natae biiuges mihi, nubilis aetas;
uirginitas in flore tumet: iam dedita messi
digna cupida uiris: tulerit quam uestra uoluptas.
(Carmen de Sodoma, 51–4)[2]

(Now, if you young men think it is right to waste your modesty, I have in
my house two daughters of marriageable age. Their virginity has burst forth
into bloom; they are ready for the harvest. They are worthy of the desire of
men; let your passion pluck them.)

There is plenty of evidence to suggest that biblical commentators found
Lot's offer of his two daughters extremely dubious—'not to be
imitated',[3] so Augustine warned his readers—but for the *Gawain*-poet
and the poet of *De Sodoma* the end of reforming Sodomites thoroughly
justifies the means. Lot in *Cleanness* proudly markets his wares. In fact,
only his own stake in the praise he lavishes on his daughters gives him
pause: 'In Sodamas, *þaȝ I hit say,* non semloker burdes'. Strangely
enough, what emerges from that concessive phrase 'if I say so myself' is
not moral compunction but parental pride.

The *Gawain*-poet's sexual morality is quite straightforward: heterosexuality is good; homosexuality is distasteful. The harvest imagery which
Lot uses to advertise his daughters calls to mind the grounds on which
medieval theologians had reached this verdict: sex between members of
the same sex cannot issue in offspring, sex between a man and a woman
can. It is better, it follows, to prostitute one's daughters than to condone
homosexuality. Shocking as it seems to us, it is a conclusion that would
have raised few eyebrows in a period when the same logic inclined the
compilers of manuals of confession to the view that masturbation
(unproductive) is a more serious sin than raping a nun (productive)
(Tentler 1987, 142).

Yet what ought to convince us of the superiority of heterosexual
intercourse in *Cleanness* is not so much the arguments of the theologians
as the evidence of common sense and good taste. In Lot's view heterosexuality is good because it feels good, and homosexuality is bad because
it feels bad. As Elizabeth Keiser notes, 'cleanness, for the *Gawain*-poet, is
what men of refined sensibility like best' (Keiser 1980). While the
absence of casuistry in *Cleanness* may compare favourably with confessors'

2. *Carmen de Sodoma*, ed. R. Peiper, *CSEL* 23 (Vienna: Akademie der Wissenschaften,
1891), 212–19.
3. Augustine, *Contra mendacium*, PL 40, 530.

manuals, it would be misleading to suggest that the *Gawain*-poet was a more enlightened thinker on matters of sexuality than his contemporaries. It is true that he does not shrink from attributing to God a long eulogy on the pleasures of heterosexual sex, in the course of which God is allowed to wax lyrical about the 'play of paramore3':

And þe play of paramore3 I portrayed myseluen,

And made þerto a maner myriest of oþer.
When two true togeder had ty3ed hemseluen,
Bytwene a male and his make such merþe schulde come,
Wel-ny3e pure paradys mo3t preue no better.

(700–4)

(And the revelry of love I devised myself, and I added thereto a practice most pleasant of all: that, when two true ones had joined themselves to one another, such joy should come between a man and his wife that paradise itself might almost prove no better.)

But this speech which the poet puts in God's mouth should not be regarded (as some critics do) as a sign of an unusually permissive mind. First, the poet's association of marital sex and paradise is not, as it might first appear, unorthodox or daring. Marriage, so many medieval theologians observed, had the distinction of being the first of the seven sacraments in human history, ordained by God when Adam and Eve were still in Eden. Many writers had therefore linked the joys of marriage explicitly with those of paradise (Tavormina 1995, 129–33). Thus, Langland in *Piers Plowman* suggested that marriage allows people to have 'heaven on earth':

And thus was wedlok ywro3t and God hymself hit made;
In erþe þe heuene is; hymself was þe witnesse.

(B IX. 117–18)[4]

The *Gawain*-poet's comparison of marital sex with paradise probably belongs to this tradition of thought. Moreover, it must be remembered that this flattering comparison follows hard on the heels of God's condemnation of sodomy (688–96). The glorification of straight sex in *Cleanness* cannot and should not be separated from the poet's contempt for homosexuality; the praise of the one goes hand in hand with the denigration of the other.

Homosexuality and heterosexuality are, however, only one of many

---

4. Ed. A.V.C. Schmidt (London: Everyman, 1995).

meanings that cluster around the words cleanness and uncleanness. The reason why Lot's visitors are 'unclean' partners for the Sodomites lies not only in the fact that they are 'yonge men' (881). They are also angels, and as such belong to a different ontological category. The Sodomites pose a double threat to the order of things: a confusion both of members of the same sex that ought to be kept apart, and of members of two incompatible kinds of creatures, the one human, the other heavenly. Homosexuality is thus an act of cosmic implications, for the elision of the proper separation between men also undermines the order of God's hierarchical chain of being.

The spectre of this double crisis of categories links the story about Sodom and Gomorrah with the *Gawain*-poet's retelling of the Flood. Following the Bible, the *Gawain*-poet describes the union of the 'sons of God' with the 'sons of man' (Genesis 6: 2), but *Cleanness* departs from the Bible by presenting the cross-breeding of two different sorts of creatures as the consequence of sexual depravity among Adam's descendants:

> And þenne founden þay fylþe in fleschlych dedeȝ,
> And controeued agayn kynde contrare werkeȝ,
> And used hem vnþriftyly vchon on oþer,
> And als with oþer, wylsfully, upon a wrange wyse.
>
> So ferly fowled her flesch þat þe fende loked
> How þe deȝter of þe douþe wern derelych fayre,
> And fallen in felaȝschyp with hem on folken wyse,
> And engendered on hem ieaunteȝ with her iapeȝ ille.
>
> (265–72)

(Then they established filth in carnal deeds, and invented, against nature, immoral acts, and practised them unproductively on each other, and also with others, wilfully, and wrongly.

Their flesh was so wondrously defiled that the devils noticed that the daughters of men were very attractive, and they coupled with them in the manner of humans, and begot on them giants with their foul play.)

The phrase 'iapeȝ ille', we remember, crops up again in *Cleanness* to describe the sexual practices of the Sodomites, and the similarity between the two *exempla* is significant. In the poet's account of the Flood, too, homosexuality has cosmological repercussions. Intercourse with the wrong sex is an act of defilement that invites the fallen angels down to copulate with humans (Schmidt 1988, 111). Once brought into being, pollution cannot be contained. The uncleanness produced by the miscegenation between the sexes instantly spills over into other areas, into language, where *'ferly* fowled' is taken for 'derelych *fayre*', and into God's hierarchy of creatures, where angels descend to the level of human beings. Expanding our definition of uncleanness accordingly, we might say that uncleanness is a confusion of the categories of God's creation (Spearing 1987).

This broader view allows us to make sense of the *Gawain*-poet's explanation for the punishment meted out to Lot's wife. Escaping from the burning city, Lot and his relatives are warned not to look behind them. In the Bible, Lot's wife ventures a quick glance at the fireworks behind her and is changed into a pillar of salt. Why salt? The author of Genesis did not think the question needed explaining, but the *Gawain*-poet found an ingenious answer. Lot's wife, he writes, had been foolish enough to serve the angels salt at the dinner the evening before, in spite of her husband's orders to the contrary. The idea was not entirely new, and the *Gawain*-poet may have come across it in the glosses on Lot's wife's metamorphosis by the early-fourteenth-century Franciscan Nicolas of Lyra, known as the *Postilla*, which were copied in the margins of numerous later-medieval manuscripts of the Bible:

> And the Jews say it was because she had sinned the night before by using salt; so that the punishment might correspond to the sin.[5]

Still, the use of salt seems a trivial sin. Lot's wife for one does not give the matter of salt much thought. This is how the *Gawain*-poet portrays her as she makes up her mind to add some extra flavour to her sauce:

> Bot ȝet I wene þat þe wyf hit wroth to dispyt,
> And sayde softely to hirself: 'þis vnsauere hyne
> Loueȝ no salt in her sauce, ȝet hit no skyl were
> Þat oþer burne be boute, þaȝ boþe be nyse.'
>
> Þenne ho sauereȝ with salt her seueȝ vchone,
> Agayne þe bone of þe burne þat hit forboden hade,
> And als ho scelt hem in scorne þat wel her skyl knewen.
> Why watȝ ho, wrech, so wod? Ho wrathed oure lorde.
>
> (821–8)

(But all the same I think that Lot's wife acted wrongly, and she said silently to herself: 'This unsavoury lot do not like salt in their sauce, but it would not be right if another person would have to do without it, when these men are ill-bred.'

Then she salted all of their dishes, against the command of the man who

---

5. Translated from *Textus Biblie cum Glosa ordinaria & Nicolai de Lyra postilla* (Basel, 1506–8).

had forbidden it. And so she scorned those who knew very well what she was up to. Why was the wretch so mad? She angered our lord.)

Lot's wife has no intention of making allowances for the dietary requirements of her guests. Their fastidiousness is wittily dismissed as 'vnsauere' (meaning both 'unflavoured' and 'uncivilized'), a pun that neatly discloses the all too recognizable tendency to treat tastes different from one's own as a symptom of cultural inferiority. Convinced as she is of her own culinary refinement, Lot's wife reaches for the salt, like a committed carnivore slipping a cube of beef stock into the dish for her vegetarian friends.

The guests are, for Lot's wife, no different from her husband or herself. And this explains the grave consequences of her disobedience. Unaware that her guests are angels, she expects them to take pot luck like ordinary human beings. The problem of whether ordinary food might not be 'unsavorie ... to spiritual Natures' had Adam deeply worried in Milton's *Paradise Lost* (V, 401–2), and for good reason, for, as Adam realizes, the possible discrepancies in diet and digestion touch on the larger question of the differences between celestial and human beings. No less than the Sodomites who would treat the angels as suitable sexual partners, Lot's wife fails to make the proper distinction between different kinds of creatures. Her fate, to be turned into a pillar, aptly demonstrates the terrible vengeance God inflicts on the 'unclean'. For her failure to make the right distinctions between humans and angels, she is transformed, like the Sodomites who survive as ashes inside apples or as the grime of the Dead Sea, into an unnatural and repulsive object: a heap of salt, human in shape, but inorganic in matter, licked, as the *Gawain*-poet writes, by the 'bestes' of the area (1000).

IMITATING GOD

God is the only character who is omnipresent in the *Gawain*-poet's *exempla*, and in considering the confusion of categories which, as I have suggested, underpins the notion of 'uncleanness', we need to be attentive to the poet's powerful vision of the dangers that attend transgressions of the ontological divide between God and man. Medieval biblical commentators, who preferred to think of God as immutable, disembodied and patient, might well have been shocked by the way the *Gawain*-poet presents God. We meet him in various moods in *Cleanness*, overwhelmed by anger, upset by the degeneracy of his creatures, and then sorry about having lost his temper with them:

> Hym rwed þat he hem vprerde and raȝt hem lyflode,
> And efte þat he hym undyd, hard hit hym þoȝt;
> For quen þe swemande sorȝe soȝt to his hert,
> He knyt a couenande cortaysly with monkynde þere ...
>
> (561–4)

(He regretted that he had raised them and given them life, and afterwards he thought he had been too severe in unmaking them. For when the painful sorrow sank to his heart, he made a courteous covenant with mankind.)

At other times God confesses himself disgusted and physically sick at the sight of human filth:

> With her vnworþelych werk me wlates withinne;
> Þe gore þerof me hatȝ greued and þe glette nwyed;
> I schal strenkle my distresse and strye al togeder,
> Boþe ledeȝ and londe and alle þat lyf habbeȝ.
>
> (305–8)

(In my body I am disgusted by their shameful deeds. The gore of it has harmed me and the filth has made me sick. I will give vent to my distress and destroy everything, both people and lands and everything that is alive.)

The *Gawain*-poet is exceptional among medieval writers in portraying God as someone who is occasionally overcome with nausea and bouts of ill temper. It is an instance of an originality that is entirely due to the poet's courage to read the Old Testament accurately, and to see how uncannily familiar God, especially the God of Genesis, actually is: now furious, now repentant, sometimes hungry, as when he tucks in at Abraham's picnic at Mamre, sometimes so pleased with his creatures as to show a genuinely compassionate side.

Medieval commentators spent a great deal of time screening God's strong personality from themselves and their audience behind the well-tried method of allegorical interpretation. God appears familiar, they argued, not because there is some way in which he is like us, but because he adopts a human guise to accommodate himself to our puny minds. The anthropomorphic guise is not for real; it exists only 'in a manner of speaking'. I shall argue in a later section that one of the reasons why such an abstract understanding of God's nature did not suit the *Gawain*-poet is that he attempts to present human or divine hatred of 'unclean' actions as an entirely *natural* response. God and the poet in

Cleanness are never repelled by filth as a result of moral or intellectual deliberation. Uncleanness is what makes God and decent humans sick. As such, the poet's idea of what is clean and unclean is placed beyond rational debate. As far as the poet is concerned, it is a matter on which the body rather than the brain makes its decision.

A second reason for God's immediacy in *Cleanness* lies in the simple fact that the Old Testament stories which he used show God not as a remote deity but as one who interacts, often face to face, with human beings. He is like us, not simply in experiencing intensely physical responses to filth, but like us, too, in being directly involved in the world, in talking to human beings, warning them, even turning up on their doorstep in person. But, as I shall show in this section, God in the Old Testament *exempla* carefully polices the boundaries that separate him from his creatures; and perhaps his humanization makes the need to do so all the more urgent.

The *Gawain*-poet's insistence on the categorical differences between God and mankind may seem to sit oddly with his advice that we should strive to be like God: 'confourme þe to Kryst, and þe clene make' (1067). But likeness does not cancel out difference. On the contrary, it is predicated on the recognition of difference. For how could God be like man, and how could man be like God, if they were in fact identical? The error of Lucifer who desires to 'be lyke to þat lorde þat þe lyft maked' (212), of Adam and Eve who eat the forbidden fruit to acquire a God-like knowledge of good and evil (241–4), and of Nebuchadnezzar who fancies himself to be 'as he þat hyȝe is in heuen' (1664), is that they would be like God without recognizing the unlikeness that makes this imitation possible in the first place. They aim, in the words of Thomas Aquinas, at the 'likeness of equality' rather than that of 'imitation':

> Their sin is not simply wanting to be like God by knowledge, but in wanting it inordinately, that is, above one's measure. On the verse 'O God, who is like thee?' Augustine comments that he who wills to owe nothing to God wills perversely to be like God.
>
> (*Summa Theologiae*, 2a2ae.163.2)[6]

The episodes in which God humbles creatures who 'will perversely to be like God' are too numerous for me to analyse in detail, and I want to limit myself to the *Gawain*-poet's most detailed portrayal of 'perverse likeness' in the story of Belshazzar, who organizes an extravagant feast

6. Ed. T. Gilby et al., 61 vols (London: Blackfriars, 1963–75).

designed for the single purpose of self-glorification and indulgence. From start to finish the feast is modelled on the wedding feast which the lord lays on to celebrate his son's wedding in the parable from Matthew 22: 7–14 and Luke 14: 16–20. Orderly and generous, the lord's wedding feast is an apt image for God's kingdom of heaven, which it represents by analogy. Like the wedding feast, Belshazzar's festivities are referred to as a 'mangerie' (cf. 53 and 1365), but of the generosity and decorum that characterize the feast in the parable, Belshazzar's own feast is merely a diabolical imitation, with Belshazzar himself in the role of God.

Out to make an impression, he treats his guests to a spectacular display, enhanced by sensational and ingenious audio-visual effects, rendered for us in the poet's minute and indefatigable descriptions:

> Þenne watȝ alle þe halle flor hiled with knyȝteȝ,
> And barouneȝ at þe side-bordeȝ bouned aywhere,
> For non watȝ dressed vpon dece bot þe dere seluen,
> And his clere concubyneȝ in cloþes ful bryȝt.

> When alle seggeȝ were þer set, þen seruyse bygynnes;
> Sturne trumpen strake, steuen in halle;
> Aywhere by þe wowes wrasten krakkes,
> And brode baneres þerbi, blusnande of gold.

> Burnes berande þe bredes vpon brode skeles,
> Þat were of syluveren syȝt, and seves þerwyth;
> Lyfte logges þerouer and on lofte coruen,
> Pared out of paper and poynted of golde;

> Brode baboynes abof, besttes anvnder,
> Foles in foler flakerande bitwene,
> And al in asure and ynde enaumayld ryche;
> And al on blonkken bak bere hit on honde.
>
> (1397–1412)

(Then the floor of the hall was covered with knights, and barons were present in numbers at the side-tables. For no one was seated on the dais apart from the great man himself and his pretty concubines in resplendent clothes.

When all the people were seated, the service began. Shrill trumpets were blown, a clamour in the hall, and all the time the flourishes resounded from the walls. Broad banners hung from the trumpets, shining with gold.

There were men carrying the roasts and the stews on broad dishes, of silver appearance. They were covered with high houses, carved on top, cut out of paper, and painted over with gold;

Huge grotesques on top, and animals underneath, and in between birds fluttering in the foliage. And all was enamelled in azure and priceless indigo blue. And everything was carried in by servants on horseback.)

As soon as the audience have taken their places, Belshazzar's show begins, an extravagant production in which concubines are dressed up as ladies, and platters of food as houses and castles, fancifully decorated with imitation baboons and sculptures of fluttering birds. And in the middle of this stage Belshazzar himself sits enthroned, the centre of the guests' and his own attention.

Belshazzar, the poet leaves no doubt about it, has a sense for the dramatic and the artistic. Confident in his powers to transform matter into art, he turns concubines into ladies, guests into spectators, and finally even the sacred vessels into the stage-props of his theatre. But while the poet's captivation by the glossy surfaces of Belshazzar's art of illusion is a tribute to Belshazzar's creativity, it is also a reminder that this creativity is *only* superficial. Belshazzar's art is mimetic; it imitates objects, substances like gold and silver, animals, people. This is true not just for the decorations on the platters of food or for the concubines that have to pass for ladies—'þat ladies wer called' (1352)—but for Belshazzar's world as a whole. His feast is a parody of the wedding feast, he himself apes God, and his palace in Babylon is a miniature of the Heavenly City. Compare the proportions of Belshazzar's city with God's in *Pearl*:

Þe cyté stod abof ful sware
As longe as brode as hyȝe ful fayre.
> (*Pearl*, 1023–4)

(Above it the city stood in perfect symmetry and beauty, as long as it was wide and as broad as it was high.)

Þe place þat plyed þe pursaunt wythinne
Watȝ long and ful large, and euer ilyich sware,
And vch a syde vpon soyle helde seuen myle,
And þe saudans sete sette in þe myddes.
> (1385–8)

(The place that was enclosed by the wall was long and broad, and always symmetrical, and each side was seven miles long, and the sultan's seat was set in the middle.)

But while the similarities between God in his heavenly city and Belshazzar are visible to the audience, Belshazzar himself believes that his 'burȝ of Babiloune' is unique: 'þe biggest ... þat nauþer in heuen ne on erþe had no pere' (1336). He is misguided, of course; not for modelling his creations on God's originals, but for refusing to admit that imitation is all that they are. In his delusions of grandeur and originality, Belshazzar copies and mimics, fashions objects and identities that are finally only supplements to God's prior act of creation, of which Belshazzar is himself the product, not the producer.

But the creatureliness which Belshazzar disowns returns with a vengeance. Belshazzar's organizational skills are soon caught out by the unexpected appearance of a hand that scribbles strange letters on his wall. The moment is an exquisite example of the stinging irony of which the *Gawain*-poet was so fond, the irony that punctures the illusion of control felt by so many of his protagonists by driving in the point that they are not running the show. Belshazzar is flabbergasted, and reduced to a puppet:

> His cnes cachches to close and cluchches his hommes,
> And he with plattyng his paumes displayes his leres,
> And romyes as a rad ryth þat rorez for drede,
> Ay biholdand þe honde til it had al grauen,
> And rasped on þe roz woze runisch sauez.
>
> (1541–5)

(His knees knock together and his arms and legs double up, and he tears open his cheeks by beating his palms against them, and he bellows like a frightened bull that roars for fear, looking all the while at the hand until it had finished etching, and had scraped strange sayings on the rough wall.)

As ever, his response is excessive and histrionic, but he is this time no longer in command of his performance. Belshazzar's pompous theatre has been absorbed into a divinely-run comedy, where Belshazzar, once the director, must play the clown for our and God's amusement.

Belshazzar's apparently boundless creative energies are spent on a vain attempt to shake himself free of his own creatureliness and, by the same token, to reduce the Creator to an object of his own making. Belshazzar's inversion of the relations between God and man culminates in the 'abomynaciouns' of idolatry (1173): the worship of man-made gods:

> Bot fals fantummes of fendes [he] formed with handes,
> Wyth tool out of harde tre, and telded on lofte,
> And of stokkes and stones, he stoute goddes callz,
> When þay ar gilde al with stone and gered wyth syluer.

And þen he kneles and calleȝ and clepes after help;
And þay reden him ryȝt, rewarde he hem hetes,
And if þay gruchen him his grace, to gremen his hert,
He cleches to a great klubbe and knokkes hem to peces.

(1341–8)

(But with his hands he formed false images of devils, made with tools out of
hard wood, of stocks and stones, and raised on high. When they had been
gilded with precious stones and adorned with silver, he called them mighty gods.

Then he kneels and calls out to them for help. And if they advise him cor-
rectly, he promises them rewards, and if they begrudge him grace, and anger
his heart, he reaches for a big club and knocks them to bits.)

Human beings fashioning gods: this sin is inexcusable. It undermines
religion by raising the scandalous possibility that gods (and by implication God himself) might be human constructs, rather than the other way
around. Idolatry is an abomination, not in the first place because idol-
aters do not worship the proper God, but because their invention of a
god might set believers thinking about the origins of their own.

But *Cleanness* raises this uncomfortable possibility only so that it may
be the more persuasively refuted. Belshazzar's treatment of his gods
anticipates the very form that this refutation will take. If his artifacts
please him, he rewards them, if they do not, he 'knokkes hem to peces'.
Little does Belshazzar know that this imitation of the way God behaves
towards his creation will prove entirely accurate. When the feast is over
and Belshazzar is asleep in his bed, he is clubbed to death by his God-
sent enemies. 'That same night Belshazzar is slain', reads the Book of
Daniel. The *Gawain*-poet did not leave the nature of Belshazzar's death
as vague, believing no doubt that poetic justice was served if God were
to treat his handiwork in the exact same way that Belshazzar treated his:

Baltaȝar in his bed watȝ beten to deþe,
Þat boþe his blod and his brayne blende on þe cloþes.

(1787–8)

(Belshazzar was beaten to death in his bed, so that both his blood and his
brain stained the blankets.)

The irony of the moment lies in the revelation that Belshazzar has imitated God well: as Belshazzar broke his artifacts, so God breaks his. At
the same time Belshazzar's death underlines the difference between a
mortal human who plays God and the authentic and indestructible
Creator himself, the unbridgeable gap that separates being *like* God from
being God, the likeness of imitation from the likeness of equality.

THE BEAUTY OF DESTRUCTION

God's answer to 'perverse likeness' is destruction, a drastic measure whose effectiveness lies in the simple fact that destructibility constitutes the most fundamental difference between the Creator and his creatures. In a brutally simple way, God's punishment of rulers and races—of Zedekiah and the inhabitants of Jerusalem, of Belshazzar and the Babylonians, of the Sodomites, or of the antediluvians—drives home his irreducible otherness precisely when his anger, his disgust, or his bad temper make him seem all too human. If God in *Cleanness* shares some of our emotions, he differentiates himself from us to the extent that he inflicts, but does not suffer, pain and punishment. For much of the poem, this is the main difference between God and his creatures: he is at the other end of some destructive weapon.

The *Gawain*-poet devotes some of his most chilling descriptions to God's acts of vengeance. They focus mercilessly on the death and despair of human beings, and on God's firm resolve to unmake, to kill or to disintegrate. The best example is the poet's account of the Flood, probably modelled on a biblical epic that became a school text in the Carolingian period (Glauche 1970, 30), and whose influence on vernacular writings stretched right up to Milton's *Paradise Lost* (Nodes 1985, 5–10), Avitus of Vienne's *De spiritalis historiae gestis* (c. 500). I quote first Avitus, and then the *Gawain*-poet's adaptation:

> ... Tum maior strepitu tanto mortalibus aegris
> Fit metus, ascendunt turres et celsa domorum
> Culmina praesentemque iuvat vel tempore parvo
> Sic differre necem. Multos, dum scandere temptant,
> Crescens unda trahit, quosdam montana petentes
> Consequitur letoque fugam deprendit inanem.
> Ast alii longo iactantes membra natatu
> Defessi expirant animas, aut pondere nimbi
> Obruta flumineas conmixta per aequora lymphas
> In quocumque bibunt morientia corpora monte.
> Aedibus inpulsis alii periere ruina
> Inque undas venere simul dominique domusque.
> It fragor in caelum sonitu collectus ab omni
> Quadrupedumque greges humana in morte cadentum
> Augent confusos permixta voce tumultus.
>
> (476–87)[7]

---

7. Ed. R. Peiper, Monumenta Germaniae Historica, Auctores Antiquissimi VI (Berlin: Weidmann, 1883).

(Then the fear of the desperate mortals was even greater than their clamour: they clambered up towers and the highest roofs of their houses, which at least helps them to postpone their deaths for a little while. Many are swallowed up by the flood while they try to climb up, and the flood follows those who make for the mountains and overtakes the fruitless flight with death. Others give up the ghost having exhausted their limbs in a prolonged swim, or, overwhelmed by the mass of rain, their dying bodies, swirled through the waters, drink the river-streams on every mountain slope. Others are killed by the fall of their collapsing houses, and both houses and their owners land up in the flood. A clamour goes up to heaven, made up of the cries of all. Joining with the voices of humans are herds of four-footed animals, who add to the confused uproar as they fall in death.)

Water wylger ay wax, woneȝ þat stryede,
Hurled into vch hous, hent þat þer dowelle.

Fyrst feng to þe flyȝt alle þat fle myȝt;
Vvche burde with her barne þe byggyng þay leueȝ
And bowed to þe hyȝ bonk þer brentest hit wern,
And heterly to þe hye hylleȝ þay aled on faste.

Bot al watȝ nedleȝ her note, for neuer cowþe stynt
Þe roȝe raynande ryg, þe raykande waweȝ,
Er vch boþom watȝ brurdful to þe bonkeȝ eggeȝ,
And vche a dale so depe þat demned at þe brynkeȝ.

Þe moste mountayneȝ on mor þenne were no more dryȝe,
And þeron flokked þe folke for ferde of þe wrake.
Syþen þe wylde of þe wode on þe water flette;
Summe swymmed þeron þat saue hemself trawed,

Summe styȝe to a stud and stared to þe heuen,
Rwly wyth a loud rurd rored for drede;
Hareȝ, hertteȝ also, to þe hyȝe runnen,
Bukkeȝ, bauseneȝ, and buleȝ to þe bonkkeȝ hyȝed,

And all cryed for care to þe kyng of heuen;
Recouerer of þe creator þat cryed vchone.
Þat amounted þe mase, his mercy watȝ passed,
And alle his pyte departed fro peple þat he hated.

(375–96)

(The water grew wilder, and destroyed houses; it rushed into each house and seized all who lived in it.

At first all those who could took to flight; all women left their homes with their children, and rushed to the hills where they were highest, and frantically they went up the slopes.

But all their effort was useless, for the furious rain and the wild waves would not stop until all the valleys were brimful to the edge of the hills, and the deepest dales were overflowing at the brink.

Even the biggest mountains on the land were no longer dry, but the people gathered on them for fear of the vengeance. Then the wild animals of the wood floated on the water. Some tried to swim, thinking they might save themselves.

Some climbed to a high place and stared at the heavens, roaring loud and pitifully for fear. Harts and deer ran to higher grounds, bucks, badgers, and bulls ran up the mountains.

And all shouted out of distress to the king of heaven; everyone cried for relief from the Creator, but that was pointless, for his mercy had passed, and all his pity was withdrawn from the people he hated.)

There is nothing comparable to this in the Old Testament, which mentions briefly that 'all flesh died' (Genesis 7: 21). But death in Avitus and *Cleanness* is no longer the sudden and apparently painless force of the Old Testament; it is a process—slow, deliberate, and remorseless. People can see it coming, and flee hysterically. The flood reduces them to animality, compelling them to act on a basic instinct for survival that is stronger than the knowledge that there is no hope for escape. Their luck has run out, and the *Gawain*-poet states God's indifference with devastating certainty: 'And alle watȝ his pyte departed fro peple þat he hated.'

There follows in *Cleanness* a bathetic description of human beings clutching each other as death approaches, conquering their animal instinct for survival for a final grand and selfless gesture:

Frendeȝ fellen in fere and faþmed togeder,
To dryȝ her delful deystyne and dyȝen alle samen;

Luf lokeȝ to luf, and his leue takeȝ,
For-to ende alle at oneȝ and for euer twynne.
(398–401)

(Friends came together and embraced one another, to meet their doleful destiny and die all together.

Lovers look to their lovers, and take their leave, to end all at once and part forever.)

The *Gawain*-poet lingers on these final moments of human beings with extraordinary empathy. Sympathy might have been the appropriate word for it, if it were not for the fact that this spectacle of human distress is itself of the poet's making, observed by the unblinking eye of an omniscient and detached narrator whose powers of description are never hampered by emotion. Like God who, to the astonishment of human beings, has stopped caring for his creation, the passage closes in on the final throes of these human beings with a disturbingly dispassionate gaze.

Destruction, however, represents for the *Gawain*-poet not only a regression into chaos. It is the way in which God in this poem tidies up after the filth left by human beings, so that he can recommence the work of creation on a clean slate. Destruction clears the way for a new order; it purges the confusion caused by humans by dividing them on the basis of the simplest of considerations: what will live and what will not live. If the water of the Flood dissolves the distinctions on which cleanness depends, it also establishes a new boundary between the creatures inside the ark and those outside it. It cleanses, or 'washes' as the *Gawain*-poet puts it (323). For all the apparent havoc that God's vengeance wreaks, it simultaneously rejuvenates by wiping out the traces of a world become unclean.

As any reader of *Cleanness* will know, destruction fascinated the *Gawain*-poet, perhaps because he was attracted by the decisiveness and simplicity with which it answers chaos and confusion. Killing some and saving others, God solves the human muddle by breaking his creation down to the largest common denominator: life itself. Annihilation in *Cleanness* is a return to basics. Walter Benjamin might have been speaking about the *Gawain*-poet when he wrote that the destructive person is stirred by 'the realization of how immensely the world is simplified when tested for its worthiness of destruction. This is the great bond embracing and unifying all that exists. It is a sight that affords the destructive character a spectacle of deepest harmony' (Benjamin 1978).

Destructibility in *Cleanness*, however, does not only cut through the intolerable complexities and entanglements of God's creatures. It simultaneously restates God's alterity. Destructibility may be the 'great bond embracing and unifying all that exists', but it does not, in *Cleanness*, embrace God. It divides the indestructible God from mankind, the eternal Creator from what he has made and can therefore unmake.

Even when God is at his most homely, the *Gawain*-poet's sense of his categorical unlikeness never deserts him. God's visit to Abraham is a case in point. It depicts God at his most domestic, enjoying Abraham's hospitality and Sarah's cooking, almost, but not quite, like a human being:

And God as a glad gest mad god chere,
Þat watʒ fayn of his frende and his fest praysed;
Abraham, al hodleʒ, with armeʒ vpfolden,
Mynystred mete byfore þo men þat myʒteʒ al weldeʒ.

Þenne þay sayden as þay sete samen alle þrynne,
When þe mete watȝ remued and þay of mensk speken:
'I schal efte hereaway, Abram,' þay sayden,
'ȝet er þy lyueȝ lyȝt leþe vpon erþe;

And þanne schal Sare consayue and a sun bere,
Þat schal be Abrahameȝ ayre, and after hym wynne
With wele and wyth worschyp þe worþely peple
Þat schal halde in heritage þat I haf men ȝarked.'

Þenne þe burde byhynde þe dor for busmar laȝed,
And sayde sotyly to hirself Sare þe madde:
'May þou traw for tykle þat þou terme moȝteȝ,
And I so hyȝe out of age, and also my lorde?'

. . . . .

Þenne sayde oure syre þer he sete: 'Se! so Sare laȝes,
Not trawande þe tale þat I þe to schewed.
Hopeȝ ho oȝt may be harde my handeȝ to work?
And ȝet I avow verayly þe avount þat I made;

I schal ȝeply aȝayn and ȝelde þat I hyȝt,
And sothely sende to Sare a soun and an hayre.'
Þenne swenged forth Sare and swere by hir trawþe
Þat for lot þat þay laused ho laȝed neuer.

'Now innogh, hit is not so,' þenne nurned þe dryȝtyn,
'For þou laȝed aloȝ, bot let we hit one.'

(641–70)

(And like a happy guest, God made good cheer. He was pleased with his friend and praised the meal. Abraham, hoodless, and with arms uplifted, served food before those men that wield all powers.

Then they said as they were sitting together, all three of them, when the food had been removed and they made polite conversation: 'I will come again, Abraham, before the light of your life is extinguished.

And then Sarah will conceive and bear a son, who will be Abraham's heir, and will beget after him with good fortune and honour the worthy people, who will inherit what I have granted to men.'

Then the woman scornfully laughed behind the door; the foolish Sarah said slyly to herself: 'Can you believe that you could fertilize me through wantonness, I being so much over age and my husband, too?'

Then our lord said from where he was sitting, 'See, Sarah is laughing; she does not believe the story I told you. Does she think there is anything too difficult for my hands to do? But I reaffirm in truth the promise that I made;

And I shall quickly return and do as I promised, and truly I will send Sarah a son and an heir.' Then Sarah rushed forth and swore by her faith that she never laughed at any of the words they had said.

'Now, enough, it is not so', the lord responded, 'you laughed quietly, but let us leave it at that.'

As in the source, Genesis 18: 10–15, God appears in this passage in the form of *three* visitors. The biblical passage alternately refers to Abraham's visitor(s) in the third person singular (he) and the third person plural (they), as if God were continually shifting shape, revealing himself now as one person, and at other times as three. The *Gawain*-poet would have understood this enigma as the mystery of the Trinity, in which God is both one *and* three. The crucial scriptural source for the doctrine of the Trinity is the First Epistle of John 5: 7 'And there are Three who give testimony in heaven, the Father, the Word, and the Holy Ghost. And these three are one.' Biblical commentators were fond of 'solving' this mystery of the 'three-in-one' by pointing out that the three guests speak to Abraham in perfect unison. The *Gawain*-poet attempts something similar when he describes the three visitors as speaking *una voce*, in perfect simultaneity: 'þenne þay sayden as þay sette *samen alle þrynne* ... I schal efte hereaway.'

The sense of mystery emerges, however, from a scene that could hardly be more domestic. The three guests speak in unison, not 'to give testimony in heaven', but 'when þe mete watз remued', that time after dinner when guest and host can speak without food and drink getting in the way of pleasant conversation. Is it strange that in this homely setting Sarah fails to be impressed by her husband's guests, and laughs 'byhynde þe dor' at their ridiculous suggestion that she will still conceive a child when her and Abraham's playing days are long since gone? Again God's response is at once entirely 'other' and strikingly familiar: 'other' because he has *seen* and *heard* Sarah's sneer from a position in which it cannot humanly be visible and audible, familiar because God tactfully lets Sarah off the hook when she protests her innocence: 'Now innogh, hit is not so,' þenne nurned þe dryзtyn, / 'For þou laзed aloз, bot let we hit one.'

The charmingly human tone has been felt to detract from God's mysteriousness (Spearing 1970, 60), but I believe David Wallace is right when he suggests that 'the very arbitrariness of God's excursions into human modes of feeling and expression makes him seem even less knowable and more enigmatic, dangerous, and unpredictable' (Wallace 1991, 95). God, after all, does not give up his omniscience when he drops his charges against Sarah; he decides, in his infinite condescension, not to take advantage of his omniscience. The renunciation of his otherness is, in other words, purely symbolic. What safeguards his alterity in this *exemplum* is not, as medieval theologians would have argued, that his participation as a human being is only metaphorical, but that this participation is, for God, a matter of choice. He is an author who can write himself into a plot as a character without being caught up in its events, and human characters deal with him at the considerable risk of being written out.

The episode in which Abraham bargains with God on behalf of the Sodomites suggests the precariousness of man's dealings with this character of God. Hoping to save Sodom and Gomorrah from the total destruction God has in mind, Abraham appeals to God's reputation for mildness and justice. It is not in God's nature to destroy the innocent along with the wicked; therefore, if God should find fifty innocent people, Abraham asks him, might he not save the city? God grants Abraham his request, and Abraham proceeds to bargain God down from fifty to forty-five, from forty-five to thirty, then to twenty, and from twenty down to ten.

On the evidence of other medieval retellings of the Bible, such as Peter Comestor's *Historia Scholastica* or Peter Riga's *Aurora*, in which this scene is either deleted or drastically condensed, the *Gawain*-poet's interest in this episode was rather rarefied. His retelling is long (713–80), and like his source inevitably somewhat repetitious, but I think it deserved his attention, since the episode that sees God haggling with Abraham about numbers and participating, as it were, on an equal footing, is also one of the most powerful expressions in the Bible of the *inequality* between the two. While Abraham has every reason for bargaining with God about the lives of his fellow creatures, and is committed to his role in the bargain because it is the only way he can affect the future, this bargain is for God in the final analysis only a game. I mean by this that, unlike Abraham, God has absolutely no need to play the bargaining game. As the Creator he can do what he likes. This of course means that he may choose to abide by Abraham's rules of fair play, but he does so entirely gratuitously, in the way that human beings may submit to the rules of a game without being constrained to do so.

Even more than the Book of Genesis, the *Gawain*-poet reminds his audience that God's participation in the negotiations over the Sodomites depends entirely on his goodwill. Consider some of the lines the *Gawain*-poet gave to Abraham, almost all of which are additions to his scriptural source:

'Aa! blessed be þow,' quoþ þe burne, 'so boner and þewed,
And al haldeȝ in þy honde, þe heuen and þe erþe;
Bot, for I haf þis talke, tatȝ to non ille
Ȝif I mele a lyttel more, þat mul am and askeȝ.'

(733–6)

Þen Abraham obeched hym and loȝly him þonkkeȝ:
'Now sayned be þou, sauiour, so symple in þy wrath.
I am bot erþe ful euel and vsle so blake,
For-to mele wyth such a mayster as myȝteȝ hatȝ alle.

Bot I haue bygonnen wyth my God, and he hit gayn þynkeȝ;
Ȝif I forloyne as a fol, þy fraunchyse may serue.'

(745–50)

'Ah! Now blessed may you be,' said the man, 'who are so kind and gracious,
and hold all in your hand, both the earth and the sea, but, since I have begun
talking, do not be offended if I—who am dust and ashes—speak a little
longer.'

...

Then Abraham bowed to him, and thanked him humbly: 'Now blessed may
you be, saviour, who are so mild in your anger. I am only vile earth and
black ashes, to speak with such an all-powerful lord.
    But I have started this with my God, if it pleases him. And if I should go
astray like a fool, your generosity may help.')

These stanzas give us a good impression of the length to which
Abraham's self-humiliation and his flattery of God will stretch. At every
possible moment, Abraham compliments God for playing his part in the
negotiations so well, at each turn he apologizes for protracting the negotiations a little longer, and begs God not to become impatient. And
Abraham has every reason for humouring God, considering he has to
keep up God's interest in a settlement in which he is entirely disinter-
ested.
    The *Gawain*-poet did not gloss over Abraham's temerity in taking on
God in a game of give and take. Despite his ostensible humility,
Abraham is imposing his will on God who, at least in *Cleanness*, is clearly
unhappy with Abraham's idea of saving the city, and lets Abraham know
he is:

'Nay, þaȝ faurty forfete, ȝet fryst I a whyle,
And voyde away me vengaunce, *þaȝ me vyl þynk*.'

(743–4)

('No, if forty are to be lost, I will stay my hand for a while, and forgo my vengeance, though I think it is vile.')

In the style of the grovelling courtier who is looking for the prince's favours, and knows he must not push his luck, Abraham's words to God pass cautiously from self-abasement to self-assertion. 'I am unworthy of your favours', Abraham can be heard saying, before pressing on to his next request. His self-abasement aims at concealing the hazardous position of equality which he assumes as God's partner in a bargain. And God's power emerges both from the fact that Abraham believes that such concealment is necessary, that one cannot *openly* treat God as an equal, and from the painful truth that Abraham's humility topoi ('I ... þat mul am and aske3') are in fact an entirely accurate assessment of man's relation to God: dust we are and to dust we will return. What is really rhetorical about the bargaining episode, then, is not Abraham's humility, but God's co-operation.

The *Gawain*-poet underlined this point by adding to his biblical source Abraham's desperate plea to God to spare at least his kinsman Lot. It had occurred to other writers that Abraham might express some concern about his family. An example is the Middle English poem *Genesis and Exodus*, in which Abraham raises the matter as follows:

> Tho adde Abram is herte sor,
> For Loth his newe wunede thor.
> 'Louerd,' quad he, 'hu saltu don,
> If thu salt nimen wreche thor on;
> Salt thu nogt the rigt-wise weren,
> Or for hem the tothere meth beren?'
> Quad God, 'find ich thor ten or mo,
> Ic sal meþen þe stede for þo.'
>
> $(1039–46)$[8]

(Then Abraham's heart was aggrieved, because of his nephew Lot who lived there. 'Lord', he said, 'what will you do if you take vengeance on them. Will you not spare the righteous, or have mercy for the sake of those others?' God said: 'If I find there ten righteous men, I will save the city.')

The passage is representative of the tendency of medieval biblical poets to condense the bargaining episode. *Cleanness* shares with *Genesis and Exodus* Abraham's intercession on behalf of Lot, but the *Gawain*-poet imagines the moment altogether differently than the poet of *Genesis and*

---

8. Ed. R. Morris, EETS OS 7 (London: Trübner, 1873).

Exodus. In the latter poem God answers. In *Cleanness*, however, he is already on his way to inspect the scene of the crime, so that Abraham must shout in order to make himself heard; whether in vain or not we do not know, since God gives no reply:

> And als he loked þere as oure lord passed,
> 3et he cryed hym after with careful steuen:
> 'Meke mayster, on þy mon to mynne if þe lyked,
> Loth lenge3 in 3on leede, þat is myn lef broþer.
>
> He sytte3 þer in Sodomis, þy seruaunt so pouere,
> Among þo mansed men þat han þe much greued;
> 3if þou tyne3 þat toun, tempre þyn yre
> As þy mersy may malte, þy meke to spare.'
>
> Þen he wende3 his way, wepande for care,
> Towarde þe mere of Mambre, mornande for sorewe;
> And þere in longyng al ny3t he lenge3 in wones,
> Whyl þe souerayn to Sodomas sende to spye.
> (769–80)

(And as he looked to where our lord went, he cried after him with an anxious voice: 'Meek lord, please remember your servant. Lot lives in this city; he is my beloved brother.

He dwells there in Sodom, your poor servant, amongst those wicked men who have offended you so much; if you destroy the town, temper your anger, as your mercy may soften it, to spare your humble creature.'

Then he went his way, weeping anxiously, towards the border of Mamre, crying for sorrow. And there he stays all night, in hope, while the sovereign sent messengers to Sodom to spy.)

The *Gawain*-poet's final twist to the bargaining episode leaves Abraham and the audience in no doubt about who is in charge. Abraham, in despair, calls out to God, but receives no assurance. The time has come when God has stopped playing the game, and has ceased to be Abraham's partner in a dialogue which it is in Abraham's interest to pursue. God's reticence communicates what we might have known all along, that God is not constrained to enter into a dialogue or negotiations, that the need to bargain is entirely one-sided. Abraham's dependence on God's co-operation is not—and never was—matched by a corresponding dependence on the part of God. True, God may have given Abraham many answers, but his ultimate silence reveals that he was never *answerable* to him. With this hint God descends into Sodom and Gomorrah, while Abraham, uncertain of God's next move, dissolves in tears.

Such are the differences between the Creator and his creatures. God may, of course, symbolically suspend them, but his suspension is simply a manifestation of his complete freedom of action.

CLEANNESS AND KNOWING ONE'S PLACE

As we have seen, destruction separates the obedient from the disobedient, and God from man. Separation and the restoration of order are directly linked to the poet's theme of uncleanness. For the *Gawain*-poet, and for us, what is dirty or clean depends on a set of ingrained assumptions about the way the universe is ordered, about where in this order things belong and where they are out of place. Earth on a kitchen table is dirt. It is clean in a garden. There is nothing dirty about food on a plate, but it may be transformed into dirt when we spill it on our clothes. Dirt, as the anthropologist Mary Douglas puts it, is '*matter out of place*' (Douglas 1968, 35), and for the poet this 'matter out of place' includes human beings such as Belshazzar or the Sodomites who do not know their place.

The poet's paraphrase of the Parable of the Wedding Feast will illustrate the relativity of uncleanness. To mark the occasion of his son's wedding, a rich lord invites his acquaintances to a feast. When his friends invent various transparent excuses for not being able to attend, the lord orders his messengers to invite anyone they should meet, regardless of status or appearance. Eventually the hall is filled with a colourful assembly of guests, all properly dressed for the occasion, some seated better than others, and some dressed more richly than others, as status requires:

> Wheþer þay wern worþy oþer wers, wel wern þay stowed,
> Ay þe best byfore and bryʒtest atyred,
> Þe derrest at þe hyʒe dese, þat dubbed wer fayrest,
> And syþen on lenþe biloogh ledeʒ inogh ...
>
> (113–16)

(Whether they were noble or of lower birth, they were well placed; the best always in front, and in the brightest attire, and the noblest, who were best dressed, sat at the high table, and then in the hall below many others ...)

But the order and hierarchy of the feast, its *clannes*, is threatened by the presence of a labourer who is wearing his everyday clothes:

> Bot as he ferked ouer þe flor he fande with his yʒe
> Hit watʒ, not for halyday honestly arayed,

A þral þry3t in þe þrong, unþryuandely cloþed,
Ne no festiual frok, bot fyled with werkke3.

(133–6)

(But as he walked across the floor his eye fell on someone who was not properly dressed for this holy day, a churl in the midst of the crowd, poorly
clothed, not wearing a garment for a feast, but one stained by his labour.)

Offended by the man's negligence, the lord commands his torturers to
throw him into his dungeon. Are the labourer's clothes dirty? Not when
he wears them at work on an ordinary day, but in the lord's hall on a
'halyday' his clothes are unclean. And the lord cleanses them for good
when he expels the man to the dungeon where no dress code applies.

The *Gawain*-poet's horror at the guest's impropriety may seem excessive to us. In the five centuries that separate us from *Cleanness*, time and
place have lost much of their sacred character. Few of us experience a
'holiday' as a time that is of a different order than any other day of the
week. We treat space with the same neutrality, and few experience a
radical sense of discontinuity when opening the door of a church and
stepping into a 'hallowed' zone. But we may at least understand our
incomprehension of the poet's sense of justice better when we realize
that it is precisely for desecrating time and space, for making no qualitative distinctions between them, that the guest in the Parable of the
Wedding Feast is punished:

Þe abyt þat þou hat3 vpon, no halyday hit menske3
. . . . .
Þou praysed me and my place ful pouer and ful nede,
Þat wat3 so prest to aproche my presens hereinne.

(141–7)

(The clothes you have on do not do honour to the holy day. You pay your
respect to me and my place poorly and meagrely, having been so hasty to
approach my presence in this place.)

'Prest' is here clearly used in the sense of hasty or overhasty. But it has
another sense, that of 'priest', a sense which the *Gawain*-poet must have
wanted us to have in mind, since line 147 echoes the poet's earlier definition of priests in lines 7–8 as 'renke3 of relygioun þat reden and syngen
/ And *aprochen* to hys *presens*, and *preste3* arn called' ('religious men who
read and sing and approach his presence and are called priests'). This
alternative sense of 'prest' is called up so that we signal its exclusion. The
play on the word is what Christopher Ricks calls an 'anti-pun', 'a device

by which another sense of the word is called up only to be fended off'
(quoted in Schmidt 1988). Another example of this device is in lines
695–6, where the poet also draws attention to the conspicuous absence
of one of the senses of a word:

> Vch male matȝ his mach a man as hymseluen,
> And fylter folyly in fere on femmaleȝ wyse.

> (Each male took as his partner a male like himself, and joined wantonly
> together in the manner of a female.)

'Mach' and 'fere' can both mean 'wife', but clearly not in the context of
these lines (Schmidt 1988). The exclusion of this legitimate sense is the
very crime with which the antediluvians are charged, just as the 'prest'
guest stands accused for not being priestly: he has no respect for the
holy, he is 'prest' in the wrong sense of the word.

Holiness must be approached with caution and with reverence, it may
not be encroached upon as if it were nothing out of the ordinary. For
religious man, 'space is not homogeneous; he experiences interruptions,
breaks in it; some parts of space are qualitatively different from others'
(Eliade 1959, 20). To respect such discontinuities is to honour the
'sacred' in the original sense of that word, as something 'separate'.
'Sacred' derives from Latin *sacrare* ('to set apart'); its opposite 'profane'
derives from Latin *pro-fanum* ('outside the temple', and hence 'without
restricted access'). Acts of separation and of lumping together owe their
resonances in *Cleanness* to the fact they either acknowledge or deny the
sacredness of creation.

Without exception, acts of separation distinguish the 'clean' characters
in the poem from the 'unclean'. Christ can break a loaf of bread into
two pieces more 'cleanly' than the sharpest knife. Lot seals off one space
from the other by closing doors and gates:

> He went forth at the wyket and waft hit hym after,
> Þat a clyket hit cleȝt clos hym byhynde.
>
> (857–8)

> (He went out by the gate and closed it after him, so that a catch fastened it
> firmly behind him.)

The Sodomites by contrast jostle and bustle about, and threaten to
engulf Lot in the hubbub. The angels come to Lot's defence by erecting
a secure boundary which the Sodomites cannot pass beyond:

> Þus þay þrobled and þrong and þrwe vmbe his ereȝ,
> And distresed hym wonder strayt with strenkþe in þe prece,

Bot þat þe ȝonge men so ȝepe ȝornen þeroute,
Wapped vpon þe wyket and wonnen hem tylle,
And by þe hondeȝ hym hent and horyed hym withinne,
And steken þe ȝates ston-harde wyth stalworth barreȝ.

(879–84)

(Thus they jostled and milled around and crowded close around him, and the violence of the crowd would have hurt him very severely, if the young men had not boldly run outside, flung open the gate and gone to the rescue. They grabbed him by the hands, hurried him back in, and barricaded the doors securely with sturdy bars.)

The characters in the final *exemplum* also divide into those who lump together and those who separate. The consecrated vessels are robbed from their 'precious place' (1282) in the temple of Jerusalem and brought 'hamppred togeder' (1284) in cases to Nebuchadnezzar, who restores their holiness by setting them apart in his treasury:

He trussed hem in his tresorye in a tryed place,
Rekenly, with reverens, as he ryȝt hade ...

(1317–18)

(He placed them in his treasury in a well-chosen place, properly and with reverence, as was right ...)

But before long they are profaned, put to common use, by Belshazzar who has them fetched from the treasury, set without distinction—'al aliche' (1477)—on his altar, and then encourages his guests to make a run for them: 'rennkkes in þat ryche rok rennen hit to cache' (1514).

The symbolic significance of space confers a wealth of meaning even on an apparently trivial act such as the arrangement of food on a picnic cloth. This is how Abraham sets the table in the *Gawain*-poet's adaptation of Genesis 18: 8:

Þe burne to be bare-heued buskeȝ hym þenne,
Clecheȝ to a clene cloþe and kesteȝ on þe grene,
Þrwe þryftyly þeron þo þre þerue-kakeȝ,
And bryngeȝ butter wythal and by þe bred setteȝ.

Mete messeȝ of mylke he merkkeȝ bytwene,
Syþen potage and polment in plater honest ...

(633–8)

(The man hastened to take off his hat, took a clean cloth and cast it on the grass, then swiftly he put on it the three unleavened loaves, and brought the butter and placed it beside the bread.

He put appropriate cups of milk in between, followed by the pottage and stew in a suitable bowl.)

The poet follows Abraham meticulously as he puts each item in its proper place. The word used to describe Abraham's organization of space is 'merkkeʒ', a word pregnant with meanings, many of which go back to the Old English 'mearc' (a mark or a boundary). The best-known use of the word is the description of Grendel and his mother as 'mearc-stapan' (literally 'boundary-stalkers') in *Beowulf* (1348), a phrase that captures exactly what scares us in the monstrous: its indeterminacy, its 'in-betweenness', the way it inhabits neither the realm of the human, nor that of the non-human, neither the wilderness nor the hall, but the fuzzy boundary (*mearc*) between the two. These are overtones that *Cleanness* exploits. The poet uses the verb 'merkken' elsewhere in the poem to refer to God's act of creation, the act of circumscription and separation *par excellence*: 'he man vpon molde merked to lyue' (558). When Abraham 'merkkez bytwene', he creates order out of randomness as God did in the beginning. On a smaller scale, Abraham also repeats the careful distribution of matter by Noah, who follows God's precise instructions about the ark's internal and external design. He allocates the various species of animals, pair by pair, to different rooms and cubicles in his ship; he then ensures an orderly disembarking, a 'skylly skyualde' (529), when he lets them loose on dry land. And Noah, in his turn, re-enacts on a smaller scale God's creation of the world, the division and separation of an originally formless chaos into water and earth, light and day, live matter and dead matter, woman and man.

As Abraham lays the table, so God structured the world. Abraham's seemingly insignificant act encapsulates the poet's entire ethic of clean-ness. It reaffirms the poet's view of the cosmos as an order where all things have their proper places, and where nothing may be out of bounds.

EMBODYING CULTURE

'I am simply laying the table,' Abraham might object, and as far as he is concerned, that might indeed be what he thinks he is doing. But to con-cede Abraham the point is not to say that his physical movements do not have wider moral implications. It should alert us to the possibility that people can assimilate an ethic to such an extent that they forget that they carry it with them, and carry it out. I am not under the illusion that I am describing Abraham's experiential reality when I claim that he is organizing the world in a way analogous to God. The reason why such an interpretation would be perverse is that I am restoring what seems natural to the level of culture, whereas Abraham has done *exactly the opposite*: he has incorporated culture so fully that it now comes naturally.

In spelling out the logic that holds the many stories about cleanness and uncleanness in this poem together, meanings that encompass the physical, the moral, and the cosmological, I have similarly described the poem from the perspective of an outsider. As A.C. Spearing was the first to point out, the links between, for example, Belshazzar's profanation of the vessels, Lot's wife salting her guests' meal, and sodomy, become visible once it is understood that uncleanness is an offence against a sense of order (Spearing 1987). It owes its reach and cosmological implications to the fact that it is a 'by-product of a systematic ordering and classification' —to the fact that it is a product of culture rather than nature.

We have seen how Spearing's anthropological approach allows us to grasp the poem's overall coherence and its interest in boundaries, categories, separations, transgressions and confusions. However, the approach does *not* place us inside the *Gawain*-poet's 'whole world of thought and feeling' as Spearing suggests (Spearing 1979, 178). On the contrary, it demystifies that world, in the same way that we demystify Abraham's actions when we lay bare the cultural dimensions behind his innocent setting of the table. Seeing cleanness and uncleanness as culturally determined is useful inasmuch as it makes it possible for us to appreciate (at least intellectually) why the poet should attach labels of *clanness* and *fylthe* to situations where we think they do not apply. But we should not confuse this 'cultural' view of cleanness and uncleanness with the view put forward by the poet. For the reason why the *Gawain*-poet associates various transgressions against the order of things with physical filth is not to denaturalize uncleanness but to naturalize culture, to inculcate in his audience the proper measure of 'natural' disgust at the kinds of behaviour that the poet finds reprehensible. His ideal reader is not a cultural anthropologist but someone like Abraham, who has literally come to embody the poet's set of values, and who knows what is clean and unclean not after pondering its cultural implications but simply because he does or does not feel disgusted.

The poet's strategy in *Cleanness* is to provoke in his readers an intensely physical response to moral issues, as if they were matters over which the body rather than the brain had jurisdiction. It is in the light of this project that the purposeful confusion or interchangeability in *Cleanness* between physical and moral pollution must be understood. Generations of critics and editors have tried to disentangle moral *clannes* in this poem from physical *clannes*, an attempt to which the work owes its distinct modern titles: *Cleanness* (emphasizing the physical) and alternatively *Purity* (emphasizing the moral). But the confusion between the moral and the visceral is deliberate. The *Gawain*-poet breaks down the distinction between the two in order to cultivate in us a somatic revulsion against moral impurity that can be felt as naturally and unselfconsciously as the queasy feeling at the sight of physical filth.

The collapse of the moral and the physical senses of *clannes* is an effect on which the success of the poet's pedagogy depends, and the passages which show the poet attempting to present his ethical judgements as 'natural' bodily reflexes are numerous. The man whose deeds are 'unclean', the poet writes, is like the disgusting guest in the Parable of the Wedding Feast who turns up in filthy rags. What is the point of the comparison if not to prompt us to treat an evil-doer with the same loathing as a man who does not wash his clothes? The *exemplum* of the Flood likewise presents antediluvian sexual practices as 'gore' and 'glette', as filth that upsets God's stomach rather than his sensibilities:

> With her vnworþelych werk me wlateʒ withinne;
> Þe gore þerof me hatʒ greued and þe glette nwyed ...
>
> (305–6)

> (In my body I am disgusted by their shameful deeds. The gore of it has harmed me and the filth has made me sick.)

In the *exemplum* of Sodom and Gomorrah, the Sodomites are singled out for this kind of treatment. Taking a wider view of their sin we might say that the Sodomites confuse the categories of God's creation, but the poet is trying to instil in us a repugnance that is again overwhelmingly somatic, as if the Sodomites were rebelling against our gastric juices rather than our sense of right or wrong. Rather than listening to what the Sodomites have to say for themselves, the poet simply reduces their words to filth and stench:

> Whatt! þay sputen and speken of so spitous fylþe;
> What! þay ʒeʒed and ʒolped of ʒestande sorʒe,
> Þat þe wynd and þe weder and þe world stynkes
> Of þe brych þat vprayde þose broþelich wordeʒ.
>
> (845–9)

(Listen to this! They talked and spoke of such vile filth. Listen how they roared and bellowed about festering filth, so that the wind and the air and the world stank of the stench thrown up by those wretched words.)

The *Gawain*-poet knew all too well that there is nothing that seems more natural than the feeling of sickness that seizes us at the sight of *fylþe* or the smell of *brych*. It makes any attempt to empathize with the Sodomites impossible. And that, of course, is the point. Disgust, wrote George Orwell, places an 'impassable barrier' between us and the 'unclean':

> For no feeling of like or dislike is quite so fundamental as a *physical* feeling. Race-hatred, religious hatred, differences of education, of temperament, of intellect, even differences of moral code, can be got over; but physical repulsion cannot. You can have affection for a murderer or a sodomite, but you cannot have an affection for a man whose breath stinks; habitually stinks, I mean.
>
> (Orwell 1937, 129–30)

It might well be objected that even the kind of 'spitous fylþe' exhibited by the Sodomites in *Cleanness*—bad breath, bad odour and vomit—is not truly absolute, dependent as it is on assumptions learnt from our youngest days about what the boundaries of our bodies are, about what should stay inside the body, and about when and where excretions may be allowed to exit. But the argument that the nausea which the Sodomites arouse in the poet and his ideal readers is socially constructed is to resist the poet's attempt to convert our bodies into the safe-deposit of his cultural prejudices. 'Breþe' (stench), 'bryche' (vomit) 'clater', 'dyn', 'fylþe', 'ȝeȝen' (to scream), 'flot' (scum), 'foul', 'froþande', 'gore', 'ȝelpen' (to bellow); this is only a small sample of the sickening vocabulary in which the poet couches his disapproval of transgressions of the boundaries he imposes on what human beings may and may not do. It is a vocabulary which tries to get under our skin, which bombards our sense of taste, smell, vision, touch, and hearing so that we may come to experience this disapproval as an entirely 'natural' or 'automatic' response.

The trick of good pedagogues, writes Pierre Bourdieu, is that they treat the body as a memory:

> [They] entrust to it in abbreviated and practical, i.e. mnemonic, form the fundamental principles of the arbitrary content of the culture. The principles embodied in this way are placed beyond the grasp of consciousness, and hence cannot be touched by voluntary, deliberate transformation, cannot even be made explicit.
>
> (Bourdieu 1977, 94)

The pedagogy of *Cleanness* is of this kind. When we have forgotten that uncleanness is what offends against the poet's view of the world, and experience it, like God or like the poet, as a pain in the bowels, *Cleanness* will have done its job. We might for once be better off not trying to be this text's ideal readers.

Bibliography

PRIMARY SOURCES

'ABC on the Passion of Christ', ed. F.J. Furnivall, *Political, Religious, and Love-Poems*, EETS OS 15 (London: Trübner, 1866).

Abelard, Peter, 'O quanta, qualia sunt illa sabbata', *PL* 178, 1786–8.

Ambrose, *De excessu fratris sui Satyri*, *PL* 16, 1289–1317.

Aquinas, Thomas, *Summa Theologiae*, ed. T. Gilby et al., 61 vols (London: Blackfriars, 1963–75).

Augustine, *Contra mendacium*, *PL* 40, 517–48.

— *De patientia*, ed. and trans. Gustav Combès (Paris: Desclée de Brouwer, 1948).

— *Sermo 53*, *PL* 38, 364–72.

— *Sermo 87*, *PL* 38, 530–9.

— *De sermone Domini*, ed. A. Mützenberger, *CC* 35 (Turnhout: Brepols, 1967), 1–15; trans. D.J. Kavanaugh, *The Fathers of the Church*, vol. 11, (New York: Fathers of the Church, 1951), 19–32.

Avitus, *De spiritalis historiae gestis*, ed. Ruldof Peiper, Monumenta Germaniae Historica, Auctores Antiquissimi VI (Berlin: Weidmann, 1983).

Bevington, David (ed.), *Medieval Drama* (Boston: Houghton Mifflin, 1975).

Boniface, *De octo beatitudinibus*, *PL* 89, 850–2.

Brewer, Elisabeth (ed.), *Sir Gawain and the Green Knight: Sources and Analogues* (Woodbridge: Boydell and Brewer, 1992).

Bruno Astensis, *Commentaria in Matthaeum*, *PL* 165, 63–314.

Carmen de Jona et Ninive, ed. Rudolf Peiper, *Cypriani Galli poetae*, *CSEL* 23 (Vienna: Akademie der Wissenschaften, 1891), pp. 221–6; trans. S. Thelwall, *Tertullian, The Ante-Nicene Fathers*, vol. 4 (Buffalo: Christian Literature Publications Company, 1887), 127–9.

Carmen de Sodoma, ed. Rudolf Peiper, *Cypriani Galli poetae*, CSEL 23 (Vienna: Akademie der Wissenschaften, 1891), pp. 212–19; trans. S. Thelwall, *Tertullian, The Ante-Nicene Fathers*, vol. 4 (Buffalo: Christian Literature Publications Company, 1887), 129–32.

Cato, *Distichs*, in *Minor Latin Poets*, LCL, eds J. Wight Duff and Arnold M. Duff (Cambridge, Mass.: Harvard University Press, 1934).

Chaucer, Geoffrey, *The Riverside Chaucer*, ed. Larry D. Benson et al., (Boston: Houghton Mifflin, 1987).

Chrétien de Troyes, *Le Chevalier au lion (Yvain)*, ed. Mario Roques, CFMA (Paris: Champion, 1982); trans. D.D.R. Owen, *Chrétien de Troyes: Arthurian Romances* (London: Everyman, 1978).

Cleanness, ed. J.J. Anderson (Manchester: Manchester University Press, 1977).

Clopper, Lawrence M. (ed.), *Chester*, Records of Early English Drama (Toronto: University of Toronto Press, 1979).

Dante Alighieri, *The Divine Comedy*, ed. and trans. Charles S. Singleton, Bollingen Series (Princeton: Princeton University Press, 1973).

Destruction of Troy, eds G.A. Panton and David Donaldson, 2 vols, EETS OS 39, 56 (London: Trübner, 1869–74).

Didot-Perceval, ed. William Roach (Philadelphia: University of Pennsylvania Press, 1941); trans. D. Skeels, *The Romance of Perceval in Prose* (Seattle: University of Washington Press, 1961).

First Continuation, ed. William Roach, vols I–III of *Continuations of the Old French Perceval of Chrétien de Troyes*, 5 vols (Philadelphia: Pennsylvania University Press, 1949–83); trans. Nigel Bryant, *Perceval: The Story of the Grail* (Cambridge: Brewer, 1986), pp. 98–135.

Gascoine, George, 'Certain Notes of Instruction Concerning the Making of Verse', in *Elizabethan Critical Essays*, ed. G. Gregory Smith, 2 vols (Oxford: Oxford University Press, 1904), I, 46–57.

Genesis and Exodus, ed. Richard Morris, EETS OS 7 (London: Trübner, 1873).

Geoffrey of Monmouth, *Historia Regum Britanniae*, ed. Neil Wright (Cambridge: Brewer, 1984); trans. L. Thorpe, *History of the Kings of Britain* (London: Penguin, 1966).

Giacomino da Verona, *The De Jerusalem Celesti and the De Babilonia Infernali by Fra Giacomino da Verona*, ed. Esther Isopel May (London: Oxford University Press, 1930).

Gower, John, *The English Works of John Gower*, ed. G.C. Macauley, 2 vols, EETS ES 81, 82 (London: Oxford University Press, 1900–1).

Grene Knight, ed. Elizabeth Brewer, *Sir Gawain and the Green Knight: Sources and Analogues* (Woodbridge: Boydell and Brewer, 1992).

Guillaume de Lorris and Jean de Meun, *Roman de la Rose*, ed. Armand Strubel (Paris: Librairie Générale Française, 1992); trans. Charles Dahlberg, *The Romance of the Rose* (Princeton: Princeton University Press, 1971).

Hilton, Walter, *The Ladder of Perfection*, trans. Leo Sherley-Price (Harmondsworth: Penguin, 1988).

Honorius Augustodunensis, *Elucidarium*, PL 172, 1109–76.

Jerome, *In Jonam*, ed. and trans. Yves-Marie Duval (Paris: Editions du Cerf, 1985).

John of Bromyard, *Summa praedicantium* (Nuremberg, 1518).

Lancelot do Lac: The Non Cyclic Old French Prose Lancelot, ed. Elspeth Kennedy, 2 vols (Oxford: Clarendon Press, 1980); trans. Corin Corley, *Lancelot of the Lake*, World's Classics (Oxford: Oxford University Press, 1989).

Langland, William, *The Vision of Piers Plowman: A Critical Edition of the B-Text*, ed. A.V.C. Schmidt (London: Everyman, 1995).

Latini, Brunetto, *Li livres dou tresor*, ed. F.J. Carmody (Berkeley: University of California Press, 1948).

Lull, Ramon, *The Book of the Lover and the Beloved*, ed. and trans. Kenneth Leeds (London: Sheldon Press, 1979).

Malory, Thomas, *Sir Thomas Malory: Works*, eds. Eugène Vinaver and P.J.C. Field, 3rd edn, 3 vols (Oxford: Clarendon Press, 1990).

Marbod of Rennes, *Naufragium Jonae prophetae*, PL 171, 1675–8.

Nicholas of Lyra, *Postilla, Textus Biblie cum Glosa ordinaria & Nicolai de Lyra postilla* (Basel, 1506–8).

Otto of Freising, *Chronica sive historia de duabis civitatibus*, ed. Walther Lammers (Darmstadt: Wissenschaftliche Buchgesellschaft, 1961).

Paston Letters and Papers of the Fifteenth Century, 2 vols, ed. Norman Davis (Oxford: Oxford University Press, 1976).

Patience, ed. J.J. Anderson (Manchester: Manchester University Press, 1969).

Pearl, ed. E.V. Gordon (Oxford: Clarendon Press, 1974).

Peter of Blois, *Sermo 42*, PL 207, 688–93.

Philip of Harvengt, *De institutione clericorum*, PL 203, 665–1206.

Pseudo-Ambrose, *Acta S. Sebastiani martyris*, PL 17, 1019–58.

Pseudo-Fulgentius, *Sermo 16*, PL 65, 878–80.

Roger of Basevorn, *The Form of Preaching*, ed. J.J. Murphy, *Three*

Medieval Rhetorical Arts (Berkeley: University of California Press, 1971).

Rupert of Deutz, *Commentariorum duodecim prophetas minores*, PL 168, 401–42.

Sir Gawain and the Green Knight, eds. J.R.R. Tolkien and E.V. Gordon, revis. Norman Davis (Oxford, 1967).

Speculum morale, attributed to Vincent of Beauvais, *Speculum majus*, 4 vols, III: *Speculum morale* (Douay, 1624).

St Erkenwald, ed. Ruth Morse (Cambridge: Brewer, 1975).

Tabula exemplorum, ed. J.T. Welther (Paris: Guitard, 1926).

Tresplaisante et recreative histoire de Perceval le galloys (Paris, 1530).

Virgil, *Aeneid*, ed. E.H. Warmington and trans. H. Rushton Fairclough, 2 vols, LCL (London: Heinemann, 1967).

Wace, *Le roman de Brut de Wace*, ed. Ivor Arnold, 2 vols, SATF (Paris: Firmin Didot, 1938–40).

Wynnere and Wastoure, ed. Stephanie Trigg, EETS 297 (Oxford: Oxford University Press, 1990).

SECONDARY SOURCES

Aers (1993) David Aers, 'The Self Mourning: Reflections on *Pearl*', *Speculum* 68, 54–73.

Anderson (1969) J.J. Anderson (ed.), *Patience* (Manchester: Manchester University Press).

Andrew (1973) Malcolm Andrew, 'Jonah and Christ in *Patience*', *MP* 70, 230–3.

  (1979) *The Gawain-Poet: An Annotated Bibliography 1839–1977* (New York: Garland).

  (1982) ' "Rome-runners" and *Patience*, line 52', *Archiv* 219, 116–19.

Andrew and Waldron (1978) Malcolm Andrew and Ronald Waldron (eds) *The Poems of the 'Pearl' Manuscript*, York Medieval Texts (London: Edward Arnold).

Axton (1977) Richard Axton, 'Folkplay in Tudor Interludes', in *English Drama: Forms and Development*, eds Marie Axton and Raymond Williams (Cambridge: Cambridge University Press), 1–23.

Baldwin (1990) Anna P. Baldwin, 'The Triumph of Patience in Julian of Norwich and Langland', in *Langland, the Mystics, and the Medieval English Tradition: Essays in Honour of S.S. Hussey*, ed. Helen Phillips (Woodbridge: Boydell and Brewer).

Barron (1965) W.R.J. Barron, '"Luf-Daungere"', in *Medieval Miscellany Presented to Eugene Vinaver*, eds F. Whitehead, A.H. Diverres, and F.E. Sutcliffe (Manchester: Manchester University Press), 1–18.

Beer (1989) Gillian Beer, *Arguing with the Past: Essays in Narrative from Woolf to Sidney* (London: Routledge).

Benjamin (1978) Walter Benjamin, 'The Destructive Character', in *Reflections*, ed. Peter Demetz and trans. Edmund Jephcott (New York: Harcourt Brace Jovanovich), 301–3.

Bennett (1979) Michael J. Bennett, '*Sir Gawain and the Green Knight* and the Literary Achievement of the North-West Midlands: The Historical Background', *Journal of Medieval History* 5, 63–88.

(1981a) '"Good Lords" and "King-Makers": The Stanleys of Lotham in English Politics, 1385–1485', *History Today* 31, 12–17.

(1981b) 'Courtly Literature and North-West England in the Later Middle Ages', *Court and Poet*, ed. G.S. Burgess (Liverpool: University of Liverpool Press), 69–78.

(1983) *Community, Class, and Careerism: Cheshire and Lancashire Society in the Age of Sir Gawain and the Green Knight* (Cambridge: Cambridge University Press).

Benson (1965a) Larry D. Benson, 'The Authorship of *St. Erkenwald*', *Journal of English and Germanic Philology* 64, 393–405.

(1965b) *Art and Tradition in Sir Gawain and the Green Knight* (New York: Rutgers University Press).

Blanch (1990) Robert J. Blanch, 'Supplement to the *Gawain*-Poet: An Annotated Bibliography', *ChR* 25, 363–86.

Blanch and Wasserman (1984) Robert J. Blanch and Julian N. Wasserman, 'Medieval Contracts and Covenants: The Legal Coloring of *Sir Gawain and the Green Knight*', *Neophilologus* 68, 598–610.

Bogdanos (1983) Theodore Bogdanos, *Pearl: Image of the Ineffable: A Study in Medieval Poetic Symbolism* (Pennsylvania: Pennsylvania State University Press).

Bonjour (1951) Adrien Bonjour, 'Werre and wrake and wonder', *ES* 32, 70–2.

Bonnard (1884) J. Bonnard, *Les traductions de la Bible en vers français* (repr. Geneva: Droz, 1967).

Borroff (1962) *Sir Gawain and the Green Knight: A Stylistic and Metrical Study* (New Haven: Yale University Press).

(1982) Marie Borroff, '*Pearl*'s "Maynful Mone": Crux, Simile, and Structure', in *Acts of Interpretation: The Text in Its Contexts*

700–1600: Essays in Honor of E. Talbot Donaldson, eds Mary J. Carruthers and Elizabeth D. Kirk (Norman, Oklahoma: Pilgrim Books), 159–72.

Boulton (1987) D'A.J.D. Boulton, *The Knights of the Crown: The Monarchical Orders of Knighthood in Later Medieval Europe* (Woodbridge: Boydell and Brewer).

Bourdieu (1977) Pierre Bourdieu, *Outline of a Theory of Practice*, trans. Richard Nice (Cambridge: Cambridge University Press).

Bowers (1971) R.H. Bowers, *The Legend of Jonah* (The Hague: Nijhoff).

Bowers (1995) John H. Bowers, 'Pearl in Its Royal Setting: Ricardian Poetry Revisited', *SAC* 17, 111–55.

Brewer (1966) Derek S. Brewer, 'Courtesy and the *Gawain*-Poet', in *Patterns of Love and Courtesy: Essays in Memory of C.S. Lewis*, ed. J. Lawlor (London: Arnold), 54–85.

Brown (1904) Carleton F. Brown, 'The Author of *Pearl*, Considered in the Light of His Theological Opinions', *PMLA* 19, 115–53.

Bumke (1986) Joachim Bumke, *Höfische Kultur*, 2 vols (Munich: Deutscher Taschenbuch Verlag).

Burnley (1979) J.D. Burnley, *Chaucer's Language and the Philosophers' Tradition* (Cambridge: Brewer).

Burrow (1965) J.A. Burrow, *A Reading of Sir Gawain and the Green Knight* (London: Routledge and Kegan Paul).

(1982) 'Sir Gawain and the Green Knight', in *Medieval Literature*, ed. Boris Ford, New Pelican Guide to English Literature 1 (Harmondsworth: Penguin), 208–23.

(1989) 'Two Notes on the Middle English *Patience*', *N&Q* 234, 300–3.

(1993) 'St Erkenwald, line 1: 'At London in Englond', *N&Q* 238, 22–3.

Bynum (1987) Caroline Walker Bynum, *Holy Feast and Holy Fast: The Significance of Food to Medieval Women* (Berkeley: University of California Press).

Carlson (1987) David Carlson, 'The *Pearl*-Poet's Olympia', *Manuscripta* 31, 181–9.

Casey (1987) Edward S. Casey, *Remembering: A Phenomenological Study* (Bloomington: Indiana University Press).

Cave (1988) Terence Cave, *Recognitions: A Study in Poetics* (Oxford: Clarendon Press).

Cawley and Anderson (1976) A.C. Cawley and J.J. Anderson (eds),

Pearl, Cleanness, Patience, Sir Gawain and the Green Knight, Everyman Library (London: Dent).

Chapman (1945) C.O. Chapman, 'Virgil and the *Gawain*-Poet', *PMLA* 60, 16–23.

Charity (1966) A.C. Charity, *Events and Their Afterlife: The Dialectics of Christian Typology in the Bible and Dante* (Cambridge: Cambridge University Press).

Charland (1936) Th. Charland, *Artes praedicandi: contribution à l'histoire de la rhétorique au Moyen Âge* (Paris and Ottawa: Institut d'Études Médiévales d'Ottawa).

Childs (1983) Wendy Childs, 'Anglo-Italian Contacts in the Fourteenth Century', in *Chaucer and the Italian Trecento*, ed. Piero Boitani (Cambridge: Cambridge University Press), 65–88.

Coldstream (1981) Nicola Coldstream, 'Art and Architecture in the Late Middle Ages', *The Later Middle Ages*, ed. Stephen Medcalf (London: Methuen), 225–90.

Coward (1983) Barry Coward, *The Stanleys, Lords Stanley and Earls of Derby: 1385–1672* (Manchester: Chetham Society).

Davidson (1994) Clifford Davidson (ed.), *The Iconography of Heaven* (Kalamazoo, Mich.: Medieval Institute Publications).

Davies (1971) R.R. Davies, 'Richard II and the Principality of Chester', in *The Reign of Richard II: Essays in Honour of May McKisack*, eds F.R.H. du Boulay and C.M. Barron (London: Arnold), 256–79.

Dean (1987) Christopher Dean, *Arthur of England: English Attitudes to King Arthur and the Knights of the Round Table in the Middle Ages and the Renaissance* (Toronto: University of Toronto Press).

Dinzelbacher (1979) Peter Dinzelbacher, 'Klassen und Hierarchien im Jenseits', *Miscellanea Mediaevalia* 12, 20–40.

Donner (1989) Morton Donner, 'Word Play and Word Form in *Pearl*', *ChR* 24, 166–83.

Douglas (1968) Mary Douglas, *Purity and Danger: An Analysis of the Concepts of Pollution and Taboo* (London: Routledge).

Doyle (1982) A.I. Doyle, 'The Manuscripts', in *Middle English Alliterative Poetry and Its Literary Background*, ed. David Lawton (Cambridge: Brewer), 88–100.

Du Boulay (1970) F.R.H. Du Boulay, *An Age of Ambition* (London: Nelson).

Duggan (1986) H.N. Duggan, 'The Shape of the B-Verse in Middle English Alliterative Poetry', *Speculum* 61, 564–92.

Duncan (1992) Ian Duncan, *Modern Romance and Transformations of the Novel* (Cambridge: Cambridge University Press).

Duval (1973) Yves-Marie Duval, *Le Livre de Jonas dans la littérature Chrétienne grecque et latine* (Paris: Etudes Augustiniennes).

Edwards (1990) Elizabeth Edwards, 'Amnesia and Remembrance in Malory's *Morte Darthur*', *Paragraph* 13, 132–46.

Eldredge (1975) Laurence Eldredge, 'The State of *Pearl*-Studies since 1933', *Viator* 6, 171–93.

(1981) 'Sheltering Space and Cosmic Space in the Middle English *Patience*', *Annuale mediaevale* 21, 121–33.

Eliade (1959) Mircea Eliade, *The Sacred and the Profane*, trans. Williard R. Trask (New York: Harper).

Elliott (1984) Ralph W.V. Eliott, *The Gawain Country* (Leeds: University of Leeds, School of English).

Emmerson (1992) Richard K. Emmerson, 'The Apocalypse in Medieval Culture', in *The Apocalypse in the Middle Ages*, eds Richard K. Emmerson and Bernard McGinn (Ithaca, New York: Cornell University Press), 293–332.

Fày (1975) Attila Fày, 'Marbodean and Patristic Reminiscences in *Patience*', *Revue de littérature comparée* 49, 284–90.

Finlayson (1983) John Finlayson, '*Pearl*, Petrarch's *Trionfa della Morte* and Boccaccio's *Olympia*', *English Studies in Canada* 9, 1–13.

Fish (1974) Stanley Fish, *Self-Consuming Artifacts* (Berkeley: University of California Press).

(1984) 'Authors-Readers: Jonson's Community of the Same', *Representations* 7, 26–58.

Fisher (1977) John H. Fisher, 'Chancery and the Emergence of Standard Written English in the Fifteenth Century', *Speculum* 52, 870–99.

Foley (1989) M. Foley, '*The Gawain*-Poet: An Annotated Bibliography, 1978–1985', *ChR* 23, 251–82.

Fradenburg (1986) Louise O. Fradenburg, 'The Wife of Bath's Passing Fancy', *SAC* 8, 31–58.

Friedman (1981) John B. Friedman, 'Figural Typology in the Middle English *Patience*', in *The Alliterative Tradition in the Fourteenth Century*, eds Bernard S. Levy and Paul E. Szarmach (Kent, Ohio: Kent State University Press), 99–129.

Gadamer (1975) Hans-Georg Gadamer, *Truth and Method* (London: Sheed and Ward).

Ganim (1976) John Ganim, 'Disorientation, Style, and Consciousness in *Sir Gawain and the Green Knight*', *PMLA* 91, 376–84.

Gardiner (1993) Eileen Gardiner, *Medieval Visions of Heaven and Hell: A Sourcebook* (New York: Garland).

Gillespie (1975) J.L. Gillespie, 'Richard II's Cheshire Archers', *Transactions of the Historic Society of Lancashire and Cheshire* 125, 1–40.

Gilson (1946) Etienne Gilson, 'La vertu de patience selon St. Thomas et St. Augustine', *Archives d'histoire doctrinale* 15, 93–104.

Ginsberg (1988) Warren Ginsberg, 'Place and Dialectic in *Pearl* and Dante's *Paradiso*', *ELH* 55, 731–53.

Glauche (1970) Günter Glauche, *Schullektüre im Mittelalter* (München: Münchener Beiträge zur Mediävistik und Renaissance-Forschung).

Gollancz (1921a) Sir Israel Gollancz (ed.), *Pearl: An English Poem of the Fourteenth Century* (London: Chatto).

(1921b) *Cleanness: An Alliterative Tripartite Poem* (London: Oxford University Press); reprinted with a translation by D.S. Brewer (Cambridge: Brewer, 1974).

Gordon (1974) E.V. Gordon (ed.), *Pearl* (Oxford: Clarendon Press).

Gradon (1971) Pamela Gradon, *Form and Style in Early English Literature* (London: Methuen).

Grant and Tracy (1984) Robert M. Grant and David Tracy, *A Short History of the Interpretation of the Bible* (London: Fortress Press).

Hill (1967) Ordelle G. Hill, 'The Late Latin *De Jona* as a Source for *Patience*', *Journal of English and Germanic Philology* 66, 21–5.

(1968) 'The Audience of *Patience*', *MP* 66, 103–9.

Holbert (1981) John C. Holbert, '"Deliverance belongs to Jahweh": Satire in the Book of Jonah', *Journal for the Study of the Old Testament* 21, 59–81.

Hughes (1968) Robert Hughes, *Heaven and Hell in Western Art* (Frankfurt am Main: Lohse).

Jacob (1968) E.F. Jacob, 'To and from the Court of Rome in the Early Fifteenth Century', in *Essays in Later Medieval History* (Manchester: Manchester University Press), 58–78.

Jacobs (1972) Nicolas Jacobs, 'Alliterative Storms: A Topos in Middle English', *Speculum* 47, 695–719.

James (1951) M.R. James, '*Pictor in carmine*', *Archaeologica* 94, 141–66.

Kean (1967) P.M. Kean, *The Pearl: An Interpretation* (London: Routledge and Kegan Paul).

Keen (1990) Maurice Keen, *English Society in the Later Middle Ages, 1348–1500* (Harmondsworth: Penguin).

Keiser (1980) Elizabeth Keiser, 'The Festive Decorum of *Cleanness*', in

Chivalric Literature: Essays on Relations between Literature and Life in the Later Middle Ages, eds Larry D. Benson and John Leyerle (Kalamazoo: University of Western Michigan Press), 1–24.

Kelly (1992) Douglas Kelly, *The Art of Medieval French Romance* (Madison: University of Wisconsin Press).

Kennedy (1986) Elspeth Kennedy, *Lancelot and the Grail: A Study of the Prose Lancelot* (Oxford: Clarendon Press).

Kennedy (1987) Ruth Kennedy, '"A Bird in Bishopswood": Some Newly Discovered Lines of Alliterative Verse from the Late Fourteenth Century', in *Medieval Literature and Antiquities: Studies in Honour of Basil Cottle*, eds Myra Stokes and T.L. Burton (Woodbridge: Boydell and Brewer), 71–87.

Ker (1955) W.P. Ker, *Medieval English Literature* (London: Oxford University Press, first edn 1912).

Kermode (1979) Frank Kermode, *The Genesis of Secrecy: On the Interpretation of Narrative* (Cambridge, Mass.: Harvard University Press).

Kirk (1978) Elizabeth D. Kirk, '"Who suffreth more than God": Narrative Redefinition of Patience in *Patience* and *Piers Plowman*', in Schiffhorst (1978), 88–104.

Lawton (1978) David A. Lawton, '*Scottish Field*: Alliterative Verse and Stanley Encomium', *Leeds Studies in English* 10, 42–53.

(1989) 'The Diversity of Middle English Alliterative Poetry', *Leeds English Studies* 20, 143–72.

Leclerq (1974) Jean Leclerq, 'Aux origines bibliques du vocabulaire de la pauvreté', in *Études sur l'histoire de la pauvreté*, ed. Michel Mollat, 2 vols (Paris, Publications de la Sorbonne), I, 35–44.

Lee (1977) Jennifer A. Lee, 'The Illuminating Critic: The Illustrator of Cotton Nero A.x.', *Studies in Iconography* 3, 17–46.

Legge (1936) Dominica Legge, 'A fuer de guerre', *Medium Aevum* 5, 121–2.

Loomis (1959) Roger Sherman Loomis, 'Arthurian Influence on Sport and Spectacle', in *Arthurian Literature in the Middle Ages*, ed. Roger Sherman Loomis (Oxford: Oxford University Press), 553–9.

Luttrell (1958) Claude Luttrell, 'Three North-West Midland Manuscripts', *Neophilologus* 42, 38–50.

(1979) '*Sir Gawain and the Green Knight* and the Versions of Caradoc', *Forum for Modern Language Studies* 15, 347–60.

Macrae-Gibson (1970) O.D. Macrae-Gibson, '*Pearl*: The Link-Words and the Thematic Structure', *Neophilologus* 52 (1968), 54–64; repr.

in *The Middle English Pearl: Critical Essays*, ed. John Conley (Notre Dame: University of Notre Dame Press), 203–19.

Madden (1839) Sir Frederic Madden (ed.), *Syr Gawayne: A Collection of Ancient Romance Poems* (London: Taylor).

Mann (1983) Jill Mann, 'Satisfaction and Payment in Middle English Literature', *SAC* 5, 17–48.

(1986) 'Price and Value in *Sir Gawain and the Green Knight*', *Essays in Criticism* 36, 298–318.

(1994a) 'The Power of the Alphabet: A Reassessment of the Relation Between the A and the B Versions of *Piers Plowman*', *Yearbook of Langland Studies* 8, 21–50.

(1994b) 'Sir Gawain and the Romance Hero', in *Heroes and Heroines in Medieval Literature: A Festschrift Presented to André Crépin*, ed. Leo Carruthers (Woodbridge: Boydell and Brewer), 105–17.

(1994c) 'Allegorical Buildings in Mediaeval Literature', *Medium Aevum* 63, 191–210.

Markus (1971) Manfred Markus, *Moderne Erzählperspektive in den Werken des Gawain-Autors* (Regensburg: Carl).

Mathew (1968) Gervase Mathew, *The Court of Richard II* (London: Murray).

McDannell and Lang (1988) C. McDannell and Bernard L. Lang, *Heaven: A History* (New Haven: Yale University Press).

McGovern (1971) William McGovern, 'The Enforcement of Informal Contracts in the Later Middle Ages', *California Law Review* 59, 1145–83.

McIntosh (1963) Angus McIntosh, 'A New Approach to Middle English Dialectology', *ES* 44, 1–11.

Middleton (1978) Anne Middleton, 'The Idea of Public Poetry in the Reign of Richard II', *Speculum* 53, 94–114.

(1982) 'The Audience and Public of *Piers Plowman*', in *Middle English Alliterative Poetry and Its Literary Background*, ed. David Lawton (Cambridge: Brewer), 101–23.

Mollat (1986) Michel Mollat, *The Poor in the Middle Ages*, trans. A. Goldhammer (New Haven and London: Yale University Press).

Moorman (1963) Charles Moorman, 'The Role of the Narrator in *Patience*', *MP* 61, 90–5.

Morey (1993) James H. Morey, 'Peter Comestor, Biblical Paraphrase, and the Medieval Popular Bible', *Speculum* 68, 6–35.

Mullally (1988) Evelyn Mullally, *The Artist at Work: Narrative Technique in Chrétien de Troyes*, Transactions of the American Philosophical Society 78, 4 (Philadelphia: American Philosophical Society).

Nodes (1985) Daniel J. Nodes (ed.), *Avitus, The Fall of Man* (Toronto: Centre for Medieval Studies).

Nolan (1977) Barbara Nolan, *The Gothic Visionary Perspective* (Princeton: Princeton University Press).

Oberman (1957) Heiko Oberman, *Archbishop Bradwardine: A Fourteenth-Century Augustinian* (Utrecht: Drukkerijen Uitgeversmaatschappij).

Ong (1947) Walter J. Ong, 'Wit and Mystery: A Revaluation', *Speculum* 22, 310–41.

Orwell (1937) George Orwell, *The Road to Wigan Pier* (London: Heinemann, repr. 1965).

Parkes (1992) M.B. Parkes, *Pause and Effect: An Introduction to the History of Punctuation in the West* (Aldershot: Scolar Press).

Payne (1989) Roberta L. Payne, '*Pearl*: A Revaluation of Its Relationship with the *Divina Commedia*', in her *The Influence of Dante on Middle English Dream-Visions* (New York: Peter Lang), 27–58.

Pearsall (1955) Derek Pearsall, 'Rhetorical *Descriptio* in *Sir Gawain and the Green Knight*', *MLR* 50, 129–34.

Pellistrandi (1974) Christine Pellistrandi, 'La pauvreté spirituelle', *Etudes sur l'histoire de la pauvreté*, ed. Michel Mollat, 2 vols (Paris, Publications de la Sorbonne), I, 275–94.

Peterson (1974) Clifford J. Peterson, 'The *Pearl*-Poet and *St. Erkenwald*: Some Evidence for Authorship', *RES* 25, 49–53.

Pilch (1970) Herbert Pilch, 'Das mittelenglische Perlengedicht: Sein Verhältnis zum Rosenroman', *Neuphilologische Mitteilungen* 65 (1964), 427–46, transl. as 'The Middle English *Pearl*: Its Relation to the *Roman de la Rose*', in *The Middle English Pearl: Critical Essays*, ed. John Conley (Notre Dame: University of Notre Dame Press), 163–84.

Preus (1969) James Samuel Preus, *From Shadow to Promise: Old Testament Interpretation from Augustine to the Young Luther* (Cambridge, Mass.: Harvard University Press).

Prickett (1986) Stephen Prickett, 'The Paradoxes of Disconfirmation', in his *Words and The Word: Language, Poetics, and Biblical Interpretation* (Cambridge: Cambridge University Press), 149–73.

Putter (1995) Ad Putter, *Sir Gawain and the Green Knight and French Arthurian Romance* (Oxford: Clarendon Press).

(forthcoming) 'Sources and Backgrounds for Descriptions of the

Flood in Medieval and Renaissance Literature', to appear in *Studies in Philology*.

Rayé (1964) Jean Rayé, 'Tempête et littérature dans quelques textes Chrétiens', in *Oikoumene: Studi paleocristiani in onore del Concilio Ecumenico Vaticano II* (Catania: University of Catania), 61–75.

Robbins (1943) Rossell Hope Robbins, 'A Gawain Epigone', *MLN* 9, 361–6.

Robertson (1980) D.W. Roberston, 'The Heresy of *Pearl*', *MLN* 65 (1950), 152–5; repr. in his *Essays on Medieval Culture* (Princeton: Princeton University Press), 215–17.

Robinson (1982) Ian Robinson, '*Pearl*: Poetry and Suffering', in *Medieval Literature*, ed. Boris Ford, New Pelican Guide to English Literature 1 (Harmondsworth: Penguin Books), 224–34.

Ruberg (1965) Uwe Ruberg, *Raum und Zeit im Prosa-Lancelot* (Munich: Wilhelm Fink Verlag).

Russell (1988) J. Stephen Russell, *The English Dream-Vision: Anatomy of a Form* (Columbus: Ohio State University Press).

Salter (1966–7) Elizabeth Salter, 'The Alliterative Revival', *MP* 64, 146–50, 233–7.

(1983) *Fourteenth-Century English Poetry* (Oxford: Clarendon Press).

(1988) *English and International: Studies in the Literature, Art and Patronage of Medieval England*, eds Derek Pearsall and Nicolette Zeeman (Cambridge: Cambridge University Press).

Scarry (1985) Elaine Scarry, *The Body in Pain: The Making and Unmaking of the World* (New York: Oxford University Press).

Schiffhorst (1978) Gerald J. Schiffhorst (ed.), *The Triumph of Patience: Medieval and Renaissance Studies* (Orlando: University Presses of Florida).

Schleusener (1971) Jay Schleusener, 'History and Action in *Patience*', *PMLA* 86, 959–65.

Schmidt (1988) A.V.C. Schmidt, '*Kynde Craft* and the *Play of Paramorez*': Natural and Unnatural Love in *Purity*', in *Genres, Themes, and Images in English Literature*, eds Piero Boitani and Anna Torti (Tübingen: Gunter Narr), 105–24.

Schotter (1984) Anne H. Schotter, 'Vernacular Style and the Word of God: The Incarnational Art of *Pearl*', in *Ineffability: Naming the Unnamable from Dante to Beckett*, eds Peter S. Hawkins and Anne H. Schotter (New York: AMS Press), 23–34.

Seymour (1993) M.C. Seymour, *Sir John Mandeville*, Authors of the Middle Ages (Aldershot: Variorum).

Shippey (1971) T.A. Shippey, 'The Uses of Chivalry: *Erec* and *Gawain*', *MLR* 66, 241–50.

Shoaf (1981) R.A. Shoaf, 'God's "Malyse": Metaphor and Conversion in *Patience*', *Journal of Medieval and Renaissance Studies* 11, 261–80.

(1990) '*Purgatorio* and *Pearl*: Transgression and Transcendence', *Texas Studies in Literature and Language* 32: *Beatrice Dolce Memoria, 1290–1990: Essays on the Vita Nuova and the Beatrice-Dante Relationship*, ed. David Wallace, 152–68.

Silverstein (1964) Theodore Silverstein, 'The Art of *Sir Gawain and the Green Knight*', *University of Toronto Quarterly* 33, 258–78.

Simmel (1950) Georg Simmel, 'The Secret and the Secret Society', in *The Sociology of G. Simmel*, ed. Kurt H. Wolff (Glencoe, Ill.: Free Press), 307–76.

(1960) 'The Adventure', in *Georg Simmel, 1858–1918*, ed. Kurt H. Wolff (Columbus: Ohio State University), 243–58.

Simpson (1975) A.W.B. Simpson, *A History of the Common Law of Contract* (Oxford: Clarendon Press).

Simpson (1990) James Simpson, *Piers Plowman: An Introduction to the B-Text* (Harlow: Longman).

Sklute (1973) Larry M. Sklute, 'Expectation and Fulfillment in *Pearl*', *Philological Quarterly* 52, 663–79.

Smalley (1984) Beryl Smalley, *The Study of the Bible in the Middle Ages* (Oxford: Blackwell).

Spearing (1970) A.C. Spearing, *The Gawain-Poet: A Critical Study* (Cambridge: Cambridge University Press).

(1987) '*Purity* and Danger', in his *Readings in Medieval Poetry* (Cambridge: Cambridge University Press), 173–94.

Spitzer (1988) Leo Spitzer, 'The Addresses to the Reader in the *Divina Commedia*', in *Leo Spitzer: Representative Essays*, eds Alban K. Forcione, Herbert Lindenberger, and Madeline Sutherland (Stanford: Stanford University Press), 178–204.

Stainsby (1991) Meg Stainsby, *Sir Gawain and the Green Knight: An Annotated Bibliography 1978–1989* (New York: Garland).

Stanbury (1987) Sarah Stanbury, 'Space and Visual Hermeneutics in the *Gawain*-Poet', *ChR* 21, 476–89.

Stanesco (1988) Michel Stanesco, *Jeux d'errance du chevalier médiéval* (Leiden: Brill).

Stokes (1983–4) Myra Stokes, 'Suffering in *Patience*', *ChR* 18, 354–63.

Strawson (1974) P.F. Strawson, *Freedom and Resentment and Other Essays* (London: Methuen).

Strohm (1986) Paul Strohm, 'The Social and Literary Scene in England', *The Chaucer Companion*, eds Piero Boitani and Jill Mann (Cambridge: Cambridge University Press), 1–18.

(1989) Paul Strohm, *Social Chaucer* (Cambridge, Mass.: Harvard University Press).

Tavormina (1995) M. Teresa Tavormina, *Kindly Similitude: Marriage and Family in Piers Plowman* (Woodbridge: Boydell and Brewer).

Tentler (1977) Thomas N. Tentler, *Sin and Confession on the Eve of the Reformation* (Princeton: Princeton University Press).

Thomasch (1989) Sylvia Thomasch, 'A *Pearl* Punnology', *Journal of English and Germanic Philology* 88, 1–20.

Todorov (1970) Tzvetan Todorov, *Introduction à la littérature fantastique* (Paris: Éditions du Seuil), trans. Nicholas Howard, *The Fantastic* (Cleveland and London: Case Western Reserve, 1973).

Trigg (1990) Stephanie Trigg (ed.), *Wynnere and Wastoure*, EETS 297 (Oxford: Oxford University Press).

Turville-Petre (1977) Thorlac Turville-Petre, *The Alliterative Revival* (Cambridge: D.S. Brewer & Rowman and Littlefield).

(1989) *Alliterative Poetry of the Later Middle Ages: An Anthology* (London: Routledge).

Twomey (1994) Michael W. Twomey, '*Cleanness* 1057–64 and the *Roman de la Rose*', in *Loyal Letters: Studies on Mediaeval Alliterative Poetry and Prose*, eds L.A.J.R. Houwen and A.A. MacDonald (Groningen: Egbert Forsten), 167–86.

Vantuono (1972) William Vantuono, 'The Structure and Sources of *Patience*', *MS* 34, 401–22.

(1975) 'A Name in Cotton Nero A.X.', *MS* 37, 537–42.

(1984) *The Pearl Poems: An Omnibus Edition*, 2 vols (New York: Garland).

Wallace (1991) David Wallace, '*Cleanness* and the Terms of Terror', in *Text and Matter: New Critical Perspectives of the Pearl-Poet*, eds R.J. Blanch, M.Y. Miller, and J.N. Wasserman (New York: Whitson), 93–104.

Watts (1984) Anne Chalmers Watts, '*Pearl*, Inexpressibility, and Poems of Human Loss', *PMLA* 99, 26–40.

Weiss (1991) Victoria Weiss, '*Sir Gawain and the Green Knight* and the Fourteenth-Century Interlude', in *Text and Matter: New Critical Perspectives of the Pearl-Poet*, eds R.J. Blanch, M.Y. Miller, and J.N. Wasserman (New York: Whitson), 227–42.

Whatley (1986) Gordon Whatley, 'Heathens and Saints: *St. Erkenwald* in its Legendary Context', *Speculum* 61, 330–63.

Whitaker (1984) Muriel Whitaker, *Arthur's Kingdom of Adventure* (Woodbridge: Boydell and Brewer).

(1990) *The Legends of King Arthur in Art* (Woodbridge: Boydell and Brewer).

Williams (1970) David Williams, 'The Point of *Patience*', *MP* 68 (1970), 127–36.

Wilson (1976) Edward Wilson, *The Gawain-Poet* (Leiden: Brill).

(1979) '*Sir Gawain and the Green Knight* and the Stanley Family of Stanley, Storeton, and Hooton', *RES* 30, 308–16.

Wittgenstein (1953) Ludwig Wittgenstein, *Philosophical Investigations* (Oxford: Blackwell).

Woods (1985) S. Woods, *Natural Emphasis: English Versification from Chaucer to Dryden* (San Marino: Huntington Library).

Woolf (1957) Rosemary Woolf, 'The Effect of Typology on the English Mediaeval Plays of Abraham and Isaac', *Speculum* 32, 805–25.

Zavadil (1962) J.B. Zavadil, 'A Study of Meaning in *Patience* and *Cleanness*' (Unpublished Dissertation, Stanford University).

Index